Interviews and Encounters with Stanley Kunitz

Interviews and Encounters with Stanley Kunitz

Edited by Stanley Moss

All inquiries and permission requests should be addressed to: The Sheep Meadow Press, P.O. Box 1345, Riverdale-on-Hudson, New York 10471.

This book has been composed in Linotron Galliard

Typeset and printed by Princeton University Press on acid-free paper. It meets the guidelines for permanence and durability of the Committee on Production Guidelines for Book Longevity of the Council on Library Resources.

Library of Congress Cataloging-in-Publication Data

Kunitz, Stanley, 1905-
    Interviews and encounters with Stanley Kunitz / edited by Stanley Moss.
        p. 230 cm.
    Includes bibliographical references (p. 6) and index.
    ISBN 0-935296-79-4 : $22.50
    1. Kunitz, Stanley, 1905- —Interviews. 2. Poets, American—20th century—
Interviews. I. Moss, Stanley, 1936-   .
II. Title.
PS3521.U7Z466   1993   92-19621
811'.52—dc20   CIP

Acknowledgments

Contents first appeared in the following publications:

Act of the Mind: Conversations with Contemporary Poets (University of Alabama Press, 1983), *American Poetry Review, Contemporary Literature, Garden Design, The Iowa Review, New Directions, Nimrod, The Paris Review, Provincetown Arts, Publishers Weekly, Salmagundi, The Craft of Poetry: Interviews from the New York Quarterly* (Doubleday, 1974), *Translating Poetry: The Double Labyrinth* (Macmillan, 1989), *Yale Literary Magazine.*

Editor's Note

Various good ghosts helped make this book. I want to give special thanks to Geoffrey O'Brien for his heart and head, and for working day after day as if he were bringing swans to the Liffey. Special thanks go to Bruce Smith for his editorial input and thanks to Sharon Kraus and Katie Roiphe for care in tasks others might have considered thankless.

S.M.

Contents

Introduction — *Stanley Moss*   ix

A Tribute — *Marie Howe*   xv

Language Surprised — David Lupher (1968)   1

Speaking of Craft — William Packard (1970)   10

Tongues of Fallen Angels — Selden Rodman (1971)   19

Myths and Monsters — Cynthia Davis (1972)   31

Imagine Wrestling with an Angel — Robert Boyers (1972)   44

Periodicity — Michael Ryan (1974)   56

The Taste of Self — Christopher Busa (1977)   68

Living the Layers of Time — Richard Jackson (1978)   92

Translating Anna Akhmatova — Daniel Weissbort (1982)   99

The Poet in His Garden — Christopher Busa (1984)   117

The Buried Life — Caroline Sutton (1985)   123

Life between Scylla and Charybdis — Michael Ryan (1985)   128

To My Teacher — Louise Glück (1985)   137

Lighting the Lamp — Francine Ringold (1986)   141

A Visit to the Poet's Studio — Susan Mitchell (1988)   144

Dancing on the Edge of the Road — Bill Moyers (1989)   155

Roots and Place — Jonathan Blunk and Fran Quinn (1989)   165

Transcending the Self — Grace Schulman (1990)   179

"I'm Not Sleepy" — Esther Harriott (1990)   185

Appendix: A Sampling of Poems Discussed in the Text   193

Biographical Note   227

Contributors' Notes   229

Bibliography   231

Index   237

Introduction

Interviews and Encounters with Stanley Kunitz will be kept close at hand by young poets as a survival kit. Others who care about poetry and the life of the imagination will read and re-read the book to clear the head, and there is always hope a few indifferent to poetry and the meaning of the word "poet" may read the book as an awakening.

W. H. Auden pointed out that without the poetry of C. P. Cavafy, some of his own poems would not exist. There is a large devil's party of American poets and a few from overseas, notably some of the Russians, who have recognized a like debt to Stanley Kunitz. By now, there are scores of volumes by three generations of American poets that are substantially different because of the personal, critical attention given them by Kunitz. The poetry of Theodore Roethke and a congregation of poets from the far-flung districts of American poetry come to mind. This book of interviews also records separate "encounters," remembrances of Kunitz by three younger poets: Michael Ryan, Louise Glück, and Marie Howe. In each case, Kunitz, as poet, teacher, friend, and sphinx, confronts the poet on a road to Thebes with his or her own legendary self. A like encounter is also described by the poet-critic Susan Mitchell in her essay on Kunitz's poetry, which is, I believe, the best set piece on Kunitz we have.

I cannot imagine any of our other poets giving so much time to this kind of digging and gardening. None of his contemporaries has lived so long. Kunitz has a love of the young and a need to father. He blooms with questions, his own to himself and those of others. Readers will understand why Kunitz is seen by many as a paradigm of the creative artist, a model and example to whom any artist—poet, painter, or whatever—can go for aid and courage. This is a book that should set Kunitz's critics and biographers straight.

William Blake, one of Kunitz's influences and political heroes, wrote:

Allegory addressed to the intellectual powers while it is altogether hidden from the corporal understanding is my definition of the most sublime poetry.

Of course, the crucial companion book to this volume is Kunitz's collected poetry of sixty-five years, his song. *Interviews and Encounters* gives us Kunitz's other knowledge, his wisdom, his teaching, his "corporal understanding," his speech, something not ruled by beat, rhythm, or meter. Here is the news of Kunitz's method, his social and political practice, the useful superstructure of understanding, sacred and profane facts the poems kick away, the artless human touch he asks for in and out of poetry. We hear Kunitz responding to other human beings. They are also present, organically part of the book, with varying gifts for questioning. This, then, is Kunitz's book, of a fleshly order compared to Kunitz's poetry, born of a process distantly related to theater. It is worldly, not transparent; it is a well, not a vessel.

Kunitz's first book of poems bears the epigraph from Blake, "For the tear is an intellectual thing"; Kunitz proclaimed with his first published breath the inseparability of the intellect and the passions. Passion and intellect would remain part of the atomic structure of every Kunitz poem, its physical being covalently bonded to the knowledge that from birth we are simultaneously living and dying, bonded to rhythm and beat, and to the periodicity of the heart, tides, menses, pulsars. Kunitz replies to a question from Michael Ryan:

> This awareness of periodicity is what gives us the sense of a universal pulse. And any art that does not convey that sense is a lesser art. In poetry, it leads us, as Coleridge very definitely saw, toward an organic principle. I suppose that perception by Coleridge is the most profound assertion ever made about the nature of poetry . . .

Kunitz's poetry practices what this book preaches. Here are some answers to separate questions:

> All myths are the same, all metaphors are the same metaphor; when you touch the web of creation at any point, the whole web shudders.

> History—the experience of the human race—is the subject of poetry.

> A poet needs to keep his wilderness alive inside him.

When Kunitz was young and ripening, T. S. Eliot's objective correlative was the rage. On the other side of the Channel, that you reached by boat after a rough voyage, Valéry celebrated his festival of the intellect, observing the human mind (his own) in the act of thinking. From reading his poetry and notebooks we learn much, but we know nothing more of his person than we did before. Auden, bowing to Valéry, commented: "The formal restrictions of poetry teach us the thoughts which arise from our needs, feelings, and experiences are only a small part of the thoughts of which we are capable," and his poetry would prove his point. Kunitz responded more deeply to Yeats and to all poetry that contained what he (after Hopkins) called "the taste of self." One has a tendency to think of a poem with the taste of self as being a metaphysical lyric, but Dante's *Divine Comedy* is, of course, a supremely personal poem. The influence of Dante on Eliot is clear; Dante's influence on Kunitz's poetry is a different matter: it is more internal; there is kinship, but no echo. Susan Mitchell has something to say about that in this book. In the three poems from which I quote in this essay, two of them written some sixty years apart, I sense Dante guiding from just beyond the page. Each of the passages, by the way, was chosen for other reasons, not to show this kinship.

When Yeats died in 1939, leaving "the Irish vessel empty of its poetry," the vessel of English and American poetry was full and overflowing with the poetry of Wallace Stevens, Robert Frost, W. C. Williams, T. S. Eliot, Marianne Moore, and W. H. Auden. Kunitz was left with himself and prophecy:

> Father, the darkness of the self goes out
> And spreads contagion on the flowing air.
> I walk obscurely in a cloud of dark:
> Yea, when I kneeled, the dark kneeled down with me.

Almost every poem Kunitz has written is in some way devotional. He tells us in a crucial interview with Christopher Busa:

> Jewish cultural aspiration and ethical doctrine entered into my bloodstream, but in practice I am an American freethinker. . . . I said a few minutes ago that I had no religion, but I should have added that I have strong religious feelings. Moses and Jesus and Lao-tse have all instructed me. And the prophets as well, from Isaiah to Blake . . . three of the poets who most strongly influenced me— Donne, Herbert, Hopkins—happen to have been Christian churchmen.

Kunitz's poetry, without directing us to any religion, makes us aware of our own unarticulated religious feelings, our own blunted spirituality, if you like. When the beauty of his devotional poems enters us we are full of wonder; it somehow divines us, to use a term Kunitz has used elsewhere. He teaches us, with Blake, that "imagination is a portion of the divine principle," "everything that lives is holy."

When Theodore Roethke, another prophetic poet, the poet of Kunitz's generation closest to him, speaks with a language that once was Christian, I am full of wonder:

> Was it light?
> Was it light within?
> Was it light within light?
> Stillness becoming alive,
> Yet still?
>
> A lively understandable spirit
> Once entertained you.
> It will come again.
> Be still.
> Wait.

And when Delmore Schwartz writes at his best:

> Someone is harshly coughing on the next floor
> . . . it is God, who has caught cold again

I am full of wonder. As a way of speaking of Kunitz, I am speaking of others. I admire Auden's "For the Time Being"; I admire its poetic and religious architecture, and I love to hear Auden's voice. But I do not enter the poem emotionally, perhaps because I do not choose to, and I am not drawn into its beliefs or moved by its religious particulars. When I read Auden's "Thank You, Fog," a devotional poem in praise of life and God in which belief seems inarticulate, my feelings are awakened and I am willing to praise his foggy God. Beyond revelation, great devotional poetry reveals to our ordinary selves the formal wonders of the universe. Here is Kunitz:

OPEN THE GATES

> Within the city of the burning cloud,
> Dragging my life behind me in a sack,
> Naked I prowl, scourged by the black
> Temptation of the blood grown proud.
>
> Here at the monumental door,
> Carved with the curious legend of my youth,
> I brandish the great bone of my death,
> Beat once therewith and beat no more.

> The hinges groan: a rush of forms
> Shivers my name, wrenched out of me.
> I stand on the terrible threshold, and I see
> The end and the beginning in each other's arms.

In Kunitz's poetry and in his life (he is a man with "a leaf in his head") there is an especially intimate relationship between himself and nature. In his hardest hours he goes to his garden or to animals. His knowledge of the natural world is like W. C. Williams's knowledge of the people and history of Paterson, hands on and in. Such gardening is, I think, a form of devotion—his garden and poetry cross-pollinate. Part of the beauty of Kunitz's garden in Provincetown is Florentine, part English, part Chinese, part God knows what.

Thirty years ago, Theodore Roethke was staying with me at Fifty-seventh Street. He went off one evening, the not quite finished manuscript of *The Far Field* in his pocket to show it to Stanley Kunitz. Roethke put on a blue serge suit and my homburg for the occasion. Just before dawn he rolled back in. "What did Stanley say?" I asked.

"He liked it a lot."

Then a look of pain crossed his face and I knew that Ted, who had been in the mood to be crowned Heavyweight Champion and nothing less, was disheartened. I thought Kunitz had found something not quite right, that he had been demanding and not just celebratory (In a year or so, Roethke was dead, and Kunitz would write a loving explication in depth of the poems from *The Far Field*). Suddenly Roethke said, talking half to me and half to the world, "Stanley Kunitz is the most honest man in America!"

By that I think Roethke meant that Kunitz in his poetry sees the human condition more truthfully than anyone in America, that his poetry is without "effects," and that in Roethke's life Kunitz was the human being who spoke to him most truthfully.

A few days ago, at our last meeting, Kunitz showed me a new poem, "Proteus." I read it to him aloud because I thought that was the only way I would understand it. Here are the concluding lines:

> But now he was heavy in his heart, and languid,
> sensing the time had come to leave his flock.
> Must he prepare himself once more for the test?
> He could not recollect the secret codes
> that gave him access to his other lives.
> Half-listening to the plashing of the oars,

a disembodied chorus from the sea,
he shut his dimming eyes
and did not stir. These were the dreaded boatmen
racing to his side, and these their hairy hands.
He heard barbaric voices crying, "Prophecy!"

—Stanley Moss
April 1992

A Tribute to Stanley Kunitz

*At the dedication of the Stanley Kunitz Common Room
Fine Arts Work Center, Provincetown, Massachusetts*

Stanley has taught hundreds of students, not only at Columbia, where I met him, but throughout the world. Some are right here today. It is staggering to speak for all of us. Earlier in the day, when I was fussing with the ending of this tribute, Michael Ryan approached me, laughing, and said, "It's simple, cut *off* the ending," and we both laughed, knowing that's what Stanley would say. A few minutes later, Lucie Brock-Broido joined us and suggested, "End with an image and don't explain it." And we all laughed again. One of the miracles of Stanley's teaching is that when any of us who know him and love him meet, we feel, between us, an instant and deep connectedness, which is our common love for him. In that way, his tribe multiplies, connecting and reconnecting. How can I tell you what he's taught us? I can't stand here and tell you that he fussed with my commas and line breaks. He changed my life. He changed the lives of so many of us. How can I speak for us all? I can't.

But no true teaching happens without love, and it is about love that I wish to speak today.

Stanley once said, "I dream of an art so transparent that you can look through it and see the world." And he taught us to love this world, to learn the names of the rocks and plants and animals. He taught us that we are not alone, that the world is noisy with a breathing chain of being, a web in which we live, and that every molecule of it matters.

He taught us to love the places we had come from, places many of us were trying to forget, Pittsburgh or Rochester or the streets of New York, the very meadows and backyards we had struggled to get out of once and for all. He taught us to love that geography, the "testing-trees" of our own childhood, the original dirt and water and matter of our first lives.

And in that way he taught us to love our own stories, what we had hidden, what we had been ashamed of. He taught us to turn into those obsessions that haunted us and hurt us, to turn into their "deeper dark." And we looked at his own work and saw that he had done so, and that he had made of those turnings, poetry. And we took courage and tried.

He said, "My struggle is to use the life in order to transcend it, to convert it to legend." And, believing him, we allowed our own small stories to take on the power of myth, the primitive, intimate struggles of parents and children, men and women, friend and friend, the dead and the living. And we learned that myth is not atrophied, but embedded in this world, living and luminous, and it healed us and helped.

He said, "The heart breaks and breaks and lives by breaking."

And he showed us a poetry of feeling, crucial to actual living, embracing both the rapture and the dread, and we saw, in his work, that they were not two things, but one, and a gift to us.

He said, "I am not done with my changes." And we, his arrogant and defensive students, watched his own work change, and we were humbled, and we tried better to listen, not only to criticism, but to the more quiet changes in our own inner lives. Because we saw that he had done so, and that his spirit had grown bigger.

He said, "We have to make our living and dying important again, and the living and dying of others. Isn't that what poetry is all about?" And hearing him say that so simply, so utterly, we were relieved and answered, yes.

Stanley Kunitz is a great teacher. No true teaching happens without love. If every act of love is a blessing, what blessings in this room then. In his name, in the name of all he taught us, in a common room where young artists and writers will gather for countless years to come, where his spirit will live forever.

—Marie Howe
July 29, 1989

NOTE

For the convenience of the reader, certain poems referred to in the text are collected in an Appendix. Those poems are marked in the text by an asterisk.

Language Surprised

by David Lupher

David Lupher: One of your definitions of poetry is "language surprised in the act of changing into meaning." Many poets, however, regard language as an embarrassment. They believe that "meaning" can be found by such shortcuts as drugs or free association, rather than by exploration and exploitation of words. Do you feel that the search for these shortcuts is ill-fated?

Stanley Kunitz: What I meant by that remark of "language changing into meaning" is simply that I am differentiating there between the language of statement, of fact, and that language which is largely unconscious, which is drawn from the unconscious itself, and which therefore is not yet in the form of explication—and *should* not be, in terms of my concept of the poem. The poem is always changing into meaning, but is not meaning itself. In a sense the exploration of the unconscious that seems so essential to the act of the poem is a form of, let us say, hallucination. So I am not disagreeing at all with your premise.

DL: You have said that "one of the difficulties of the modern poet is that the sacredness of things, the sense of that sacredness, has been lost." Would you elaborate on this?

SK: Well, I think we see it around us every day of our lives. All the great words have been sullied: courage, honor, truth, patriotism, even the word "virtue". These are words that have lost their shining—and in that sense have lost their sacredness. One of the functions of the poet is certainly to give back to the virtues and the words that attach to them their original luster and redeem them from the marketplace.

DL: But wouldn't you agree that to some extent this has always been the case, this debasement of important words?

SK: I would say that we live in a cynical age, and that perhaps the great words suffer more attrition in our time than in other times—perhaps because we are a more self-conscious people.

DL: I was wondering if perhaps the cataclysmic events of this century have done something to help this attrition?

SK: Oh, yes. I would definitely agree.

1

DL: I wonder, though, about your own preoccupation with disorder in poetry. Among my favorite lines of yours are, "Absurd though it may seem, / Perhaps there's too much order in this world; / The poets love to haul disorder in, / Braiding their wrists with her long mistress hair."

SK: That goes back to my sense of the poem as language changing into meaning. Actually language comes to one in a shapeless rush. It's a montage, an overlapping of imagery, of feelings, words, sensations which have not yet been reduced to order. Part of the freshness of the poem comes from leaving some of that primordial dew on it, not polishing the language down to the point where it becomes something made, not something born. In that sense I do think there is a great love in the poet for disorder which operates in tension with the great order of syntax and of prosody. So he has both of these operating at the same time. But I don't believe in a poetry that is absolutely conscious. Consciousness to me is order, and the unconscious life of the poet is the great sea in which he has to swim.

DL: How do poems come to you?

SK: Given my whole aesthetic, the poem is difficult to find, and it does not lie exposed on the surface of the brain. It has to be reached for, dug for, and that is always a slow process. It really requires a deep interiority, which is hard to come by. One of the difficulties of writing a poem is to wash the mind of the day, and that has to be done before you can even get near a poem. And this is my criticism of a good deal of the poetry of our time: that the minds haven't been washed, the minds that made them.

DL: How do form and meaning relate when you write a poem?

SK: I never think of meaning as anything separate from the act of poetry. If you find the poem, you have found the potentialities of meaning that are implicit in the language.

DL: What is the sincerity of the poet?

SK: Sincerity rests in the capacity to be as ruthless with oneself as with others. One is insincere in the writing of a poem if one does not go to all the trouble of finding it where it lies hidden, if one is satisfied with circumlocution or easy dodges, tricks, surprises, sensations. Insincerity is usually an example of a superficial quest for an effect rather than for truth.

DL: It seems to be that many poets feel that if they substitute pure confessionalism for sincerity they are doing the job.

SK: I don't mean confessionalism, for confession can be too easy, too glib, or a contrived effect. In that case, no matter how blatant the confession may be, no matter how open one is to others, there is something false and unreal at the center. I think there has been too much reliance on the shock effect of confession in a good deal of modern poetry; the vogue of confessionalism is just about over. To be a poet at all is to confess a difference; the rest is a torment and a discipline.

DL: Your own love poetry is certainly among the finest in the language, and I remember that on television recently you said to Yevtushenko that you were glad he writes love poetry, for when poets stop writing love poetry, they might as well quit.

SK: Then you'd better turn to prose. Well, I . . . one can't talk about it. All poetry is born of love, and the moment one doesn't have love enough for the world, or love enough for others—at that point one is dead as a poet.

DL: I know that most younger poets feel that if they are not being "original" they are not being worthwhile. How do you feel about originality per se?

SK: Every poet has his own idiosyncrasies; he has his own, let us say, central sources, his own pastness which is different from any other past, and the originality of any poet consists to a considerable degree in finding those key images which forever haunt him, which make him different from others. It is not to be found in seeking originality, for that is what everybody else is doing and it is not an original pursuit.

DL: How would you trace the evolution of your own style?

SK: It is hard to say. Every artist, as Malraux has said, is born into a style. That style is a compound of all the artwork of a generation. There is a voice that belongs to each epoch in history, and it is different from any other voice. That one naturally inherits. Then the problem is to find within that style, that generational style, the individual quality which is the sum of all one's differences, and this is a quest that takes a lifetime. As one matures and changes, the voice must change too. It cannot remain the voice of a young man of twenty-five when you are sixty. Your preoccupations are different, even your sensibilities have been modified. In my own case I notice that in the poetry I am writing now, I am moving toward a much more open style than I used in my earlier work. I somehow no longer feel right within a tight structure, and I'm trying to crack it. This is a deliberate act, it is the way I feel about the poem when I start attacking it.

DL: It seems to me that your earlier work, especially that in *Intellectual Things*, was almost metaphysical.

SK: It was. My influences during that period were primarily metaphysical, particularly Donne . . . also Herbert, to a degree. But at the same time Hopkins was a strong influence on me—and Blake. I was not really ever a son of Eliot, and thought of myself as someone writing in a counterstyle—even though he, too, had some metaphysical sources.

DL: Several of the poems since *Passport to the War* are dramatic monologues. Are you continuing this?

SK: Yes. The new poems that I am working on now and hope to finish this year for a new book are largely dramatic monologues, and they tend to run anywhere from a hundred, a hundred and fifty, to two hundred lines. That seems to be their natural span.

DL: You think a longer poem is . . .

SK: Well, that's part of the openness that I am seeking at this moment. In other words, when I want compression I tend these days to write epigrams, and I work in these two different modes, really, most of the time.

DL: The epigrams are something new for you, aren't they?

SK: Yes. The epigrams that I have been . . . "jotting down," really, have been very contemporary in their allusions, political, very direct. They're not essentially metaphorical.

DL: Speaking of political poems, you have said that under a dictatorship a poet needs to write "soapbox" poems. However, wouldn't you agree that even outside of a dictatorship political poems tend to be soapboxish and distressingly bad? I am thinking especially about Vietnam War poetry.

SK: The reason is that in the political poem or any topical poem there tends to be a certain obviousness. The emotion and the attitude are fairly coarse-grained by their very nature. For example, to write a poem against the war in Vietnam, an act that has tempted almost every poet, hardly seems worth doing because there is no interest, there is nothing to be gained by putting it into a poem. The feelings are simply too obvious to make for poetry. The meaning is already there before you write the poem, so that you're really writing *about* something rather than writing something.

DL: But I noticed that your poem "The Mound Builders" has been published in an antiwar anthology. Would you really term it an anti–Vietnam War poem? It was a little pre-Vietnam anyway, wasn't it?

SK: Let's see . . . I think it was just about the time of our commitment of military advisers to Vietnam and our resumption of nuclear testing. I was thinking about the limits of power and the possibility of nuclear war. This happened to coincide with my visit to the South, where I saw the remains of an older civilization, and out of this the poem began. So it is a poem that has some political background, but it is not a political poem.

DL: What first attracted you to the work of Andrei Voznesensky?

SK: Well, I suppose that there is a certain freshness of idiom, a vitality, a quality of contemporaneity in the work. Aside from that, there was the accident of meeting him and liking him as a human being, and I find the same attractive qualities in his work as I do in him as a person. Also, there's a curious bond, I think, between American and Russian literature. When I was there last year [1967] I sensed a great curiosity and affection for American writers. They couldn't get enough. They wanted to know who was writing, what our poetry sounds like. It was refreshing to find so much responsiveness in a whole generation of writers. Our reception of Voznesensky and Yevtushenko and the continual production of books about Russia and anthologies of Russian literature indicate our reciprocity in that area.

DL: Who were the poets you met over there? What were they like?

SK: I met by request practically every writer of importance in Russia today—with the exception of Solzhenitsyn, whom I couldn't get to, perhaps because they didn't want me to—but otherwise I saw everybody I wanted to see, and that would include practically everyone you have heard of and then a large number of young writers who are unknown here: young poets in their twenties and thirties, and many of them not getting published, partly because of their political views, partly because so many of them are refusing to write in the vein of socialist realism and are turning back to the mode of the lyric, which the state is not really interested in, in fact which the state opposes. The state is in a curious way afraid of the lyric mode, because it represents an individual voice, as opposed to a collective one.

DL: Why is it that, despite the current boom in the publishing of new poetry, the so-called man in the street in America is as distant from poetry as ever, if not more than ever?

SK: I don't think the man in the street has ever been a reader of poetry in this country. There is a myth of a popular art, but actually there has been no popular poetry since the nineteenth century "fireside poets"—and then, you know, the bad newspaper poets of the modern era. But for a popular art the man in the street finds, let us say, folk rock in its various manifestations, or the Beatles, adequate to his needs. He has no particular desire to read poetry, which he thinks is too complicated for his understanding.

DL: But he won't claim that the Beatles are poetry?

SK: Well, the Beatles are a form of . . . well, an art form, and to me extraordinarily interesting.

DL: You're a believer in specialized knowledge for the poet. Why is this?

SK: I suppose this all stems from my belief in particularity, in, as Blake called them, the "minute particulars" of a poem. That hardness of detail, that precision of detail is very important to me. And I think it is an advantage for the poet not always to be immersed in poetry, not to become incestuous with his own art. It is a great help to him to have some knowledge, some hard grains of knowledge about something completely different from the art with which he is coping. If he is, for example, involved in modern physics or in agriculture or horticulture or any other specialty, if he studies the life of the whale, for example, and knows as much about it as Melville did, this all in the end becomes grist for him and gives to his work that particularity which in the end will sustain him. I think too much poetry is airy. It is spun only out of the need to write the poem and is not nailed into the foundations of the life itself.

DL: When you mentioned whales I was wondering if you were thinking of your poem "Ambergris"?

SK: No, I was thinking of a later poem I've been working on. Up in the Cape last summer a whale came up on the beach and was live when I found him, a sixty-three-foot whale. The tide went out, and I went up to the whale, which was lying there, obviously in agony, and was making the most terrifying noises—groaning . . . he was groaning—and I put my hand on his flanks, and I could feel the life inside that whale. And while I was standing there, suddenly he opened his eye, and it was a big, red, cold eye, and it was staring directly at me. Then it closed, and he died. . . . Anyhow, that made me mention whales, and I've been thinking about whales.

DL: Your areas of specialized knowledge, then, are zoology and horticulture?

SK: I would say that horticulture has always been a passion of mine. I've always been involved in some sort of gardening, and I now have two gardens, one in the city, and one in the country. These are very important to me. I couldn't live in the city without a garden.

DL: I've often wondered how you can live in New York City. Have you acquired a love for the place?

SK: No, I've always hated the idea of living in New York. I tried it two or three times before and never managed to last more than a year, but now I find that by living in the Village and having my garden I can manage to exist. I also have, under the present circumstances, more space. I hated the sense of being cramped. The city is a difficult place. But I don't consider myself to be an urban person at all and have no real affection for the city. And I know that when I write poems I am always returning to the land, the landscape—the in-scape, if you want to call it that.

DL: You pride yourself on being something of a chef. You've said that your inventiveness in cooking without recipes . . .

SK: Well, that's a specialized knowledge too.

DL: Certainly, but I wonder if you consider this in a way also a poetic process?

SK: Yes, to me it's a very creative act. For example, to know what to do with fish, which is generally treated so badly even in good restaurants. Furthermore, there's a certain subtlety about seasoning. And the palate itself is very important to me—touch and taste, I suppose, are my strongest senses. So that although I am not a gross eater, I like something that is a bit exotic and piquant on my plate.

DL: What are your triumphs?

SK: I guess I'm best in the preparation of fish and the handling of veal, both of which require a light hand. I won't give you any recipes.

DL: I'll try without them. I understand that another of your hobbies is modern painting. Do you yourself paint?

SK: My wife is a painter. I suppose most of my friends are painters and sculptors. I find them very congenial as human beings—more so than poets, although I've had great friends among the poets too, still have—but I do enjoy their openness, their congeniality, their conviviality: this I find in the world of the painter much more than in the world of literature. I have long had more than a casual interest in sculpture as a medium. Years ago, before it was recognized as a mode of sculpture, I was playing with wire construction. And in more recent years I have been working with boxes, assemblages. Sometimes I have to escape from language. Language can be crucifying. I'm happy when I'm working with my hands.

DL: It always pleases me to think that the two American poets whose work I love the most were close friends. I wonder now if you would tell me about your friendship with Theodore Roethke?

SK: Well, that's a long story. I don't know what I can say, except that it was an association that began when we were both young men. I had just published my first book of poems. Roethke discovered it and one day suddenly appeared at my place in the country, early in the evening, I remember, and there he was, knocking at my door, a big shambling fellow with a copy of my poems in his hand. I think that for the rest of our lives we really had a sense of true fellowship, comradeship, even when we were at opposite ends of the continent. And even if we didn't see or write to each other for years, nevertheless, it was important to both of us to know that the other was there, passionately caring about poetry and about the work of the other. We were helpful to each other in a way that two poets can be who share some of the same values and loves. And to me he was always the most important poet of my generation, even when he was unknown.

DL: What sort of man was he?

SK: An extraordinarily sensitive and vulnerable being was locked in his large frame. For most of his adult life he tried to conceal from others, even from his intimates, that he was a manic-depressive, subject to periodic breakdowns. One never knew whether to expect the Ted who was shy and inarticulate, even humble, or the alter ego who was boastful and contentious. The best conversations with Ted occurred around three or four in the morning, after plenty of booze. Some of his stock anecdotes—about escapades with gangsters during the Prohibition era and heroic shoot-outs and pugilistic encounters—improved with each telling. Despite his fierce competitiveness, he was a wonderfully loyal friend. Poetry was for him a sacred passion that bound him to his peers. He loved to read poems aloud, stuff that he had copied out and carried around with him—stuff so precious you felt complimented by his wanting to share it with you. Of all the poets I've known he had the best ear. We prided ourselves on having read everything and used to play a game in which we challenged each other in turn to identify the author and date of a poem chosen for its obscurity as much as for its merit. Over the years we became so expert at the game that even when we failed to guess the author, we almost never missed the date of composition by more than ten years. Poets like to think of themselves as one of a kind, but every generation has its telltale style.

DL: Is it true that you're the one who caught him on Sir John Davies' "Orchestra," which led to his "Four for Sir John Davies?"

SK: Yes, that's true. Somehow he had missed out on that Elizabethan treasure. I still recall the night I read it to him and the expression on his face. I felt as though I had hit a home run!

DL: In a conversation with W. H. Auden during his visit to Yale last December, I asked him why you have received so much less of a following than you have deserved from 1930 to the present day. He replied, "It's strange, but give him time. A hundred years or so. He's a patient man. He won't mind waiting." *Will* you mind waiting?

SK: No. I've waited a good many years. I can wait—a hundred more.

New Haven/1968
[*Yale Literary Magazine*, May 1968]

Speaking of Craft

by William Packard

William Packard: A few years ago, many of our poets were also serious critics. Today there doesn't seem to be the same interest in critical theory that there was when Mr. Ransom, Mr. Winters, Mr. Brooks, and Mr. Warren—

Stanley Kunitz: Oh well, it's part of the revolt against the establishment, which is also a revolt against conventions and standards, including critical standards.

WP: And it seems also as if some poets are their own aestheticians, such as Mr. Olson. Now, does this take part of a poet's energy, part of what used to be given to him?

SK: Yes, but on the other hand it means that the possibilities are more open; that nobody is required to write in the prevailing style or in the voice of the master. The danger, of course, is in thinking that anything goes in the new dispensation.

WP: Perhaps there will be a swing back; perhaps there will be new criticism after this period is over.

SK: I suspect there will be. These are energetic and confusing times. There will have to be an evaluation of the work of a whole generation. In fact, it is already happening—look at the spate of freshly minted anthologies. I note, by the way, that reputations are being shuffled faster than ever.

WP: This must be one of the freest periods of your whole career, in terms of what can be done.

SK: Freer than ever—but tied to the same old carcass! Incidentally, I can't think of it as a career. To me it's a life.

WP: Mr. Auden has complained about the abuses of this period, that there seems to be a lack of interest in history on the part of some young poets, a lack of interest in meter, in craft, in prosody. He was very concerned, distressed.

SK: Who will be left to admire his great craft? When I first began to teach, in the late forties, it seemed quite obvious that instruction in prosody was part of a workshop discipline. Today the young are mostly indifferent to such matters; not only indifferent but even strongly antipathetic. They praise novelty, spontaneity, and ease, and they resist the very concept of form, which they relate to mechanism and chains. Few understand that, for a poet, even breathing comes under the heading of prosody.

WP: You once said that the originality of any poetry consists to a large degree in the poet's finding his own key images, those that go back to his roots and traumas. Can a poet talk about these images?

SK: Not unless he's very sick, or very foolish. Some poets are both. One oughtn't to try to explain everything away, even if one could. It's enough to reconcile oneself to the existence of an image from which one never gets very far. No matter how one turns or where one travels in the mind, there inescapably it is, sending out vibrations—and you know it's waiting, waiting to be seized again.

WP: Several years ago, you said that certain themes—those of the quest, the night journey, and death and rebirth—preoccupied you.

SK: I must have been reading Jung then. Those are archetypes built into the structure of the mind.

WP: In discussing "Father and Son"* in the Ostroff book (*The Contemporary Poet as Artist and Critic*), you referred to your sister, and to the big house on the hill, and you said, "They belong to that part of my life which I keep trying to rework into legend." What does that mean?

SK: What the alchemists meant when they spoke of converting dross into gold.

WP: The voice in the poem you call simply "Poem" is intensely personal, and at the same time the events described have a sense of universal myth behind them.

SK: When I wrote that poem I was young and ignorant. But even then, as now, I wanted to get below the floor of consciousness, to wipe off the smudge of the day. The poems I like best, I suppose, are the ones that are steeped in "the taste of self"—Hopkins's phrase. Such poems are hard fought for.

WP: What do you feel about improvisations, about randomness as a prime creative principle?

SK: My advice to myself is, Trust in your luck, but don't trust in it absolutely. I recall that after a couple of excruciating experiences as an amateur mycologist, John Cage saw that though the principle of chance operations was good enough for his music, it could not be extended to his mushroom hunting without killing him. Was he aware of the irony implicit in that revelation? Maybe he didn't pursue his insight far enough.

WP: So far, *The New York Quarterly* is more or less dependent on the quality of the poems that are submitted to us. What do you feel about the level of the poems that are appearing in the *Quarterly*, and what should we do to improve the quality? We're always looking for that one poem that will be "below the floor of consciousness," as you have said.

SK: Standards were easier to maintain in an aristocratic society. Emerson said somewhere that democracy descends to meet. All the modern arts are being threatened by the cult of the amateur. And being nourished, too. You have to know the difference between naiveté and simplicity, novelty and originality, rhetoric and passion. The most insidious enemy of the good is not so much the bad as it is the second-best. I mean particularly, in this context, the inferior productions of first-rate reputations. Anyone can see that we have plenty of talent around—what civilization had more? The trouble is that our gifts are not being used well. On the face of it, our literature reflects a mediocre or silly age, sometimes an angry one. When are we going to wake up to the fact that it's tragic?

WP: Have you had any experience with editing, with magazines?

SK: The only magazine I ever edited, after the Classical High School *Argus* (Worcester, Massachusetts), was a library periodical. But last year [1969] I became editor of the Yale Series of Younger Poets, succeeding the late Dudley Fitts. That means reading some five hundred book-length manuscripts a year. Nobody believes me, but I actually make an effort to read every one of them, though not necessarily every page. It's a responsibility I refuse to unload on others, because—who knows?—the most miraculous, most original work of all might get weeded out in the first round, as sometimes happens in competitions of this kind. At least half the submissions can be put aside at once as hopelessly inept or maudlin—usually both. It isn't asking much of a manuscript that it prove reasonably competent and tolerably readable, but I've learned that no more than one hundred out of the five hundred can be expected to pass that test. Eventually it becomes clear that there are only three or four manuscripts, maybe, in the lot from which any sort of fire breaks each time you turn to them. As far as I am concerned, these finalists are all winners, and I wish the rules of the game didn't require me to make an arbitrary choice. I have always hated the business of ranking poets. What was it Blake said? "I cannot think that Real Poets have any competition. None are greatest in the Kingdom of Heaven."

WP: You have said that you used to play technical games, and do craft exercises. Have any of your poems come out of one of those games?

SK: Not that I can recall. But, of course, there is a game element in all poetry. In the very act of writing a poem one is playing with language, playing with the capacities of the mind to hold together its most disparate elements. The object of the game is to fuse as many of one's contradictions and possibilities as one can.

WP: Before we began to record our interview, you said that most of your poems have begun with something that was "given" to you, a very strong opening voice. Doesn't, then, the challenge of realizing the poem require a great understanding of craft in extending the impulse through to the end? So many poems by mediocre poets seem to start beautifully and then are not brought off.

SK: Practically all my poems start with something given to me, that is, a line or a phrase, or a set of lines, that takes me by surprise. When that happens, the challenge is to accept the blessing and go along with it. Only in the process of writing the poem do you discover why the gift was bestowed on you and where it will lead you. Craft is there to sustain and fortify the original impulse, and to preserve the momentum, now by letting go, now by pulling back. Sometimes you find in the end you have to throw out the very lines that gave the poem its start, because they have become embodied in the whole act of the poem and are no longer necessary. Sometimes they require modification, because they may not have come to you perfect. For example, in "End of Summer,"* the opening lines, as they announced themselves to me, were "*The* agitation of the air, / *The* perturbation of the light." At a certain point in the revision my ear told me that the four definite articles thickened the lines unpleasantly. I changed them to "*An* agitation of the air, / *A* perturbation of the light"— much more open, airy, fluid.

WP: Now surely this process of rewriting and trying to fulfill the intention of the given lines must require a full understanding of verse and prosody. This is the whole reason for craft.

SK: As I indicated earlier, prosody isn't just metrics. It's closer to biology than to mechanics. It involves everything that has to do with the making of a poem, the way it moves, the way it sounds, the way it lives from word to word, the way it breathes.

WP: It is interesting to hear that the beginnings of your poems often consist of "inspired" material, because so much attention has been paid to the way you have ended your poems—particularly those that turn at the end in a line or two in a way that seems both to come out of the poem and to be something new. Do you ever begin the writing of a poem with the ending?

SK: Occasionally I am astonished to find, through all the devious windings of a poem, that my destination is something I've written six months or a year or two years before, and that is what the poem's been seeking out. The mind's stuff is wonderfully patient.

WP: This process of retention, of being able to carry these lines for years and years, requires a tremendous memory. Is there ever any confusion with lines that have been written by other poets? Do you ever find yourself not sure if you wrote a line?

SK: In the beginning, sometimes, I would say to myself, I wonder—is this line really mine? And I discovered quite soon that if I questioned it, the only thing to do was to forget it, because the mind has its own conscience, which has to be trusted. A little doubt is all you need to know.

WP: You keep a notebook of quotations that mean something to you. Has an entry from that notebook ever inspired a poem of yours? Or, do you ever incorporate other people's words into the body of a poem?

SK: The mind is a prolix gut. That's a phrase I suspect I stole from Woodrow Wilson, of all people, though I can't be sure. All poets are thieves—or magpies, if you want me to be euphemistic. The imagination keeps looking for information to digest, and digestion is a process of reconstitution. I don't really care much for paste-and-scissors jobs.

WP: Do you consciously try to control the speed of lines in your poems? In "Benediction," the line "God drive them whistling out" has speed and force, and in the same poem the line "No shy, soft, tigrish fear" is suspended and slow.

SK: The variable pulse of a poem shows that it is alive. Too regular a beat is soporific. I like to hear a poem arguing with itself. Even before it is ready to change into language a poem may begin to assert its buried life in the mind with wordless surges of rhythm and counterrhythm. Gradually the rhythms attach themselves to objects and feelings. At this relatively advanced stage, the movement of a poem is from the known to the unknown, even to the unknowable. Once you have left familiar things behind, you swim through levels of darkness toward some kind of light, uncertain where you will surface.

WP: It's improbable, isn't it, that this kind of experience would ever be given in sum to a poet, without the long struggle, without the long process of—

SK: I wish it were easier. How I envy prolific poets!

WP: To go back to your underwater metaphor for the creative process, what is the sensation at the point of surfacing?

SK: Joy. As though a burden had been removed. One is freer than before.

WP: Then a false ending to a poem would be an attempt to create this result without actually achieving it.

SK: If you fake it, your rhetoric betrays you.

WP: Have you always written in the way you have just described?

SK: I think so. Even the earliest poems. "For the Word Is Flesh," for example.

WP: How young were you when you began to write poetry?

SK: Even in grade school I was rhyming—doggerel, mainly. But I enjoyed that. And I was reading all the bad poets, along with some good ones, and loving them equally. Words always fascinated me, regardless of whether I knew what they meant. In fourth grade, I recall, I began a composition on the Father of Our Country with the sentence: "George Washington was a tall, petite, handsome man."

WP: Which of the poets you read as a young person had the most influence on the development of your own writing? Did reading Tennyson affect the development of your ear?

SK: During my high school years I admired Keats and Tennyson for their music. One day my English teacher read Herrick in class. Later, a neighbor gave me Wordsworth's collected poems. Those were red-letter days. At Harvard I discovered the metaphysicals and Hopkins, and they shook me up. Afterwards, in the thirties, the later Yeats became important to me, and I began my long friendship with Roethke.

WP: Would you say something about your feelings concerning faith and religion? This process you describe of struggling with the given lines of a poem might almost be an Old Testament scene of Jacob wrestling with the Dark Angel in order to find God through intuition rather than through outside revelation.

SK: I suppose I am a religious person without a religion. Maybe because I have no faith, I need it more than others. And the wrestling is damn good exercise.

WP: Do you often change words in poems after they have been printed? There are two versions of "Deciduous Branch" in print—the first says "Passion" where the later one has "Summer."

SK: "Summer" made the metaphor harder and cleaner. I can't usually bear to read my early poems, but once in a while I am tempted to see whether I can make some small improvements in the ones I want to keep. I haven't the slightest interest in rewriting them *in toto*, even if I could, nor do I propose to make major changes.

WP: This brings up the matter of a poet's going back and revising, or even disclaiming, early poems which the public has already come to know. How can he blot them out? Should a poet keep trying to bring his work up to date, or should he let the record stand?

SK: A poet tends to be a perfectionist. I see no reason why he should be disqualified from trying to improve his own work, published or unpublished. As long as he's alive, it's his property. After his death, posterity will have the privilege of determining which versions of his poems, if any, it chooses to remember.

WP: What prompted you to edit those massive collections of literary biographies, *Twentieth Century Authors, European Authors*, and the rest?

SK: Simply that I had to earn a living. After college I went to work for a publisher in New York and soon discovered that I wasn't geared for an office existence. So I fled to a farm in Connecticut, where I produced a crop of herbs, flowers, and reference books. And, perennially, poems.

WP: Now you seem to be spending a good part of your time on Cape Cod, in Provincetown.

SK: I'm truly happier there. I have a great world of friends in New York, but the city depletes me. I need to grow things and to breathe clean air. Then, I have my involvement with the Fine Arts Work Center in Provincetown. A few of us have banded together, with the help of some foundation money, including a grant from the National Endowment for the Arts, to invite a selected group of young writers and artists each year to join a productive winter community up there by the sea. We give what help we can. Alan Dugan and I are the ones most concerned with the poets. And we bring in all sorts of brilliant people from the outside for weekly seminars.

WP: That sounds like an exciting program. How does one find out more about it?

SK: By writing to the Fine Arts Work Center, Box 565, Provincetown, Massachusetts, 02657.

WP: Poetry seems to be the orphan child of the arts—it is always difficult to find public support for projects involving poetry. Do you see any sign of improvement? Will a person who wants to become a poet always have to look forward to a lifetime of struggling, and working at vocations he doesn't really enjoy in order to support his art?

SK: Hasn't that usually been true? I'm not sure that a poet should expect to be rewarded for his voluntary choice of a vocation. If he has any sense at all, he should realize that he's going to have a hard time surviving, particularly in a society whose main drives are exactly opposite to his. If he chooses, against the odds, to be a poet, he ought to be tough enough, cunning enough, to take advantage of the system in order to survive. And if he doesn't, it's sad, but the world is full of the most terrible kinds of sadness.

WP: What do you think of the way in which poetry and literature have been presented to elementary school children through our present educational system?

SK: Almost anybody would have to agree that the American system of education has been a dismal failure. Certainly one of the areas in which it has most significantly failed is in teaching students how to cope with poetry. The failure begins at the grade school level. But there are some promising signs—first of all, a general recognition of the failure. The new young educators, clearly, know the essential truth about the injury done to the imagination of the child, and there are many signs of revolt against the educational system, just as there is a revolt against the political system.

WP: Many high school and college students feel that poetry has no importance for them, in their lives.

SK: So many of the young today doubt that classroom instruction in general and the reading of poetry in particular are what they need most. I can understand their negativism. They fail to see that the work of the imagination is precisely what has to be achieved if we are going to save our civilization from disaster. And that a poem, regardless of its theme, can embody for us a principle of the free mind engaged in a free action.

WP: Wasn't "The Mound Builders" written out of a political situation?

SK: Many of my poems are, but in an oblique way. By its nature poetry is hostile to opinions, and the opinions of a poet on public affairs are, in any case, of no special interest. The poems that attract me most, out of the contemporary dilemma, are the peripheral ones that are yet obviously the product of a mind engaged with history. "The Mound Builders," I can recall, came out of the resumption of nuclear testing by President Kennedy in 1962, when I was traveling through the South, and looking at the archeological traces of a civilization that flourished in this country between 900 and 1100 A.D., the greatest civilization of the Eastern seaboard, and maybe the greatest civilization north of Mexico, of which nothing now remains except a few shards. There in Georgia the inscription reads, "Macon is the seventh layer of civilization on this spot." Macon, one of the seats of racist injustice in this country. So all these elements entered into the making of the poem, including the fact that I was traveling, and reading my work, and talking to college students in the South. But most readers would say, not without justification, "It's a poem about mound builders."

WP: Are you writing dramatic monologues now?

SK: My new book has several poems that are basically dramatic in their structure. They're not quite dramatic monologues—I don't know really what to call them—but in each case there is a dramatic action incorporated in the poem, sometimes appearing and sometimes disappearing. The very last poem I wrote for the book is called "Around Pastor Bonhoeffer." Bonhoeffer, you know, was the Lutheran pastor in Germany who, after a great struggle with his conscience, joined the plot to kill Hitler. The plot failed, and he was exterminated. The conflict between his Christian principle of nonviolence and the political necessity for action seems to me a parable for our times. I myself am a nonviolent man with radical feelings about the way things are.

WP: When will that book be published?

SK: Next March.

WP: And it's called *The Testing-Tree?*

SK: With a hyphen.

New York /1970
[*New York Quarterly*, Fall 1970]

Tongues of Fallen Angels

by Selden Rodman

The Kunitz house is on Commercial Street in Provincetown, at the far end of the tourist honky-tonk with its owl-faced girls in hip-huggers and bearded men in patched dungarees looking like unemployed Christs. The house is set back from the street and above it, the steep slope ingeniously terraced with railroad ties to provide beds for the poet's potentillas, pink-eyed Susans, and lilies, a cataract of blossoms.

I began by asking Stanley about his boyhood. It wasn't biography I was after, but the story he told was so fascinating that I encouraged him to talk about his childhood. He was born in Worcester, Massachusetts, in 1905. His immigrant parents were from grain merchant families in Lithuanian Russia—"though perhaps my father, who killed himself six weeks before I was born, came from East Prussia. I've never known much about him because mother made it a forbidden subject. Why he killed himself wasn't clear. The dress manufacturing business they'd started together was going bankrupt; but there must have been another woman, too, or mother wouldn't have made the subject taboo. Not even his name could be mentioned. Mother was a great seamstress—and businesswoman—so after the double catastrophe she opened a little dry goods store and for years worked day and night to pay off the debt—she wasn't obliged to legally.

"I was farmed out, or in the hands of nursemaids."

> At breakfast mother sipped her buttermilk,
> her mind already on her shop,
> unrolling gingham by the yard . . .

"When I was ten we moved to the outskirts of the city. Our house was the last in town, bordering the old Indian trail, which I proceeded to explore in deep loneliness."

> On my way home from school
> Up tribal Providence Hill
> past the Academy ballpark
> where I could never hope to play
> I scuffed in the drainage ditch
> among the sodden seethe of leaves
> hunting for perfect stones
> rolled out of glacial time

19

into my pitcher's hand;
then sprinted lickety-
    split on my magic Keds
      from a crouching start,
scarcely touching the ground
    with my flying skin
      as I poured it on
for the prize of the mastery
    over that stretch of road,
      with no one no where to deny
when I flung myself down
    that on the given course
      I was the world's fastest human . . .

"I didn't return to Worcester until 1963 when Clark University gave me an honorary degree. And just last year [1971] I ventured back for a few days to reexplore my stamping grounds and let my memory simmer. It was terribly depressing to see the degradation of that once wild and free countryside where I'd once walked all day long without seeing another soul and tested myself by climbing the quarry's sheer rock face.

"I was lonely and fatherless, but my father *had* left a library—fairly substantial sets of Dickens, Thackeray, Tolstoy, and the like—and once I had gone through it I could take the daily four-mile walk to the big library. I would take out my quota of five books a day. I discovered poetry. A lady gave me her complete Wordsworth—perhaps one reason I never developed your distaste for Wordsworth!

"My two older sisters died young. Mother was just forty when I was born. When I was eight, she married again. My stepfather taught me most of what I know about love and gentleness. He was an Old World scholar, of no practical help to my mother, but she revered his learning and the sweetness of his character. She anticipated the modern liberated woman, being perfectly capable of managing by herself what had developed into a flourishing business based on her dress designs—I can still see the loft with its cutting tables and long rows of girls bent over their electric sewing machines. Mother never trusted anybody else to repair the machines when they were out of order. But she was always tired at the end of the day. When my stepfather died suddenly in my fourteenth year, my world was shattered. It didn't leave me with much sense of family."

"You have a great sense of Worcester," I said, "so Worcester must have had something. What with you and Charles Olson and Elizabeth Bishop all having been born there in the same decade," and I told him of my adventures five years before, driving through Worcester on the way to visit the Cummingses on Silver Lake.

"Cummings and I met late, but we had an understanding," Stanley said. "In a curiously disturbing way I am involved with his death. You know he was very naive in many ways; there was something childlike and beautiful about his presence. Marian told me afterward that on his last day at Silver Lake he was being driven around the countryside by a friend. The conversation turned to contemporary poets, and Cummings spoke warmly of me. The friend betrayed his surprise: 'Isn't he a Jew?' Cummings was indignant and replied vehemently: 'How can you possibly call him that? He's a gentleman! He went to Harvard!' And on his return home he was expressing this same complicated feeling of outrage to Marian when his heart failed him. At Marian's death I came into possession of their Victorian chairs and their houseplants—keepsakes I treasure."

I asked him to resume the story of his mother.

"What finally destroyed her," he said, "was that she couldn't bear to fire anyone. So she went bankrupt again in the Depression, and that was the end of her business career. She had fought for money and power, and she had failed—for which she could not forgive herself. She died, alert and intransigent, in the early fifties at the age of eighty-six.

"I had already graduated from Harvard [1923–27], where I won the Garrison Prize for a dreadful poem called 'John Harvard.' Very romantic-melancholy, but I suppose it anticipated my themes of Time and Mutability. The decisive moment came when a visiting professor, Robert Gay, wrote on one of the daily page-essays of 1925: 'You're a poet. Why don't you write poetry?' Of course I'd written some, for years, but I was then deep in a novel, which fortunately never saw print. At Worcester Classical High I'd edited our school magazine and contributed light verse. I saw some of those verses recently and was surprised by their technical competence—with no instruction. The great experience of those high school years was hearing Martin Post, my English teacher, read Herrick's songs—definitely not in the curriculum. On one occasion, after telling us that sounds had color, he asked us what the treble notes on the piano made us think of. I answered 'White!' And when he struck the bass: 'Deep purple turning to black!' Whereupon he announced: 'Stanley, you're going to be a poet!'—a prophecy that still astonishes me.

"In 1928 I had good jobs reporting and night-editing for the *Worcester Telegram*, but quit to try my luck writing in New York. I almost starved. Finally the H. W. Wilson Company, reference publishers to the library world, offered me a job—which I still have, sort of! It didn't take me long to discover I couldn't survive in an office and they went along with that, letting me drop out little by little, after I'd founded their *Wilson Library Bulletin* and initiated the Authors Biographical Series, of which I am now advisory editor. In 1929 I went abroad for a year. And in 1930 my first book of verse, *Intellectual Things*, was published."

"The title would have put me off even then," I said, "but how could the poems have escaped my notice completely?"

"Quite easily," he said. "There were only five hundred copies in print. But it did get some quite marvelous reviews: Zabel in *Poetry*, Yvor Winters in *The New Republic*, William Rose Benét in the *Saturday Review*, and so on. Marianne Moore had already published some poems from it in *The Dial*. But then I more or less dropped from sight, living in the country, far from literary circles, and not emerging with another book till fourteen years later—in the midst of World War II, the least propitious time for my kind of voice.

"My hundred-acre farm in Connecticut, Wormwood Hill, absorbed me. I restored the old house, raised herbs and vegetables, ploughed my fields with a yoke of white oxen, and earned enough, besides, out of free-lancing, for my subsistence. *Our* subsistence, I should say, for my first marriage, a most painful one, was then running its course. She was a poet, Helen Pearce, a great beauty. I'd met her at Yaddo in 1928—"

"Is she still alive?"

"Nobody knows! She simply disappeared."

"You have a daughter, Stanley?"

"Yes, out of my second marriage, which occupied my middle years—a good marriage, to a fine person, though it ended in divorce. Now, as you know, I'm married to Elise Asher, who's a painter and who links me to that other world, of art, where I have so many friends and where I feel so much at home. Do I regret not having children in my later years, as you have, Selden?—No, because I am so close to the young anyway, through my poetry and my teaching and my editorship of the Yale Series of Younger Poets."

We took time out for tennis and lunch, and he concluded his biography in the few minutes left to us that afternoon.

"After beating Frankie Parker in his prime," I said, "as you claim—but I still think you're pulling my leg—I'm surprised that you didn't settle for tennis as a career."

"I forgot to tell you," he laughed, "that my earliest training was as a *violinist*! It ended at Harvard where I played under Walter Piston in the Pierian Sodality—only Harvard could call an orchestra *that*!

"It was in 1936," he continued, "after the hurricane had uprooted my sugar maples, blowing my first marriage away with them, that I moved to an old stone house in New Hope, Pennsylvania. That's where Ted Roethke 'discovered' me. 'Are you Stanley Kunitz?' he said.

" 'Yes.'

" 'Well—I just wanted to say—you're—one hell of a poet!'

"When Ted was fired from Bennington ten years later, after a breakdown, he got me the job to succeed him by saying, 'I'll go quietly, if—' I was nearing the end of my army career then, having accepted conscription as a conscientious objector, refusing to kill or bear arms, but agreeing to be a medic. Once they had me in their grip, they denied there was any such agreement. It was a nightmare. I went through basic training three times. I was down to one hundred pounds, doing nothing but KP and latrine duty for more than two years. Finally I went south to Camp Monroe, where the racial tensions were fierce and I was accused of being a 'nigger-lover,' but somehow, finally, I got to the commanding officer.

" 'What do you want?' he said.

" 'I want to tell you the morale at this camp is terrible—and so is mine—Sir!' I told him also that I was constantly under surveillance, falsely accused of being a Communist—as if I were the kind of person who would ever have submitted himself to Party discipline. I proposed editing a camp newspaper for them.

" 'Why are you qualified, Private Kunitz?'

" 'Look up my history—Sir!'

"Amazingly, he let me. And more amazingly, our publication won first prize for army publications four months later. I was transferred to Gravely Point, Washington, headquarters of the Air Transport Command, in the office of Information and Education. But I refused to be commissioned as an officer."

⁂   ⁂   ⁂   ⁂   ⁂

"Poetry is not necessarily involved with statement," Stanley began the following morning when we resumed our talk. We were taking up an argument we'd been having in Seattle, where I'd spent most of my time talking to Mark Tobey, arguing that the major artist's major commitment is to his "message."

"Poetry can be the poet's ultimatum, his defiance of Chaos and Old Time," he continued. "Rothko *does* communicate grandeur, a poignant sense of the colors of the world removed from the flux, so that they *stand* and are true. They embody a vision of tragic reality."

"If Rothko had had any sense of humor at all," I said, "I'd have said 'Smile when you say that' when he tried to justify what he was doing in almost those words . . . Tragic? How?"

"As opposed to flux, resistant to mortality, refusing to surrender to mere *motion* . . . and yet ultimately doomed. We mustn't look here for the dialectic implicit in language."

"And why not, Stanley, why not? There isn't this abyss between Goya and Blake that you tolerate between Rothko and yourself."

"Painting is essentially a medium of forms and pigments, as music is of sounds, as poetry is of words."

"Bullshit! Tell that to Beethoven . . . Not that I'm denying the accuracy of your description of the bloodless little world painting has settled for, but your tone implies that you acquiesce in the limitation. How can you? Obviously you don't accept any such formalistic straitjacket when it comes to using *words*—"

"The difference is that the nature of language is conceptual."

"Couldn't we all write poems like 'Jabberwocky'?"

"Even Carroll's nonsense poems have logic and sequence—'Jabberwocky' included. Poetry cannot escape meaning. But painting, even in the ages and cultures where it is expected to be representational, is always converting its themes into a convention—subject matter does not explain greatness."

"But Stanley! Your own poems! Surely they don't deviate from this sterile abstract formula by having logic and sequence? Take such a great one as 'The War against the Trees'* with its tremendous lines:

> They struck and struck again,
> And with each elm a century went down . . .

Isn't that whole poem, apart from its transcendent language, a primer of ecology?"

"Thanks. I'm grateful for a medium that can catch the mind in motion. Painting deals with broader aggregates—quanta of perception. What is common to all the arts is the struggle to achieve an imaginary order out of the real disorder of life. One of the measures of art is the amount of wilderness it contains.

"I call poetry," he went on, "a metamedium—metaphoric, metamorphic, metabolic. It articulates shifts of being, changes and transfers of energy. This has always been so, of course, but we are much more aware of it today."

"Metabolic—" I interrupted. "Is that the meaning of Blake's

> The caterpillar on the leaf
> Repeats to thee thy mother's grief . . . ?"

"He is saying that the universe is a continuous web. Touch it at any point and the whole web quivers."

"Your recent poem on the Apollo flight,"* I reminded him, "with its ending:

> I was a stranger on earth.
> Stepping on the moon, I begin
> the gay pilgrimage to new
> Jerusalems
> in foreign galaxies.
> Heat. Cold. Craters of silence.
> The Sea of Tranquillity
> rolling on the shores of entropy.
> And, beyond,
> the intelligence of the stars.

"What's going on, Stanley?" I said, with a smile. "Don't you believe in the second law of thermodynamics?"

"One of the first questions I can remember asking," he said, "was, Where does space end? Later—as if I didn't have enough problems on earth as an adolescent to concern me—I began to worry about the running down of the universe. I still do. When I read about the latest galactic probings, I get a feeling that can only be described as a metaphysical shudder. I don't need to partake of the magic mushroom to see Shakespeare, Mozart, Michelangelo, Jesus, Buddha, you, me, everything we love, all the works of man, his cities and his dreams, pouring through a black hole in the universe, hell-bent for eternal annihilation. Time is shorter than Newton knew. What do you suppose motivates our space explorers? They may not admit it or even realize it, but they are trying to find a way to escape from the solar system before it is too late. It is the greatest of all human adventures. And the odds are all against us."

"What if we don't make it," I said, "has it all been a waste of time?"

"The act of imagination, of self-assertion, justifies itself. Do we really need a posterity of witnesses to give meaning to our existence? And who knows?" He smiled slyly, with the crow's-feet around those sad, bulging eyes contracting. "Some great salvage operation may carry our best to another galaxy. Say—twelve books?"

"Which twelve?"

"What a torment to have to choose between poetry and information! Shakespeare, Homer, Virgil, Dante, of course. But what about books of reference? Dictionaries, encyclopedias, histories, bibles, anthologies? I'm afraid I'd have a nervous collapse before rocketing off."

We got to talking about painting again, and I asked him whether any of the figurative moderns satisfied him. "Bacon—?"

"Part of me is tuned to Bacon, but in the end that compulsive pitch of hysteria turns me off."

"What does his art say to you?"

"It says, 'I suffer, I'm scared.' Art at its best has freshness and sanity—"

"Like Matisse?"

"Like Matisse. I know you don't care for him. I'm restored and glorified. Picasso's machismo overwhelms me without moving me as much. But I recognize that our age responds more readily to a muscle man."

"To come back to poems," I said, "why are yours so uniformly good?"

He didn't bat an eye. "I think of every poem I write as my *last*. Even so, I have my share of duds. Most poets write too many poems."

"Galway Kinnell, to mention one of the best, doesn't, yet the 'complete poem' never seems to emerge. Why?"

"He's still young. He needs to reconcile his myth with his life, his animal sense with his humanity. Give him time."

I told him that I'd be seeing Mailer later that month in Vermont. Did he know him?

"We've both owned homes in Provincetown for well over a decade, at opposite ends of the town—which may be symbolic! He and I had what was billed as a public dialogue in the Universalist Church a few years ago—we did it for some worthy cause. It didn't go well. As two radical types—though how different!—we couldn't find enough areas of disagreement, and that's bad for Norman, who's a counterpuncher. He couldn't manage to commit an act of aggression."

"You think that's his limitation as a writer?"

"He disappoints us more than other writers because he has conditioned us to expect so much from him. Now his ego's in the driver's seat, stepping on the gas of his obsessions. The nature of his genius is to find itself by *going*. If only he could stop, reflect, take stock of himself. . . ."

*　*　*　*　*

We all had dinner at the Kunitzes our last day at the Cape, and while Carole and the children went shopping down Commercial Street with Elise, Stanley and I talked alone for another hour. He mentioned his debate with Mailer again. "He was in the prize ring with me, waiting for me to lead. But I was playing tactical tennis, with chops and lobs. We never got into the same game!

"I was thinking of something else yesterday," he went on, "how Ted

Roethke once said ruefully, 'Stanley and I are the oldest younger poets in America.' Now I'm the oldest younger poet, I suppose. It's a long haul. America does one of two things to its poets. It either withers them with neglect or kills them with success."

"Frost included?"

"Read Thompson's biography. He was always playing a role. Something had happened to his heart."

"And Borges?"

"I was talking about United States Americans. But Borges's career is fascinating. It's almost a fairy tale of an old man's triumph. Ten years ago, who would have believed it? The explanation is that we were ready for this turning away from naturalism to fantasy, this rejection of the grandiose to focus on small scale. Kafka and Hiroshima prepared us for such a writer. The influences Borges admits to you—Stevenson, Kipling, Chesterton— are figures in a charade, part of his mystification. At his best Borges has refined the drama of his inner life to the point where it can be acted out in miniature at another level. I find his fiction more interesting than his verse. In my one conversation with him he told me that his poems 'lose nothing' through their translation into English because he writes them in Spanish— a language too mellifluous for his taste—only in order to have them con- verted into English. I'd like to hear Neruda or Paz comment on that re- mark!"

"As long as we're talking about poets who are going into this book," I said, "give me your impressions of Ginsberg. You told me you met him in Seattle in 1955, the year before I was there?"

"I was sitting in my apartment reading one night," he said. "There was a knock on the door, and there were those two slim young men in blue jeans and tennis shoes. One was Gary Snyder. The other, the one with thick glasses, handed me a manuscript and said abruptly: 'I want you to read the greatest poem of the century.' It was *Howl*, then unpublished. I read it, not without astonishment, that night. Allen's recollection, by the way, differs from mine, for he contends it was not in character for him to be so brash. For the sake of the legend I hope I'm right."

"Did they give a reading?"

"Yes, next day at the university before a small audience. Allen read *Howl*. Gary read from his *Riprap* manuscript. Some members of the faculty walked out on them. They thought the barbarians were loose."

"How important was the Beat movement?"

"It signified a good deal as a social phenomenon. And it did shake up the literary scene for a while, gave it a new infusion of blood. But most of the stuff it spawned was trash—those tons of rant! Not much remains of it. Snyder has had a more interesting development as a poet, but Allen, in his own way, has shown surprising stamina. His emergence as a cult figure is a curiously edifying example of the American success story. One of the great things about Allen is the way he gives himself wholeheartedly to his causes—drugs, Bangladesh, homosexuality, whatever. His shamelessness is a kind of nobility."

I asked Stanley if he thought poetry could be taught.

"No. But poets can be. Poets learn from poets. One of the deficiencies of American life is the poverty of communication among artists. For young writers a workshop provides a testing ground in the company of their peers. You can't give a would-be writer imagination or vision; but poetry is also a *craft*, and the miracle is that the exercise of craft can release hidden powers. The poem is the battleground between the conscious and the unconscious life. The poet must never surrender *either*, for if one or the other takes over, the tension is lost. The automatic imagination is a delusion—and a bore. A poem is a sum of triumphs over unpredictable resistances."

"Do you think youth's separation from the establishment will be good for poetry? Good for the country?"

"It's already had a tremendous effect. The power brokers fear the young, and they have good reason to. And they would fear poets, too, if they understood them. Poetry has been a counterculture since the dawn of the Industrial Revolution. Indeed, some of us have been too comfortable in our adversary status. The treason of the avant-garde was in becoming fashionable."

"What about drugs?" I asked.

"I belong to the generation that looked for ecstasy and oblivion in the bottle. My experience with drugs has been desultory, but on the whole disappointing. The writers I know who depend on drugs for their visions are a sad lot. Not that you need to be a saint to have visions worth talking about. The most effective prescription, I suspect, is to be a disciplined sinner. Perfection, as Valéry noted, is *work*.

"Imagination," he continued, "often follows a deep fatigue. You catch your second wind and suddenly you're free, all your meanings adrift on a sea of language. Incidentally, this is the exact opposite of the cold manipulation of language, for ulterior motives, by advertisers and politicians. I think that Confucius was on solid ground when he argued that civilization and right language go hand in hand. Look at the decline of our public speech since the time of *The Federalist Papers*. Since Lincoln we've had no transcendental figure in the White House, and no one—with the exception of Woodrow Wilson—who could write a decent prose sentence. In fact, hypocrisy is so ingrained in the State that our presidents do not even write their own inaugural addresses."

"Do you feel more hopeful about Israel?" I asked.

"Israel began so idealistically. But she seems to be hardening into a military posture, by force of circumstances. Like us they need an act of imagination to save them. I wish they would dare to make the impossible gesture to the displaced Palestinians, a sincere offer of repatriation. Nothing less will do. It doesn't matter how many wars the Arabs lose. If they win just once, it will be the Final Solution."

"Do they think of you as one of them, Stanley?"

"Strangely, I've never been invited to Israel. Maybe it's because I'm not usually considered to be one of the Jewish writers. I have no religion. And my interests are not parochial. But that could be said of others. Anyhow, they'd better hurry up!" [Ed.:—They did. Kunitz visited Israel in 1980]

"Do we lack a tragic sense of life, Stanley? Is that one of our liabilities?"

"There's a dark strain running through the American imagination, but the mass of our people are content with their success fantasies, their sports entertainments, and their soap operas. The children of immigrants from Europe—fugitives from the Old Country's poverty and persecution—have helped make our literature serious. And now the black and Hispanic cultures are contributing their rage and their ancestral pride. In Seattle, where you and I first met, I had a wonderful sense of being a stranger in a new land, facing toward the Orient—"

"A sort of wandering Jew?"

"I could spend the rest of my life wandering from campus to campus— if I weren't so *heavily* married!"

The jesting word was for Elise who had just come in and was smiling at him from the doorway with Carole and the children behind her.

The children were enchanted with his story of the five owls he'd domesticated in Connecticut and of the woodchuck, Slop, who forced Musing, the cat, off her favorite perch on his right shoulder, obliging her to move to the left one. "The battle took place on my back," Stanley said, "and Slop won. But from then on I couldn't get any work done at all. Could you, with *both* shoulders occupied, morning and night? . . . Well, finally Slop died. He'd gotten to love marshmallows so much he couldn't eat anything else: he swelled into a butterball, could scarcely waddle around, so finally, one day—it was inevitable—he dug a hole for himself under the back porch and climbed down into it."

He and Elise bought the house nine years ago from the estate of a semi-retired Boston madam. After dinner, while the children were playing, he took us downstairs to show us his study, Elise's studio, and a whole row of sparsely furnished workshops that had once been bedrooms.

While we were inspecting Elise's latest paintings, I remarked how much easier it is to enjoy this art than ours. "Except for children," I said, "there are no primitive poets. And a college education seems to be more of a hindrance than a help in putting a picture together. Are you happy with your teaching?"

"From my kind of teaching," Stanley said, "I learn as much as I give—maybe more. In a curious way, I feel that this generation is the first I'm close to. I'm certainly not close to my own! Are you?"

"Jim Agee was the last member of my generation I felt close to," I said. "And that was more than twenty years ago."

"This new generation," Stanley said, "shares my longtime distrust of institutions, even those that profess to love me. Not to congeal in a generational pattern is so important. Not to feel that wisdom or art has already reached a climax. As with you, my closest friends today are painters. I love their élan, their openness, their gregariousness, their physicality. Poets are such difficult people, so tied up in knots—an occupational affliction. The young know that you can't live in a trap of words. A kind of romantic pantheism is in the air. I can hear the windows opening on a world of affections."

As we drove away down Commercial Street—so aptly named!—and I caught a last glimpse of Stanley and Elise at the gate behind us, waving, I thought of the ending of "The War against the Trees":

> I saw the ghosts of children at their games
> Racing beyond their childhood in the shade,
> And while the green world turned its death-foxed page
> And a red wagon wheeled,
> I watched them disappear
> Into the suburbs of their grievous age.
>
> Ripped from the craters much too big for hearts
> The club-roots bared their amputated coils,
> Raw gorgons matted blind, whose pocks and scars
> Cried Moon! on a corner lot
> One witness-moment, caught
> In the rear-view mirrors of the passing cars.

Provincetown /1971
[*Tongues of Fallen Angels* by Seldon
Rodman. New Directions, 1972]

Myths and Monsters

by Cynthia Davis

Cynthia Davis: Mr. Kunitz, you said once to a group of students studying your poetry that no one has the "right answers" in interpretation, and that after it's published the poem belongs as much to them as to you. Are you generally reluctant to explain your poems?

Stanley Kunitz: I often don't really know what a poem means, in rational terms. There are so many currents that flow into the poem, of which the poet himself can't be totally aware. Years after you have written a poem, you come back to it and find something you didn't know was there. Sometimes, I grant, a poet can be helpful about a specific image or an obscure portion of his poem.

CD: Do you think it's helpful to talk about the circumstances that led to your writing a poem?

SK: If they can be recalled, they may, in some cases, prove illuminating. But, as a general rule, the poem ought to have released itself from the circumstances of its origin.

CD: Is that related to the idea of myth—poetry as myth?

SK: Yes, it's that, but it's also related to my feeling that the poem has to be found beyond the day, that it requires a plunge into the well of one's being, where all one's key images lie. The occasion for a poem, which may have been something quite casual, is not the true source of the poem—it has only helped to trigger the right nerves.

CD: When I asked about myth, I was thinking of the idea that I find in the poems of "The Coat without a Seam" especially, the idea that myth is something constant that can be expressed in many different kinds of circumstances, but that goes beyond circumstances—even beyond the individual. So a great poem speaks to everyone because all share a common condition.

SK: Jung spoke of archetypal images that go beyond the individual persona and that pertain to the collective history of the race.

CD: Is that a reason for your use of dream and hallucination in the poetry—to reach that archetypal material?

SK: I think of dream as an actual visitation into that world, as a clue to secrets of which one is only faintly aware in ordinary consciousness.

CD: But you wouldn't agree with the "psychic automatism" of the surrealists?

SK: No. Because I think a poem is a combination of unconscious and conscious factors. One is trying to reach a level of transcendence; at the same time, one has to keep a grip on language, not to let it run away with itself. Automatic writing is such a bore!

CD: Is your use of metaphysical techniques—exploiting the metaphor in extended conceits—one of the ways of exercising that conscious control over language, giving form to the raw materials of the unconscious mind?

SK: The image leads you out of yourself into a world of relatives. The beautiful risk to take is to extend the image as far as you can go, until it turns in upon itself. The danger is in jumping off into absurdity, but that's part of the risk.

CD: Perhaps we can consider some of these questions by talking about changes in your development. You eliminated almost half of the poems in *Intellectual Things* (1930) in later volumes. Was that because they were technically unsuccessful, or because you no longer agreed with the ideas you expressed in them?

SK: My main feeling was that they were immature. Maybe I felt a little embarrassed reading them, so I thought it would be better to drop them, that's all.

CD: I felt that many of the poems in that book placed much greater emphasis on the power of the intellect than later poems. I'm thinking of poems like "Mens Creatrix" (*IT*, p. 16), in which you seem to talk about the superiority of the intellect over the emotions. I wondered if perhaps one of the reasons for elimination of such poems was that you had changed your emphasis.

SK: I doubt it. Certainly when I was writing the poems in *Intellectual Things*, I meant to demonstrate, if I could, not that the poem was a cerebral exercise, but the contrary, that the intellect and the passions were inseparable—which is the whole point of the Blake epigraph to the book, "The tear is an intellectual thing."

CD: Then why the poems in which you talk about putting away passion, or subduing it by intellectual power?

SK: It's not a question of putting it away or rising above it. Remember, I'm thinking back a good many years, so that I wouldn't swear to this—but my recollection is that my characteristic figure at this stage, in speaking of mind and heart, was of each devouring and being devoured by the other, an act of mutual ingestion. In "Beyond Reason" (*IT*, p. 62) I spoke of taming the passions "with the sections of my mind"—as though it were a sort of dog food—but then I wanted to "teach my mind to love its thoughtless crack."

CD: One of the poems that impressed me on this theme was "Motion of Wish" (*IT*, p. 52).

SK: I'll take a look at it and see whether you're right or not. . . . Yes, I think the lines you were thinking of were ". . . wish may find / Mastery only in the mind." This poem I haven't looked at in so long, but as I read it now, I see these lines as the key to understanding of the poem: ". . . mariners eat / One lotus-moment to forget / All other moments, and their eyes / Fasten on impossible surprise." And then the end: "A man may journey to the sun, / But his one true love and companion / Sleeps curled in his thoughtful womb. / Here will the lone life-traveler come / To find himself infallibly home." But you have to consider here that the mind is the eater of the passions, and the passions rest in that mind, so that what one is asserting is a sense of the unity of all experience, not a separation.

CD: And the mind contains that sense of unity.

SK: Yes. The mind stands for the whole experiential and existential process. I think that the confusion here is to think that when I talk of mind in this volume, that I'm talking about brain. I'm not talking about brain; I'm talking about the whole process of existence.

CD: What about poems like "Very Tree" (*IT*, p. 21), where it seems that what you're saying is that you perceive the essence of the tree—its treeness—and discard its particulars? That the particulars are not important?

SK: One of my great influences was Plato, and I was very deep in Platonic lore, especially at this period of my first work. The theme is the idea of tree, treeness, as opposed to the shadow of the idea.

CD: But you're not really suggesting that particulars of experience are unimportant?

SK: You arrive at universals through the perception—the clear perception—of what Blake called "minute particulars."

CD: These earlier poems are much more abstract than your later work, aren't they?

SK: I suppose so. That may have been the Platonic influence, as much as anything else that I can think of.

CD: Did you become dissatisfied with that kind of approach?

SK: As I became more of a political being, I wanted to fasten my poems to the reality of the day. I turned away from poems that began with the grandeur of generality. I wanted to find the general through breaking the kernel of particulars.

CD: Is this why, in *Passport to the War* (1944), you make so many references to contemporary events? As concretions for your general themes?

SK: Don't you think that that is possibly simply the result of maturing a bit and having more experience of the world? At the time of writing *Intellectual Things*, I was in my early twenties and was an innocent in so many ways. I had developed intellectually more than I had emotionally or experientially.

CD: This volume, especially the war poetry, seems very different even from your later poetry.

SK: It was my darkest time.

CD: Do you still have the same feelings about the conditions of the modern world and what it does to man?

SK: I've never stopped being a dissenter. I have no use for a superior technology that breeds hatred, injustice, inequality, and war.

CD: What do you think the poet's position should be in relationship to that kind of society?

SK: Number one, he must not become a subscribing member of it. Since the beginning of the Industrial Revolution, the poet has been the prophetic voice of a counterculture. Poetry today speaks more directly to the young than ever before because they recognize its adversary position.

CD: Then you think it's more difficult to be a poet now than it was before the nineteenth century?

SK: The poet before the Industrial Revolution could identify himself with State or Church, but he certainly has not been able to do so since. That's why he is a creature apart.

CD: You often talk about guilt in *Passport to the War*. Sometimes it's played upon by society, but sometimes you seem to say that everyone carries a load of guilt around with him. What is this guilt caused by and directed at?

SK: When I speak of "The Guilty Man" (*PW*, p. 27), I don't mean someone who has sinned more than anybody else. I mean the person who, simply by virtue of being mortal, is in a way condemned; he's mortal and he's fallible, and his life is inevitably a series of errors and consequences. Since he cannot really see the true path—it is not given to him to see it, except in moments of revelation—he is denied the rapture of innocence.

CD: Like Original Sin.

SK: Without the theological furniture.

CD: Is this related to the existentialist idea of the fear of freedom?

SK: I was making noises like an existentialist before I knew what it was to be one. I keep on trying to record my sense of being alive, which means in practice my sense, from moment to moment, of living and dying at once, a condition of perpetual crisis.

CD: In particular, when I read "The Fitting of the Mask" (*PW*, p. 28), I thought of Sartre's "bad faith": the attempt to conceal one's own being from oneself.

SK: If we did not wear masks, we would be frightened of mirrors.

CD: You say in "Night Letter" (*PW*, p. 9) that you "believe in love" as the salvation from this fear of one's own being and from the evils of modern society. Are you speaking primarily of love for mankind or personal love?

SK: Abstract love is not love at all. One expresses love in relation to another—that's the germinal node. I don't really care much for people who are always talking about love for mankind and hate their neighbors.

CD: The treatment of the love theme is another difference I found between the first volume and later ones. In *Intellectual Things*, the love poetry is often about relationships that fail; it isn't until the later poetry that you really celebrate fulfilling relationships.

SK: That's more or less to be expected. After all, the disasters of early love are legendary and part of one's education. For that reason, among others, poets, in their youth tend to be melancholy. "When I was young," said Yeats, "my Muse was old; now that I am old, my Muse is young."

CD: It wasn't, then, that you had a more pessimistic conception of the relationship?

SK: I've always been an optimist about love. Three marriages are the proof.

CD: I'd like to talk a little about *Selected Poems*. Perhaps we could begin with a poem that seems central to that volume. "The Approach to Thebes" (*SP*, p. 31). That poem ends with these lines: ". . . I met a lovely monster, / And the story's this: I made the monster me." Is this just acceptance of one's fate?

SK: More than that. . . . I have a theory about monsters. I remember, a few years ago, telling Mark Rothko, who was a dear friend of mine, that every genius is a monster. Mark thought about that for some time, and then, with the typical vanity of an artist, said, "You mean I'm a monster?" I replied, "Well, I'm not talking about anybody in this room." But of course I was. The adversary artist in our time pays a price, in human terms, for his excess of ego and sensibility. He has had to sacrifice too much; he is poisoned by ambition; and he carries too big a load of griefs and shames—that's the hump on his back. You're not likely to find him open, generous, or joyous. Rothko, incidentally, killed himself by slashing his wrists not long after our discussion. I have a poem about him, entitled "The Artist,"* in *The Testing-Tree*.

CD: And the burden of monsterdom is placed on mythic heroes, too?

SK: Yes.

CD: There's one mythic hero that you seem to consider more than others, and that's Christ. Why is the Christian myth more important in your poetry than other myths?

SK: Because it shakes me more. It is the supreme drama of guilt and redemption. I have no religion—perhaps that is why I think so much about God.

CD: When you speak of myth in poetry, you mean a re-creation of the human drama embodied in religious myths such as this?

SK: Poetic myth is nourished by all the great traditions.

CD: Then you are saying that all myths attempt to do the same thing, to tell the same story.

SK: All myths are the same myth; all metaphors are the same metaphor. When you touch the web of creation at any point, the whole web shudders.

CD: And poetry has the same function as myth?

SK: Metaphorically.

CD: You draw many parallels between the poet and the mythic hero. Do you, like so many poets, see the poet as supreme example of affirmative action, of what a man can be?

SK: As I said a while back, he can be a monster. But ideally he is the last representative free man, in that he is beholden to nobody but himself and his own vision of truth. Almost anybody else you can think of is beholden to others: the pastor to his congregation; the politician to the public, the actor to his audience. But the poet, since he is not a commodity, is more blessed than others—he can strive toward the absolute purity of his art.

CD: Aren't you beholden to your publisher and your readers, at least in some measure financially?

SK: No, I don't think so. One manages to survive. If I felt for a moment that I had to write lies in order to publish, I would stop publishing. It wouldn't matter that much. I could still go on writing.

CD: You're especially concerned with the question of what it is to be a poet in "The Coat without a Seam," and nearly all of the poems in that section are new in *Selected Poems:* Why is it that you became more concerned with poems about poetry in that volume?

SK: I'm not sure that I did. Periodically one tries to redefine and reassert one's vocation—not always in obvious terms. Wallace Stevens made a career out of doing precisely that. "Poetry," he wrote, "is the subject of the poem." As you rightly perceived, I keep trying to relate poetic function with mythic or heroic destiny.

CD: You note that relationship in other sections, too, in poems like "Green Ways"* (*SP*, p. 5).

SK: I wonder whether you caught the logic of the various sections in the *Selected Poems.* They were meant to indicate my primary thematic concerns.

CD: Perhaps you would talk about a couple of those sections; for example, "The Terrible Threshold."

SK: That title—"The Terrible Threshold"—comes, of course, from one of the poems, "Open the Gates"* (*SP*, p. 41), where the poet sees "The end and the beginning in each other's arms." I think of the poems in this section as visionary experiences, culminating in a moment of illumination.

CD: In speaking to a group of students studying "Prophecy on Lethe" (*SP*, p. 61), you said that that moment was one of fleeting awareness, and that you couldn't state what that awareness was of. If you can't state what you see in that moment of epiphany . . .

SK: I don't have to state it. The awareness is in the poem, not in my memory of it. Come to think of it I don't even remember what the last lines were!

CD: "With your strange brain blooming as it lies / Abandoned to the bipeds on the beach: / Your jelly-mouth and, crushed, your polyp eyes."

SK: I see all those death images piled up on that shore. The key word, the transcendental word, for me is "blooming."

CD: There is a movement there toward a sense of identity, isn't there? First an anonymous figure floating on the stream, and at the end you speak directly to the "you."

SK: Death-in-Life. Life-in-Death. The glory of the senses . . .

CD: This is what I was trying to get at: I saw the poem as, at least partially, a myth of the birth of consciousness, moving from a Being-in-Itself state—unconscious and no perception—to that sense of identity that you have because you're conscious. And of course, a sharper awareness of your own sensuous perceptions. I don't know whether that would be valid or not.

SK: Thanks—I'll buy it. It just occurs to me that there's a comparable evolution in my later poem, "Green Ways." I hadn't seen the affinity before.

CD: And part of the point of "Green Ways" is that it is the duty of the conscious being to accept his consciousness, isn't it?

SK: More than that, he must affirm his vegetable and mineral existence, as well as his animal self.

CD: Not discarding them with consciousness, then.

SK: Accepting them, in the fullness of the life process.

CD: Could you talk a little about "The Serpent's Word" section also?

SK: Those are love poems, or deal with the love experience. The phrase is always the key to the section that it heads; here it's from the line: "Who taught me the serpent's word, but yet the word." Which takes us back to the Garden of Eden.

CD: In "The Dark and the Fair" (*SP*, p. 33), the source of that line, there's a Fair Lady and another Dark Lady, and the Dark Lady replaces the Fair. The Dark Lady is from the past; is she symbolic of the Fall?

SK: She's Lilith, in the poem.

CD: There is another poem in "The Serpent's Word" that I find more difficult than most, "As Flowers Are" (*SP*, p. 10).

SK: That poem records the changes in a field through the seasons. And at the same time, it offers by implication a metaphor of the aspects of love. From week to week each species of flower, each hue, struggles to gain possession of the field.

CD: Is that the "war" of the flowers?

SK: Yes. The yellows and whites of spring yield to the hot tones of summer, a riot of colors. The chill nights bring the lavenders in; and, with the first frost, the whole field turns bronze. It's a parable, I suppose.

CD: I think I see it now.

SK: It's not so difficult, if you listen to the music.

CD: You've said that in an open society, poetry tends to become hermetic, more difficult, and very private. Do you think this is true of your own poetry?

SK: The important question is, do I still think we live in an open society. Certainly America seems to me less open than it was. And certainly my work has undergone a sea change. Robert Lowell wrote something to the effect that I've broken with my "passionately gnarled" earlier style and am writing in a language that "even cats and dogs can understand." Perhaps in my age I've managed to untie some of the knots of my youth. I want to say what I have to say without fuss. I want to strip everything down to essentials.

CD: You talked about some of these ideas in *Passport to the War*, and that volume also had a more open style than the first one.

SK: Poets are always wanting to change their lives and their styles. Of the two, it's easier to change the life.

CD: In that last volume, *The Testing-Tree* (1971), you included several of your translations of other authors. Why did you pick those particular ones?

SK: Obviously because I liked them as poems. And because they seemed to have an affinity with my own work. For example, I've been working on the poems of Anna Akhmatova for several years—they make up my next book. I've been so absorbed in her verse that it would be surprising if I hadn't been affected by it. Incidentally, I tend to think of a book as a composition, a joining of parts into an architectural whole, not just a throwing-together of the poems as written. A book ought to have an interior logic: these few translations seemed to me to fit into the logic of this particular book. I deliberately excluded scores of others.

CD: Are they fairly strict translations?

SK: Close, but not slavishly close. Translating poetry is an exercise in paradox. "Be true to me!" says the poem to its translator. And in the next breath, "Transform me, make me new." If you follow the original, word for word, and lose the poetry—as you must, if you insist on a literal rendering—your translation is a dud. But if you find the poetry in a free act of the imagination, it's a lie. I'm reminded of the citizen in Kafka's aphorism who's fettered to two chains, one attached to earth, the other to heaven. No matter which way he heads, the opposite chain pulls him back with a jolt. That's pretty much the condition of the translator.

CD: Do you read the originals yourself?

SK: My knowledge of Russian is rudimentary. Though my parents came from Russia, I am not a Russian linguist or scholar. So I nearly always translate with somebody whom I can depend on for roots and connotations and allusions. Max Hayward helped me with Akhmatova, as he did before with Voznesensky.

CD: Did you do many translations earlier?

SK: A few . . . from French, Spanish, and Italian. I included one of my Baudelaire translations in *Selected Poems*. He was important to me.

CD: You spoke of the "internal logic" of a volume of poetry. Does *The Testing-Tree* have a definite logic for its sections, as *Selected Poems* does?

SK: A logic, but less definite, perhaps. I shuffled those poems all around. The first section is the overture, anticipating the main themes. Section two is dominated by poems of place; three, political; four deals with the role and character of the artist.

CD: The title poem seems most like your earlier poems in theme.

SK: Not in form, certainly. But that and "King of the River"* go back to the mythic.

CD: Were they written earlier?

SK: No. Quite late.

CD: Would you say, then, that your themes are the same, that you're just expressing them in a different way?

SK: A man's preoccupations and themes aren't likely to change. What changes is the extent to which he can put the full diversity of his moods and interests and information into his poems. Formal verse is a highly selective medium. A high style wants to be fed exclusively on high sentiments. Given the kind of person I am, I came to see the need for a middle style—for a low style, even, though that may be outside my range.

CD: I was interested in Robert Lowell's review of *The Testing-Tree* because I thought that he was saying, among other things, that the new poetry was more like his, more like confessional poetry.

SK: I've always been an intensely subjective poet. There's never been any shift from that.

CD: The sort of open description of autobiographical detail that appears in your last volume is generally considered confessional poetry.

SK: Confession is a private matter. Most so-called confessional poetry strikes me as raw and embarrassing—bad art.

CD: Do you think you've been influenced by any of the confessional poets? Lowell and Roethke?

SK: In the first place, you mustn't call Roethke a confessional poet. He would have vomited at the thought. We were friends for thirty years, till his death, swapping manuscripts and criticism. My friendship with Lowell dates from the publication of my *Selected Poems* in 1958. *Intellectual Things* had brought Roethke and me together—he was still unpublished. But these are more than literary friendships. In these long and deep associations it's idle to discuss who influences whom. Friendship is a sustained act of reciprocity. We have all been touched by our interchange. Vulnerable human beings affect each other; that's all there is to it.

CD: You wouldn't then put yourself in any group?

SK: Now or at any stage, I can't imagine to what group I could possibly be attached. A one-to-one relationship is the limit of my herd instinct.

CD: What earlier poets would you say influenced you greatly?

SK: Donne and Herbert and Blake were my first major influences—Donne and Herbert stylistically, Blake prophetically. I must have learned something, too, from Wordsworth's "Prelude" and his "Intimations of Immortality." For a while I steeped myself in Keats and Tennyson. After that, almost nobody until Hopkins overwhelmed me during my college years. And Yeats, of course, whom I consider to be the great master of the poem in English in this century. I suppose Eliot to a degree, though I opposed him, quarreling with his ideas, his criticism, and what I thought of as his poverty of sympathy. His theory of the depersonalization of poetry struck me as false and destructive. My work didn't fit into that picture of his at all. Both Roethke and I felt from the beginning that the Eliot school was our principal adversary. We fought for a more passionate art. Nevertheless I was so aware of his existence that even in a negative way I was influenced by him. So was Roethke. That Eliot rhythm had an hypnotic effect.

CD: I'd like to go back for a moment to the question we discussed earlier, your differences from confessional poets. Your latest volume is certainly more directly autobiographical than the others. Rosenthal justifies the use of autobiographical material in confessional poetry by the poet's assumption that the literal self is important and that it becomes symbolic of the world—what happens to the self is what the modern world does to man. How does your idea of poetry differ from that?

SK: I phrase it differently. I say that the effort is to convert one's life into legend, which isn't quite the same thing. Secrets are part of the legend. My emphasis isn't on spilling everything. It's on the act of transformation, the ritual sense, the perception of a destiny.

CD: Is it possible to see these mythic connections even if you're not a poet?

SK: I'm not contending that the poet is set apart from others. On the contrary, he is more like others than anybody else—that's his nature. It's what Keats meant by negative capability, the predisposition to flow into everyone and everything. A poetry of self-indulgence and self-advertisement is produced by the egotistical sublime—Keats's phrase again—and is simply ugly. God knows a poet needs ego, but it has to be consumed in the fire of the poetic action.

CD: Then your view is almost the reverse of the confessional one; you begin with a general idea of the human condition.

SK: The only reason you write about yourself is that this is what you know best. What else has half as much reality for you? Even so, certain details of your life can be clouded by pain, or fear, or shame, or other complications that induce you to lie, to disguise the truth about yourself. But the truth about yourself is no more important than the truth about anybody else. And if you knew anybody else as well as you know yourself, you would write about that other.

New York / March 1972
[*Contemporary Literature*, Winter 1974]

Imagine Wrestling with an Angel

by Robert Boyers

Robert Boyers: Whenever I go and visit people who are interested in poetry, there seems to be constant reference to Stanley Kunitz as the "poets' poet." Have you heard yourself described in this way? What do you think these people mean?

Stanley Kunitz: When it was said of Spenser, it was meant to be a compliment. Nowadays it would depend on the inflection. I'm a bit leery of it.

RB: I was wondering if the fact that people speak of you in these terms suggests that they have in mind another kind of poetry which is more immediately contemporary, more popular among the young on college campuses, and whether this isn't the poetry, this other poetry, that the best poets themselves consider inferior, perhaps not poetry at all?

SK: That may be so, but it's dangerous to think of poetry as being divided into two kinds—a high art and a low art. No poet can afford to be out of touch with the commonplace. In my youth I suppose I rather willed myself on being a hermetic poet. But for years I have tried to make my work more open and accessible, without sacrificing its complex inner tissue. Film, jazz, and rock have been very much a part of my world of experience.

RB: You read many poetry manuscripts. Can you give us some notions of what the younger poets, those who've not published volumes, are writing?

SK: The most notable characteristic of the poetry written by the young—in their twenties or thirties—is its variety. There is no dominant strain that I can detect. So much depends on local interest—regional associations, university teachers who happen at the moment to be available to them as models. A few years ago it seemed to me that the New York school had many adherents over the country, but I think there are fewer now—it seems to have exhausted its potentiality. Certainly Robert Bly and company have a number of acolytes who follow their precepts thundered from on high—but that's only one aspect of the scene. You can find almost as many different styles as you can find poets.

RB: In particular I was interested in one poet who was awarded the Yale Series Prize, Hugh Seidman, in many ways a remarkable poet. Now many of his poems seem to me to be haphazardly put together, and he seems to trust a good deal to what one might call the "happy accident," the chance hit, which is matched, I guess, by a great many unlucky misses. I wonder if you might speak a little bit about that kind of poetry, a poetry which includes the "happy accident."

SK: The concept of chance is inseparable from the act of poetry. Verse that is precalculated and preordained inevitably goes dead. There has to be room for accidents in the writing of a poem. You leave yourself open to the possibility of anything happening and you hope that it will work—if it doesn't, that's your hard luck.

RB: In the volume *The Contemporary Poet as Artist and Critic*, there is a symposium having to do with your poem "Father and Son,"* a very beautiful poem. There is some talk in the symposium about the line in the poem which reads "The night nailed like an orange to my brow." In the course of your response, you speak of the line as an example of that special kind of risk which poets must take, and which constitutes a kind of signature, a unique signature of the poet. Could you speak a little bit about the relationship between a good risk and a bad risk in poetry?

SK: I don't think that you can tell beforehand whether the risk is a good one or a bad one—but if you take no risks, I doubt that much will happen. I want to venture beyond what I know to be safe and correct, to grapple with a possibility that doesn't yet appear.

RB: And would you say that in taking the risk with a line that doesn't seem readily to yield its private associations even to a reader who's armed with the elementary biographical information, you would justify that risk simply on the basis of what you felt strongly at the time the poem was being composed? That is, must one always take into account the presence of the reader who perhaps won't be able to pick up the association?

SK: In the first place the poet hasn't invited the reader to become the judge of his poem—he enters the scene after the event. It is the reader's choice—he can either continue to work with the poem, or he can decide that it offers him nothing, and if he so chooses, that's his privilege. The poet ought not to complain if the reader decides that he doesn't like that particular poem, or that he can't understand it, and turns to another poem, or to somebody else's work. A poet who begins by saying, "I am myself and only myself," is in no position to demand, "You must read me and love me." My own preference is for a poetry that looks fairly simple on the surface, but that moves mysteriously inside its skin.

RB: I'm very interested also in raising the whole question of composition, the process of composition, and I've come upon all sorts of preferences in poets who come at their poems in a great variety of ways. Roethke, for instance, speaks in the *Letters* of carrying around a phrase in his pocket, scrawled on a piece of paper for a very long time, and then of allowing that single phrase or image to develop over perhaps several years, and then watching that phrase lead to others, and finally building an entire poem out of that one single image; or I think of Dylan Thomas establishing a whole string of end rhymes and then sort of backing into the poem, filling in the text that leads to the end rhyme. How do you compose a poem?

SK: I'm a night bird, so that most of my poems happen in the small hours and usually after a long struggle to clean my mind out—to get rid of the day—that's the first step. The poem usually ripples out from something buried. Perhaps you turn over the leaves of your notebook and come across a phrase five years old, or fifteen years old, that leaps out of the page—it's ready now to be played with. And then you begin pushing words and rhythms around. But to me it's mainly dredging, dredging down into the unconscious—trying to find associations, links with the whole life and with the secrets of the life, not with the obvious materials. And so the poem slowly builds. I say it over and over again—whatever I have of it—the lines with which I begin—it's a kind of incantation and maybe a form of self-hypnosis, who knows, but gradually the rhythm begins to take over, and then I know that nothing is going to stop the poem from happening.

RB: Do you think it's possible for a reader of poems, like yourself for instance, to perceive, in reading the poem for the first time, whether it was written with one approach rather than another, whether a poem suggests in its very contours, its surface contours, whether it was constructed out of an image which gave birth to others, or whether it was originally an "idea poem," emerging from a particular thematic concern, a political idea, for instance? Do poems yield that kind of information, do you think?

SK: In the kind of poem I'm talking about the stitching between thoughts and feelings is invisible. I don't really care much for "idea poems" as such. They're a form of illustration.

RB: Who were the poetic models that you adopted and followed as a young poet? Were you, for instance, taken by T. S. Eliot, as others were who came of age in the 1920s and 1930s?

SK: I was moved by him but I resisted him—I think that's the answer there—one could not help but be moved by him because he was a poetic event. Certainly "The Wasteland" shook my world at the moment of its appearance. I can still remember the thrill of picking up my copy of *The Dial* in which it appeared. Subsequently I became a kind of adversary. His definition of poetry as an objective act, a depersonalized performance, was contrary to my own conviction that the art and the life were bound together. I sought a more passionate voice. And I scorned his politics.

RB: Were there other models that you felt closer to in that time, in the twenties, for instance?

SK: Contemporaries? No. The poets who meant most to me then were Yeats (the later Yeats) and Hopkins. I studied both intensively. Hardy was another of my admirations.

RB: Did you study Thomas a good deal, later on, in the forties and in the beginning of the fifties?

SK: Not particularly—though there are five or six of Thomas's poems that I admire. You're talking now of literary fashions—something I have no use for. In the twenties and thirties one had to follow Eliot in order to have an audience. In the late thirties, into the forties, one had to be Audenesque. Then Thomas was the rage. Later the Beats had their turn. And so it goes. The easiest poet to neglect is one who resists classification.

RB: In thinking of tastes and fashions in poetry, I've often been fascinated by a number of things the late Sir Herbert Read used to say about poetry, feeling that a sort of betrayal was involved in a poet's going back over ground that had been amply covered by other poets. Do you think that there is such a thing as regression in the life of poetry, and perhaps more to the point, what is the nature of the function of innovation in poetry? Is it necessary that great poets be radical innovators? Can you conceive of a great poet who is an aesthetic reactionary?

SK: Pound more or less covered that ground when he set aside a category of inventors among the poets. They are not necessarily the strongest voices of an age, but they often have great influence. Pound affected his contemporaries more than, let us say, Yeats did, who was not an inventor, but I would be willing to say flatly that Yeats is the greater poet.

RB: You would say, then, that the whole idea of regression in the life of poetry is not really a viable notion, that it is possible to go back over old ground, and to do things which are essentially similar to what earlier poets perfected?

SK: The trouble with Read's idea is that the idea of regression, like the idea of progress, has no aesthetic relevance. The way backward and the way forward are the same. A rediscovery of the past often leads to radical innovation. We know, for example, that Picasso was inspired by African sculpture, that the art of the Renaissance is linked with the resurgence of classical myth. Poetic technique follows the same route. At the moment I can think of Hopkins, who went back to Old English for his sprung rhythm; of Pound, who tuned his ear on Provençal song; of Berryman, who dug up inversion and minstrel patter for his *Dream Songs*. These are all acts of renewal, not tired replays of the style of another period—which is the last thing I am prepared to defend. Pound was, of course, right, in his criticism of "The Wasteland" manuscript, when he dissuaded Eliot from trying to compete with Pope in the matter of composing heroic couplets. As he said, Pope could do it better. In general, a poet has to rework—not imitate—the past, and the success of his reworking is dependent on the degree of his contemporary awareness. If a poet has an ear for the living speech—whose rhythmic pattern is ever so slightly modified from generation to generation—he has at least the foundation of a style, the one into which he was born. I recall that Roethke and I used to challenge each other to guess the dates of the most obscure poems we could find. Over a long period we became so expert at the game that we almost never missed by more than ten years. It was simply because the voice, the stylistic voice, of any decade is unmistakable.

RB: Is there such a thing as a direct relation between the poet and the particular moment of his culture, conceived as a political situation? What I'm referring to is the kind of statement we've heard from Denise Levertov of late, where the claim is made that a poet who is of his time must necessarily reflect the moment of his culture, especially when that culture is in crisis and turmoil, that to indulge a strictly personal kind of poetry at a time when one's own country is engaged in destroying thousands of people in Vietnam, for instance, is to do something that is totally irresponsible and runs counter to the whole life of poetry. Does that make any sense to you?

SK: The war disgusts and outrages me, just as it does Denise, but I'm not inclined to tell other poets what they may or may not write. Each of us has to be trusted with his own conscience. The fanatic is the direct opposite of the poet. It's no accident that most of the poetry of confrontation is such appalling stuff. What could be more spiritually stultifying than an exclusive diet of antiwar or anti-Nixon tracts? An age in crisis needs more than ever to be made aware of the full range of human possibility.

RB: In that respect, what do you see as the basic function of your own art? Is it essentially designed to give pleasure, is it educative, does it serve the function of rendering the general experience more complex?

SK: Let me try to reply in a historical context. Modern poetry, in the long view, springs out of the Age of Enlightenment and the Industrial Revolution. When faith withered and the Church could no longer satisfy the universal need for otherness, poetry became the alternative medium of transcendence. The poet assumed, or reasserted—from an earlier tribal structure—an ambiguous but socially disturbing role with prophetic or shamanistic implications. One of his functions—as Blake clearly understood—was to serve as defender of the natural universe and of natural man against the greed and ambition of the spoilers and their faceless agents. Politically, I see the poet as the representative free man, the irreconcilable adversary of the nation-state.

RB: Is there any useful connection to be made, in a general sense, between age and creativity? Many have claimed that the creative powers wane with the advancing years, yet we all know of very wonderful poets who seemed to have their powers grow stronger with the passage of the years. For me, for instance, the major period of William Carlos Williams is his final period, though that is not the case, of course, with people like Eliot or Stevens. Is there any general relationship that's worth pointing to?

SK: The determining factor there is the relationship between the life and the work. Yeats has a phrase, "radical innocence," that I cherish. As I interpret it, it's the capacity for perpetual self-renewal, as opposed to a condition of emotional exhaustion or world-weariness; it's waking each day to the wonder of possibility; it's being like a child—which is not to say being childish. "There lives the dearest freshness deep down things"—Hopkins's line—that's an expression of radical innocence. With Blake, it's the very essence of his art and of his prophetic function. The poets of radical innocence stay alive till the day they die—and, even then, they take that last step as an adventure.

RB: When I think of radical innocence, I think also of Roethke's special freshness and innocence. Could you tell us a little bit about how you came to know Roethke and what he was like in your experience of him?

SK: In the mid-thirties I was living in an old stone house in New Hope, Pennsylvania—it's the setting of a number of my poems, including the one called "River Road." I can still remember Roethke standing there, a big blond hulk in a raccoon coat, with my first book of poems in his hand.

Intellectual Things had been published in 1930 and had received some attention, but I still felt almost completely isolated from the literary world. Ted was then unpublished, except for a handful of poems in magazines. The first thing he told me, after I asked him in, was that he knew several of my poems by heart; and he proceeded to prove it, after a drink or two, by reciting a couple of his favorites. Would I look at his own stuff? I would, and did. We talked through that whole night. At last I had found a friend who was as mad about poetry as I was! We were two outsiders, and we needed each other. In one respect his need was greater, since I have never been able to show unfinished work to anybody.

RB: He used to send you drafts of his poems, didn't he? How did he take to criticism and to suggestions for revision?

SK: He hated criticism, most poets do. He would sulk, he was a great sulker, and if I said a poem of his didn't work he would get into a corner and ask for another drink and put his head down and breathe heavily. Oh, his silences were forbidding. He couldn't stand being rushed. A poem had to be sweated out. Eventually he would come around to doing whatever needed to be done. No one was more of a perfectionist. And he was endlessly fascinated by technique. How he despised poets who were afflicted with what he called a "tin ear"!

RB: Do you remember the kinds of suggestions you might characteristically make to Roethke about his poems, the ones he was writing in the thirties and forties?

SK: One of Roethke's problems in the beginning was that he was so impressionable. There was a good deal of Eliot in those early poems . . . obvious echoes. An even stronger influence was his friend Louise Bogan. The other women who influenced his work, but to a lesser degree, were Elinor Wylie and Léonie Adams. Sometimes I'd find my own lines coming back to me—that was a delicate matter. Then the poems tended to be a little too fussy in their working, too neatly structured and resolved. I wanted him to pry open his interior world. In those early years of our association I tried to liberate him into his own identity. When the liberation occurred, I was overwhelmed.

RB: Has your estimation of Roethke and his work changed much over the years?

SK: In my review of *The Lost Son* for *Poetry* magazine in 1948, I announced that here was a great book, the voice of a superb imagination, and I haven't wavered from that conviction to this day.

RB: You feel as strongly about the posthumous volume, *The Far Field*?

SK: It could be argued that Roethke had already gone as far in his journey as he had strength to go. Certainly not all the poems in *The Far Field* are first-rate, but enough of them are to augment any other poet's reputation. Why do critics want to fasten on the inferior poems, the failures, of a poet? It must be in order to establish the superiority of the critical act. My only interest is in the poems that will stand.

RB: How about your relationship to Lowell, to Lowell's poetry? When did it begin, and what can you say about him, from your knowledge of his manuscripts and working habits?

SK: I didn't meet Lowell till the late fifties, when he was working on *Life Studies*. A few times the three of us—Roethke, Lowell, and myself—were together—but I don't recall them as particularly happy occasions. It's difficult to talk about someone who is close, but I can't refrain from observing that one of Cal's most extraordinary aspects is that he doesn't so much write his poems as rewrite them. Criticism is more important to him than to any artist I've ever known. His imagination feeds on it, as it does on history. His earlier associations—with Tate, Jarrell, and Elizabeth Bishop—each a poet with a fine critical intelligence—had a major impact on his development. At this stage he is uniquely himself, but his manuscripts and even his proof sheets still read like palimpsests. And he is never done with a poem, not even after you would suppose it to be finally stamped into books and anthologies. Likely as not, the next time around, it will appear in a different version, revamped word by word and line by line. His work, as well as his life, is always in progress.

RB: Do you especially care for the work of poets whose names are frequently linked with Lowell as part of the confessional school? Do you feel any kinship with poets like Snodgrass, or Sylvia Plath? Is this where the energy of our best poetry has been?

SK: I must tell you that, like most poets, I hate labels. I'm not quite sure what confessional poetry is, though certain critics have seen fit to discuss me as a late convert to that school. I guess I resent that. I've always admired a fierce subjectivity; but compulsive exhibitionism—and there's plenty of that around—gobs of sticky hysteria—are an embarrassment. Perhaps I sound more censorious than I intend. One of my premises is that you can say anything as long as it is true . . . but not everything that's true is worth saying. Another is that you need not be a victim of your shame . . . but neither should you boast about it. In this context maybe Roethke showed me a way of coping with affliction. Nearly all his adult life he was a manic-depressive, subject to intermittent crack-ups of devastating violence. In the beginning he was terribly ashamed of these episodes and tried to conceal them, even from his closest friends. When he was sent away to a mental hospital, he pretended that he had gone off on vacation. The onset of his best work coincided with his discovery that he need not feel guilty about his illness; that it was a condition he could explore and use; that it was, in fact, convertible into daemonic energy, the driving power of imagination. At the same time he began to read Jung, who clarified for him the act of psychic regression, that is, of reliving one's embryonic passage through fish-shape, frog-shape, bird-shape until one is born human. That knowledge, that deep metamorphic awareness, became the source of Roethke's strength in his major poems. What they speak of is archetypal experience—which has nothing to do with being a "confessional" poet.

RB: You've spoken of your own work in terms of the note of tragic exaltation. Can you describe what this constitutes, how you see this tonality functioning in your poems? Does it bear relation to what we get in classical tragedy, for instance?

SK: Not much—but maybe in so far as recognition is an element of Greek tragedy. It's easier to locate the feeling than to define it. I could offer some lines as touchstone: "I stand on the terrible threshold, and I see / The end and the beginning in each other's arms." Or Mandelstam, at a greater distance, saying: "Only the flash of recognition brings delight." Or Pascal invoking "the eternal silence of the infinite spaces." Not everybody detects the exaltation, for it's a far more secret thing than terror or despair. Imagine wrestling with an angel, the darkest one of the tribe. You know you're doomed to lose. But that weight on your shoulder!

RB: Do you read much besides creative or imaginative literature? Do you keep up with developments in psychoanalysis, in aesthetics, in the sciences, and so on?

SK: I try to, except for aesthetics, which seems to me an arid subject. Astrophysics has always fascinated me. And anything to do with the natural universe. Right now I'm deep in whales.

RB: But you do feel that the most exciting things at the moment are still poetry, that the work of young and coming poets is still more exciting and alive than work done in other areas?

SK: No doubt I'm prejudiced, but I honestly believe that the poetic imagination is capable of embracing the actualities of our time more fully than any other discipline, including the scientific. That's one explanation of my involvement with the graduate writing program at Columbia, with the Yale Series of Younger Poets, and with the Fine Arts Work Center in Provincetown, Massachusetts, where young writers and artists can find a loosely structured community, created for their benefit. Has anyone noticed how the poetic and scientific imaginations are beginning to draw together for mutual sustenance? Perhaps it's an instinctive alliance determined by our crisis of survival. You mentioned Seidman earlier, my first poetry choice at Yale. He was trained as a physicist, and is an expert on the computer. My second choice, Peter Klappert, was a student of zoology who planned to be a veterinarian. Michael Casey, who came back from Vietnam with his collection of *Obscenities*, was another physics major who expected to become an engineer, till the Yale award threw him off his course. Robert Hass's book isn't out yet, but its title, *Field Guide*, suggests that it isn't incompatible with the others. Love and botany are his twin preoccupations. Different kinds of intellect may be turning to poetry out of desperation, but it's a good sign, nevertheless.

RB: You mentioned last night that you've been working on a long poem. Is there any special reason why you haven't written one before now, and could you speak a little bit about the general failure of our poets to write successful long poems, in most cases even to undertake them?

SK: The problem of the long poem, like that of the novel, is related to our loss of faith in the validity of the narrative continuum. Joyce invented a technique for coping with a new time sense, but that required a super-human effort, which no longer seems consistent with an antiheroic age. The collapse of Pound's *Cantos* remains a central symptomatic event. Technically he understood the problem, as his contribution to the making of "The Wasteland" proves, but his own project was too indeterminate, and he had overreached himself in the matter of scale. As a collection of fragments, of fairly limited scope, "The Wasteland" seems better adapted for enduring the weathers of an age. I suppose the last major effort to build a solid block of marble was Hart Crane's—and "The Bridge" has its magnificence, but it is the magnificence of failure. "Mistress Bradstreet" and "Howl" are passionate apostrophes, but their architecture is too frail for the weight of their rhetoric. Berryman's *Dream Songs* and Lowell's *Notebook*—to be called *History* in its next incarnation—don't aspire to the unity of the long poem. Essentially they're poetic sequences, like the sonnet cycles of the Elizabethans. I am half-persuaded that the modern mind is too distracted for the span of attention demanded by the long poem, and that no single theme, given the disorder of our epoch, is capable of mobilizing that attention. But I am only half-persuaded.

RB: I also wanted to ask you about the whole question of obscurity in the poem, something that Randall Jarrell suggests in a number of places to the effect that in an age which is so apt to appropriate poems, to convert them into acrobats of a sort, it may in fact be the business of the poet to be obscure, to challenge this audience, to make readers uncomfortable, to make them work for whatever pleasures they can get from the poem. Do you feel any sympathy with that?

SK: During the heyday of the New Criticism, there were poets who trafficked in obfuscation, providing grist for the critics who trafficked in the explication of obfuscation. A beautiful symbiotic relationship! Poets today tend to be clearer—sometimes all too clear. I strive for a transparency of surface, but I should be disappointed if my work yielded all its substance and tonality at first reading. "Never try to explain," I say somewhere. A poem is charged with a secret life. Some of its information ought to circulate continuously within its perimeters as energy. And that, as I see it, is the function of form: to contain the energy of a poem, to prevent it from leaking out.

RB: You spoke last night at dinner of the frustrations of so many contemporary artists, and this led you to reflect on the idea of the poet as monster. Would you care to expatiate?

SK: It's a notion that enters into several of my poems—for instance, "The Approach to Thebes," and later "The Artist,"* which grew out of my friendship with Mark Rothko. So many of my attachments are to the world of painters and sculptors. I recall a conversation with Mark one evening, in which I referred to Picasso—not without admiration—as a monster. And then I added Joyce's name, for good measure. Mark was troubled by my epithet. I tried to explain to him why, in the modern arts, the words "genius" and "monster" may be interchangeable. His face darkened. "You don't mean me, do you?" he asked. Less than a year later he was dead, by his own hand. What is it in our culture that drives so many artists and writers to suicide—or, failing that, mutilates them spiritually? At the root of the problem is the cruel discrepancy between the values of art and the values of society, which makes strangers and adversaries out of those who are most gifted and vulnerable. The artist who turns in on himself, feeds off his own psyche, aggrandizes his bruised ego, is on his way to monsterdom. Ambition is the fire in his gut. No sacrifice is judged too great for his art. At a certain point he becomes a nexus of abstract sensations and powers, beyond the realm of the personal. That's when the transformation into monster occurs. I don't mean to imply that everybody is worthy of that designation—it requires a special kind of greatness . . . Sylvia Plath's, for example. If we search among the poets of an older generation for the masters who were whole, who excelled in their humanity, who fulfilled themselves in the life as well as in the work, whom can we name? Not most of "the best among us"—in Pound's words. Certainly not Pound himself, not Eliot, not Yeats, nor Frost, nor Stevens . . . the list could be extended indefinitely. I am told that Pasternak was a notable exception, and I know, closer to home, that William Carlos Williams was another. Then I have to pause. They make a shining pair. The young around us give me hope that eventually they'll have plenty of company. But the condition may well be the creation of a new society.

Saratoga Springs, New York / April 1972
[*Salmagundi*, Spring-Summer 1973]

Periodicity

by Michael Ryan

Michael Ryan: Your first book of poems, *Intellectual Things*, was published in 1930. What are your reflections on continuing to write poems seriously for almost fifty years?

Stanley Kunitz: I suppose my main feeling is that writing poetry, for me, has been like breathing. It has been the condition of my existence. I've never considered surviving without poetry. The first poems come to you out of nowhere. You don't know that you are a vessel; all you know is that you have poems that have to be written. Later, those early poems seem completely extraordinary because you realize that you were a terribly immature person emotionally. I think most people in their early or mid-twenties are not ready to take the mantle of "poet" over their shoulders and say "I am a poet." It's a little ridiculous to make that assumption at that time in your life—it may be ridiculous at any time. I think of one's feeling for language as a kind of prehensile thing; it must be in the genes. You don't know why you're writing poems, any more than a cat knows why it claws at the bark of a tree, but you're doing it. Because you have to do it. And your intellectual life, such as it is at that stage, is really something separate from your feeling for the language itself. Basically, the young poet has to model himself on the poets whom he loves, preferably not on those who happen to be in fashion at the moment.

MR: If I remember correctly, the only poet you mention explicitly in any of your poems is Marvell. There is a definite affinity to the metaphysical poets in that first volume. Would you say that was your initial influence?

SK: I was mad about the metaphysical poets. During the time when I started writing seriously, I was at Harvard, studying primarily with John Livingston Lowes. In the backgound were Irving Babbitt, whom I also worked with and who I thought was an enemy of everything I believed in, and Kittredge, who was the great scholiast of the period. But Lowes was the one who really taught poetry, and his faith was in the romantic poets, as was mine initially. There wasn't even a course in the metaphysical poets. So I came upon them independently, and they seemed closest to that particular quality of voice and mind that I cared about.

MR: One thing that strikes me in reading your first volume is your attraction to forms. Wasn't part of Eliot and Pound's influence at the time to break strict form?

SK: The poems in *Intellectual Things* date from 1927, when I was twenty-two. It's true that Eliot came to notice about 1916 or so, and so did Pound, with their first writings, but they had no reputation in the academic or general world. I proposed writing my master's thesis at Harvard on the techniques of the modern writers; the ones I included were Hopkins, Eliot, Cummings, Joyce, Marianne Moore, and, I believe, Proust. When I presented my proposal to the head of the department, Lowes, he looked at me in absolute amazement and said, "You mean to take these people seriously? Don't you know that they're only pulling our legs?" That's about where the modern movement was then. It's difficult to explain now, but historically the way into the new poetry was through the doorway of the seventeenth century, through the rediscovery of the metaphysical tradition. Tone and technique were the primary agitations.

MR: Invariably in your first book, the poems adhere to a strict rhyme scheme and metrical pattern, but in many cases the way in which the line is broken tends to conceal that. So the question arises, why use conventional form in order to subsume it?

SK: I suppose I believed in an art of limitations, in certain restrictions that the form itself imposes; however, I also believed that if you insisted upon them too strictly, if, for example, you made your rhymes so obvious that there was no escaping them, the result would be an offense to the ear. Basically I've always written according to what my ear told me, and not according to any arbitrary system of metrics or linear conventions. From the beginning, although I was writing in rhyming and metric patterns, I wanted to escape their omnipresence. So the art was one of using the conventions, but trying to move within their limits so that the conventions were not obvious.

MR: And the limitation, perhaps, forced discoveries?

SK: The setting up of a form, whatever the form may be, implies certain limitations. The problem, then, is to be as free as possible within that necessity of your choice. If you don't have boundaries, you are faced with infinity. And my assumption is that art is incapable of dealing with infinity, at least in any formal sense.

MR: Where, then, does the restriction or limitation come from when you do not write using conventional form, as in many of the poems in your most recent book, *The Testing-Tree*?

SK: I have a music haunting my ear, so that's one limitation. A second is that in writing what may look like free verse I have a system of strong beats in mind. In recent years my line has been getting shorter, partly because I'm cutting down on the adjectives—I'm usually down to two or three stresses to a line. This permits any number of syllables, within reason, as long as the ground pattern is preserved. But the controls are really in the ear itself, and I don't think they should be anywhere else. The ear must tell you if a line is too long, too short, if it lacks a backbone, if it's nerveless, if it has enough promontories, if it has tension of any kind.

MR: That system of stresses is very apparent in the title poem, "The Testing-Tree,"* and in "The Customs-Collector's Report" and "River Road," but its less obvious to me in "Robin Redbreast"* and "The Mulch."* Maybe the latter two poems are simply less incantatory.

SK: They probably are, but I think that in terms of what I call functional stressing they follow very closely a pattern the ear has determined.

MR: And that's an intuitive pattern?

SK: It is not counted. I write my poems by saying them. It's the only way I know how to write. If it doesn't satisfy my ear then I know it's wrong. So essentially I'm proceeding from the same basis I always did, which is the feeling that poetry has an allegiance to music and another allegiance to dance. The problem for the poet is to both sing and dance, and yet remain within the limits of language.

MR: A tension arises, does it not, between the impulse toward sound and the impulse toward content?

SK: That's the tragic nexus of poetry. The poem wants to be pure sound and it also wants to be straight sense, and it can never be either.

MR: Because if it's straight sense it's simply discursive prose?

SK: So why put it in a poem?

MR: And if it's pure sound, it's music?

SK: And poetry is neither, but yearns in both directions.

MR: Do you think either impulse could be identified as a primary source for the poem?

SK: The word that needs to be introduced in this context is "periodicity." This is what we learn from our immersion in the natural world: its cyclical pattern. The day itself is periodic, from morning through noon to night, so too the stars in their passage, the tides, the seasons, the beat of the heart, women in their courses. This awareness of periodicity is what gives us the sense of a universal pulse. And any art that does not convey that sense is a lesser art. In poetry, it leads us, as Coleridge very definitely saw, toward an organic principle. I suppose that perception by Coleridge is the most profound assertion ever made about the nature of poetry, which I regard as the supreme art. All the other arts, except music as composition, require some matter in order to fulfill themselves. The great thing about poetry is that your selfhood is simultaneously your instrument and your vessel. The words of a poem are like a second skin. They're not apart from the self; they're inwoven with the tissue of the life.

MR: Language also has a history apart from any individual, which leads to an inexorable fact, for me, that the poem has an existence apart from the poet. It tells him at times what to say. There is always a tension, for me, between self and history, poet and poem.

SK: I don't think that's too different from the way your body tells you you're in love, you're growing old, or you're about to die. The language tells you it has certain preordained conditions: it has, for example, syntax; it has vocabulary; it has symbolic meaning. Nobody owns it. When you touch language, you touch the evolution of consciousness and the history of the tribe. You reach for a tool, a common tool, and find to your surprise that it has a cuneiform inscription on the handle.

MR: I would like to talk more about the development of your work. Since you've already described some of the changes that have occurred in your poems in terms of form, could you talk about how your concerns or subjects have changed? In the first book, for example, there's an obsession with thought, brain, concept, and the poems are self-reflecting; in the most recent book, the poems are quieter and more involved with the external world. How do you see this development?

SK: Naturally my poems reflect my transformations, though I should hope you might detect in them some spirit or principle that persists. My early writing was dense and involuted—so, I guess, was I! Now what I am seeking is a transparency of language and vision. Maybe age itself compels me to embrace the great simplicities, as I struggle to free myself from the knots and complications, the hang-ups, of my youth. Not that I have forgotten, or want to forget, the rages of my unhappy years—they still seethe inside me. It's true that I am astonished, in my sixties, by the depth of my affection for this life. It's equally true that I am no more reconciled than I ever was to the world's wrongs and the injustice of time.

MR: You say the rage is still seething. Is that rage important to a poet, to his work?

SK: No question of that. A poet needs to keep his wilderness alive inside him. One of the prerequisites for remaining a poet after, let's say, the age of forty or fifty, is an awareness of the wilderness within oneself that will never be domesticated, never tamed. He must never avert his face completely from the terrors of that dark underworld.

MR: In the most recent book, you're obviously interested in history as a material for poems; in the first book, the analogous material is myth and theology. Do you see this development as a transference of the same impulse?

SK: I don't think it's as clear as your description implies. There are poems in *The Testing-Tree* that are just as involved with archetypes as anything I've ever done. And the historic materials, as I see them, overrun the foothills of myth.

MR: Do you see that impulse, if I can so identify your interest in myth and history, as a way out of the ego?

SK: Perhaps. The self renews and fortifies itself by falling in love with time. Otherwise it's doomed to repeat itself indefinitely. One hopes to remain open and vulnerable, to keep on being terrified by history.

MR: Do you think that the activity of writing causes most poets to be monomaniacal, in the sense that it is inherent in the activity itself that one can only write about a limited part of one's entire life?

SK: Oh, yes. In this respect, one of the chains around every poet's neck is his own development as a poet. His beginnings are largely a generational phenomenon, a combination of accidents and influences; thereafter, he builds on that foundation. Maybe at a certain point he would prefer a fresh start, but the difficulty is that he has already established the condition of his art. To change your style you have to change your life. I think almost any of the poets we value, if they had lived long enough, might have become their opposites as poets. No single kind of poetry would be sufficient for a millennium.

MR: You have not been the most prolific poet in the history of literature.

SK: God, no.

MR: That implies a way of working that is perhaps partially not determined and partially determined. Do you want to talk about that?

SK: Sure. I realize that reputations are made by volume as much as by anything else. Most of the big reputations in modern American poetry have been made on the basis of a large body of work. That doesn't happen to be my style. Over a lifetime I've written poems only when I felt I had poems to write. I do not feel apologetic about refusing to convert myself into a machine for producing verse. Sometimes I think that poets have become a nation of monsters. The anomaly is that, as one of the few survivors of my generation of poets, I'm suddenly threatening to become prolific—for me, that is.

MR: Do you think it's harder now to have that patience in relationship to the work? Insofar as the university has become the new patron in recent years, the situation for a young poet, or perhaps for any poet, is such that he must publish a book in order to teach. And not just one book, but two books, three books, and four books, sometimes all too quickly. Was the atmosphere more conducive to having that patience thirty or forty years ago?

SK: To answer your question, I'll tell you something of my history. When I was about to receive my master's degree from Harvard, I assumed that I could stay on as a teaching assistant if I wanted to, not because I was already a poet but because of my scholarship record. As it turned out, I did not stay on; I was told indirectly through the head of the English department that Anglo-Saxons would resent being taught English by a Jew, even by a Jew with a *summa cum laude*. That shook my world. It seemed to me such a cruel and wanton rejection that I turned away from academic life completely. After I left Harvard, I had no real contact with universities for almost twenty years; I worked on a newspaper, farmed, free-lanced, edited publications.

Then something completely fortuitous happened. In 1945, I was in the army—my third year—and wretched for various reasons. I was a conscientious objector who had accepted service on the premise that I would not bear arms, but the army refused to acknowledge the terms of our agreement—a nightmare from beginning to end. Out of nowhere I received a wire from Bennington College offering me a position on the English faculty as soon as I was discharged. Of course I snatched at it. One needs a revolution every few years, and in my circumstances this seemed heavensent. I knew that Roethke was at Bennington, but didn't know that he had been through a violent manic episode—one of his worst. They wanted to ease him out, but he was being difficult about it. Finally, he told them he would leave quietly on one condition: [that they] hire Kunitz. So that's how I began teaching.

I suppose my personal experience is involved with my feelings about poets in the university. On the whole I think it's stultifying for young poets to leap immediately into the academic life. They would be better off tasting the rigors of a less regulated existence. I was over forty when I began to teach, and I am grateful now for the difficult years of my preparation. And I still consider myself a free agent, moving from place to place, never accepting tenure. Blake said, "I must create a system myself or be enslaved by another man's." If a poet wants to wait thirty years to publish his next book, he should be given thirty years. What difference does it make in the eye of eternity?

MR: You published your first poems in magazines such as *The Dial* and *Hound and Horn*.

SK: That's right.

MR: How do those magazines compare to those which are published today?

SK: One of the nostalgic feelings I have now is for those publications. I remember I had just graduated from college when I sent my first batch of poems to *The Dial*. Within ten days I received a handwritten letter from Marianne Moore, who was editing *The Dial* then. It was a very simple little message to this effect: "Dear Mr. Kunitz: I have read your poems, and I do admire them. We shall be so happy to publish them." I felt I had been blessed by the gods. There are no magazines now that are even faintly analogous to *The Dial*. I don't really care where I publish anymore. Several of the young poets I know have that same feeling of diffidence. There's no publication today that gives them a sense of sanction. A great loss.

MR: Has the audience for poetry changed since that time?

SK: The audience is bigger and, I think, more knowing than it has ever been. That's the paradox. Certainly, it has spun off into scattered little urban cells and colleges; but still, it's there, everywhere you go, a community of friends, waiting, listening. When I was a college student, and for a decade or two thereafter, no contemporary poetry was taught in the universities. Poets were not asked to read, let alone to teach. The underlying assumption was that poetry, after Kipling and Amy Lowell, was not a respectable vocation.

MR: Can you compare the quality of the poetry itself?

SK: It's better now. No comparison. And so much of it! Even morons nowadays seem able to write "accomplished" poems.

MR: We do seem to have passed the age of literary giants. Do you have an explanation for that?

SK: The reason is clear. In one sense, art is inseparable from politics. In hierarchical societies, genius tends to flow to the top—it percolates down on the lesser fry from the towering few who dominate the age. As society becomes more and more democratized, the genius of the race is dispersed among larger and larger numbers. A dilution occurs, so that perhaps now there are twenty poets who together are the equivalent of a Milton. There is however, no Milton.

MR: Is that unfortunate?

SK: I doubt it. Perhaps it's a reversion to primitive societies, where everybody composes songs. Maybe we're inching back to some sort of chorus of poets—no great poets, but still, now and then, great poems.

MR: The reversion you describe calls to mind McLuhan's notion of the global village. Do you think the popular media have influenced poetry in any way?

SK: The popular media, by definition, attract the attention of most of the people most of the time—and, of course, they're easy to take. I see no reason why an oral tradition and a written tradition shouldn't coexist— they've done so for centuries. Historically the former has influenced the latter, as when the ballads entered into the stream of English romanticism. Right now the contrary is true. Bob Dylan, Leonard Cohen, Rod McKuen, for example, in a descending scale of interest, are byproducts, vulgarizations, of the literary tradition. Compare them with the jazz musicians or the gospel singers, who were authentic expressions of the folk.

MR: Do you think it's possible to integrate politics and poetry? Some of the poems in your second book, *Passport to the War*, as the title implies, do have political content. I suppose the most obvious attempt at the integration right now is in the poetry of the women's movement.

SK: You cannot separate poets from the society in which they function. The relationship between the poet and his world is an obligatory theme; no poet is granted exemption. He cannot cannibalize himself indefinitely. Even his avoidance of politics is a political gesture. The moot question is one of aesthetic strategies. When the black revolution was at its height less than a decade ago, the sympathies of most poets, I think, were with the black revolutionaries. And yet the poetry that came out of it was, for the most part, coarse and shapeless and finally unreadable. That, of course, is not to negate the virtue of the cause for which it was written. By the same token, most of the poems overtly incited by the women's liberation movement are diminished by their rant and rhetoric. Yeats was at least partly right when he said that the opposite of the poet is the opinionated man—today he would have added "and woman," despite the damage to his prose.

MR: Akhmatova's poetry has political content, does it not?

SK: She's a political poet, but in her work the politics are subsumed in the life. You're hardly aware of the political content of the poems; what moves you is her personal involvement in the issues that make the poem. For example, "Requiem," one of the masterpieces of modern Russian literature, is not a diatribe against the Stalinist terror that blighted her life and took her son from her. What it conveys is a sense of tragic landscape, the desolation of hearts in a heartless epoch. Akhmatova learned from Dante the necessity for human scale in depicting the crimes of history.

MR: How did you become interested in undertaking such a project as translating the poems of Akhmatova?

SK: Through my friendship with Voznesensky I rediscovered my own Russian ancestry, which I had almost forgotten. And suddenly I felt close to Russian poetry, as though I had been waiting to hear it for years. Then I visited Russia in 1967 as part of the cultural exchange program, and I became deeply involved in the lives and fates of her poets. Akhmatova's pure and unaffected voice is the kind of speech I value. I think I can learn from her. That's as good a reason as any for trying to translate her.

MR: Is the obligation you place on yourself as a translator to make sure that the voice comes through? Do you have to choose between a faithfulness to the literal version and the making of a poem in English?

SK: That's the crux of the problem—a contradiction of loyalties. On the face of it, there is no resolution. But that doesn't deter you from attempting the impossible.

MR: I'd like to return for a moment to something we touched upon earlier. I can't imagine how it must have been to begin writing in the literary situation of the twenties. Were you intimidated by Eliot? Or is his dominance of the poetry of the age a fiction of literary history?

SK: It's not a literary fiction at all. To be born in my generation is to have been born in the shadow of the great names that belonged to the previous generation: Eliot, Pound, Frost, Robinson, Stevens, William Carlos Williams, although he was more of a democratic spirit than the others. Living in the country, I had no literary friends except for Roethke, who visited me occasionally and with whom I corresponded, exchanging manuscripts. It didn't occur to me that the senatorial generation might be interested in what I was doing, and I didn't expect them to be. Today young poets feel perfectly free to converse with their elders, and this is one of the healthiest aspects of the contemporary scene, this conversation going on. But for my generation it was inconceivable that we would even hope for any colloquy with or recognition from our seniors. Nothing happened till I was almost fifty to abate my natural feeling of isolation. But the truth is that I've never gotten over feeling like a loner.

MR: I'm sure that friendship between you and Roethke was very important to you.

SK: Both of us needed support and encouragement. For me, Ted was a link to that world of poetry with which I had no other connection. When he came to visit me, he always brought news of other poets. I would hear about those he admired most, the ones he saw, the ones he courted. The interesting aspect of Roethke in his youth was that above all he respected formal excellence, as his early poems indicate. That's where he really learned about the freedom he could later entertain—from the restraints he practiced in his early work.

MR: I'd like to ask you about your method of working in relation to a specific poem. Would you read "The Man Upstairs?"

SK: The old man sick with boyhood fears,
           Whose thin shanks ride the naked blast,
           Intones; the gray somnambulist
           Creaks down interminable stairs,
           Dreaming my future as his past.

           A flower withers in its vase.
           A print detaches from the wall,
           Beyond the last electric bill
           Slow days are crumbling into days
           Without the unction of farewell.

Tonight there suffers in my street
The passion of the silent clerk
Whose drowned face cries the windows dark
Where once the bone of mercy beat.
I turn; I perish into work.

O Magus with the leathern hand,
The wasted heart, the trailing star,
Time is your madness, which I share,
Blowing next winter into mind . . .
And love herself not there, not there.

MR: Beautiful. That's a terrific poem.

SK: I still like it, too; it's always amazed me that none of the anthologies have ever picked up that one. They are rather incredibly imperceptive about the poems that lie at the core of one's work.

MR: The whole structure of the poem, its movement, is what makes it powerful for me, but I want to concentrate on one detail of the language: "I perish into work." A naive question, but I hope a purposeful one, How do we come up with that sort of discovery?

SK: I have a sense of using the life, of exhausting it in the work itself. The analogue, of course, is the dying image involved with sex. As far as the poet is concerned, life is always dying into art.

MR: Do you keep a notebook?

SK: Yes, I'm always putting down lines, phrases, images, even pasting clippings, anything that teases my mind. I have stacks and stacks of material that interests and excites me and I keep collecting. There's so much of it, I can never find anything specific—not if I'm looking for it, but if I'm leafing through my notebooks, something I jotted down months or years ago often catches my eye. It's been there all the time, sleeping, and at the same time it's been simmering in my own mind. And I look at it and suddenly I can see what else it's hooked to, what other buried phenomena. And at that point, when it signals its attachment to the layers of the life, I can use it.

MR: When is a poem finished for you?

SK: That's a hard question. I really say my poems, as I mentioned earlier. I keep putting down the words as I say them. Usually, after starting a poem in longhand, I type what I have, because I need to get a sense of its look on the page. And then it's a process of building up line after line, discarding the earlier versions and starting again from scratch. Any one poem can involve up to one hundred sheets of paper, because it always starts from the beginning and goes as far as it can. When it's blocked, I start all over again and try to gather enough momentum to break through the barrier. That's more or less my method of composition. When there are no more impediments on the page and my original impulse is exhausted, I go to bed. I'm a night worker.

MR: How do you teach the writing of poetry?

SK: Thoroughly. Passionately. Long ago I discarded theories. The danger of the poet-as-teacher lies in his imposing his *persona* on his students. I welcome any kind of poet; I don't care if he is my kind or not. Some of the best students I've worked with have turned out to be my own opposites. But that doesn't bother me at all.

MR: Does your idea of teaching correspond to your interpretation of your position as editor and judge of the Yale Series of Younger Poets?

SK: I think it does. My obligation there, first of all, is to read everything that is submitted; second, to be as open and fair and objective as I can. I don't look for any specific kind of poet when I read those manuscripts. I'm looking for a poet. Let me add that nobody has an inside track. All but one of the poets I've picked have been perfect strangers.

MR: Your selected prose will be published by Atlantic Monthly Press next spring—essays and conversations. Why now?

SK: Maybe it's time for me to find out whether all the stuff I've turned out on poetry and art and politics makes any sense when put together.

MR: Here's a valedictory question: Can you talk briefly about the direction your own poetry is taking now?

SK: It's fairly clear to me that I'm moving toward a more expansive universe. I propose to take more risks than I ever did. Thank God I don't have to ask anyone else's premission to do what I want to do. If I give it my imprimatur, it's OK. That's the privilege and insolence of age.

New York / January 1974
[*The Iowa Review*, Spring 1974]

The Taste of Self

by Christopher Busa

NOTE: During the winter of 1977 my Provincetown friend and neighbor Chris Busa came to New York to talk with me, over drinks, about poetry and related matters. The full account of our conversation, consolidating two afternoons of taping, eventually appeared in *The Paris Review*, Number 83, Spring 1982. This is a somewhat abbreviated version of that text, with minor editorial changes, as published in my *Next-to-Last Things: New Poems and Essays*, Atlantic Monthly Press, 1985.

S.K.

Christopher Busa: Is it an actual fact, as you indicate in "The Portrait,"* that your father killed himself in a public park some months before you were born?

Stanley Kunitz: I really didn't know too much about it. It floated in the air during my childhood. I never had any specific information. I didn't know the exact details until I happened to be in Worcester a few years ago for a reading. I went over to the city hall and asked for my father's death certificate and there it was. Age thirty-nine. Death by suicide. Carbolic acid. It would have torn his guts out. Strong stuff. I'm not sure how I learned he did it in a park. Maybe my older sister told me. That scene has always haunted me. There's a reference to it in a poem called "The Hemorrhage." He becomes the fallen king, a Christ figure. My original title was "The Man in the Park."

CB: Your father has always figured strongly in your poetry, and he continues to do so in *The Testing-Tree*. But I noticed here, for the first time, that your mother asserts a prominence.

SK: That's true. My mother has become closer to me in recent years. I understand her more than I did in the beginning. There were two strong wills in that household, hers and mine, so that our natural tensions were magnified. We held each other at a distance. She was the most competent woman I have ever known—I respected that. But it took years—after her death at eighty-six—for me to be touched by the beauty and bravery of her spirit.

CB: In *The Testing-Tree*, though, there isn't quite that portrait of her. She seems a woman of unforgiveness. She is "a grey eye peeping." She guards you joylessly. In "The Portrait" she refuses to forgive your father for killing himself.

SK: Well, she was unconcessive in many ways. And it's true that she refused ever to speak to me about my father. She obliterated every trace of him. In her very last years, at my request, she began writing her memoirs. It's a remarkable document, which I will someday use in one form or other.* She is fresh and vital writing about her childhood in Russia. And her emigration to this country. And her work as an operator in the sweatshops of New York's Lower East Side. About everything until she moved to Worcester. Until she met my father. Then she froze, and wrote no more.

CB: Where in Russia did she come from?

SK: Lithuania.

CB: Did she speak Lithuanian or Russian at home?

SK: No. She spoke English, though she was twenty-four when she came here in 1890, with no knowledge of the language. She went to night school, read a good deal, educated herself.

CB: Was there much discussion of Russian writers in your house, as a boy?

SK: Not a great deal. But there was a good library. For that period and for that middle-class world, rather exceptional. There was a complete set of Tolstoy, complete Dickens, complete Shakespeare. An unabridged dictionary. A big illustrated Bible—both Testaments. A lot of history, history of all nations. The classic books. Gibbon. Goethe. Dante's *Inferno*, illustrated by Gustave Doré. There was a sense of civilization there.

CB: You say very directly in "An Old Cracked Tune"* that "my mother's breast was thorny, / and father I had none." Is this comfortless situation based simply on her attitude toward your father or did it arrive out of your relationship with her?

SK: My mother was a working woman, absent all day—in that era a rare phenomenon. She was one of the pioneer businesswomen, a dress designer and manufacturer. I was always left in the care of others and didn't have an intimate day-to-day contact with her. When she came home in the evening, she was tired and easily vexed, impatient with my moodiness. She was not one to demonstrate affection physically—in fact, I don't recall ever

* See "My Mother's Story," in *Next-to-Last Things*, Atlantic Monthly Press, 1985, p. 74.

being kissed by her during my childhood. Yet I never doubted her fierce love for me. And pride in me for my little scholastic triumphs and early literary productions.

CB: My favorite poem of yours is "King of the River,"* and I believe my reason is that the salmon, ostensibly the subject of the poem, is half fish, half Kunitz. Could we talk a little about how the poem came into being?

SK: What triggered "King of the River," I recall, was a brief report in *Time* of some new research on the aging process of the Pacific salmon. I wrote the poem in Provincetown one fall—my favorite writing season. The very first lines came to me with their conditional syntax and suspended clauses, a winding and falling movement. The rest seemed to flow, maybe because I'm never very far from the creature world. Some of my deepest feelings have to do with plants and animals. In my bad times they've sustained me. It may be pertinent that I experienced a curious elation while confronting the unpleasant reality of being mortal, the inexorable process of my own decay. Perhaps I had managed to "distance" my fate—the salmon was doing my dying for me.

A poem has secrets that the poet knows nothing of. It takes on a life and a will of its own. It might have proceeded differently—toward catastrophe, resignation, terror, despair—and I still would have to claim it. Valéry said that poetry is a language within a language. It is also a language beyond language, a metamedium—that is, metabolic, metaphoric, metamorphic. A poet's collected work is his book of changes. The great meditations on death have a curious exaltation. I suppose it comes from the realization, even on the threshold, that one isn't done with one's changes.

CB: Isn't it true that a poet has preferences among his own poems in the same way that he has preferences among the poems of other poets? That specialness isn't always based on sheer quality. You yourself have defended a line from "Father and Son"* that critics have complained was obscure or ugly even. If I remember, the line went: ". . . the night nailed like an orange to my brow." But you felt that nails and fruit have had a long history in your consciousness and that you didn't give a damn whether someone liked it or not. Do you have any of that obstinate fondness for this poem?

SK: Some days I have an obstinate fondness for all my poems. Other days I dislike them intensely. I'll concede that the poems of mine that stay freshest for me in the long run are the archetypal ones, of which "King of the River" is undoubtedly an example. I mean archetypal in the Jungian sense, with reference to imagery rooted in the collective unconscious. I am no longer attracted to or tempted by the sort of metaphysical abstraction that led me in my youth to write—somewhat presumptuously, it seems to me now—of daring "to vie with God for His eternity." The images I seek are those derived from bodily immersion in what Conrad called "the destructive element." That salmon battering toward the dam . . .

CB: Is this a Christian God you're contending with?

SK: Call Him the God of all gods. I have no sectarian faith.

CB: Theodore Roethke mentions in one of his letters that "Kunitz called me the best Jewish poet in America." I was wondering what you meant by that.

SK: It sounds like me, but I don't remember the occasion. I was probably just teasing him about being guilt-ridden and full of moral imperatives. Besides, he had inherited some anti-Semitic reflexes from his Prussian ancestors.

CB: I'm trying to find a delicate way of asking you to comment on a rather offensive characterization of you by Harold Bloom. He includes you with several poets who he feels have evaded their Jewish heritage in their poetry.

SK: Cripes!

CB: Insofar as your poems are morally conscious they may be construed to be Jewish. The son in "Father and Son" asks his absent father to "teach me to be kind." One great aim of your work is to discover the ethical content of your own unconscious.

SK: It's obvious that Jewish cultural aspiration and ethical doctrine entered into my bloodstream, but in practice I am an American freethinker, a damn stubborn one, and my poetry is not hyphenated. I said a few minutes ago that I had no religion, but I should have added that I have strong religious feelings. Moses and Jesus and Lao-tse have all instructed me. And the prophets as well, from Isaiah to Blake—though Blake is closer to me. I had never thought of it before, but it's true that three of the poets who most strongly influenced me—Donne, Herbert, Hopkins—happen to have been Christian churchmen.

CB: Bloom's point was that the Jewish poet cannot offer his whole-hearted surrender to a Gentile precursor.

SK: Bloom should ask himself why all his poets are WASPs.

CB: In the years before 1959, when you were awarded the Pulitzer Prize, you were relatively obscure as a poet. Can I have your reasons for that?

SK: I am not and never was a prolific or fashionable poet. For a long time I lived apart from the literary world, in rural isolation. During my middle years my poems were said to be too dark and obscure, though they seem quite intelligible now. To this day I've had very little serious critical attention. Maybe I don't know how lucky I've been!

CB: I detect certain mannerisms of Eliot in some of the early poems.

SK: Eliot invented a tone of voice and put his stamp on the metaphysical mode. In my generation, the next after his, one would have to be a fool not to learn something from him. But in fundamental respects I rejected what he stood for. From the beginning I was a subjective poet in contradiction to the dogma propounded by Eliot and his disciples that objectivity, impersonality, was the goal of art. Furthermore, I despised his politics. It's ironic that a generation later, when confessional poetry, so called, became the rage, I was classified as a late convert to the confessional school. That made me laugh and shudder. My struggle is to use the life in order to transcend it, to convert it into legend.

CB: What were some of the other pressures that brought about the looser style of the poems in *The Testing-Tree*?

SK: The language of my poetry's always been accessible, even when the syntax was complex. I've never used an esoteric vocabulary, though some of my information may have been special. I believe there is such an intrinsic relationship between form and content that the moment you start writing a poem in pentameters you tend to revert to an Elizabethan idiom. "Night Letter," for example, is rhetorically an Elizabethan poem. What strikes me, as I read and reread the poetry and prose of the Elizabethans, is that they had a longer breath unit—their language was still bubbling and rich in qualifiers, in adjectives and adverbs. The nouns and verbs of Shakespeare couldn't, by themselves, fulfill the line and give it enough richness of texture for the Renaissance taste. I acquired a taste for that kind of opulence of language, but as the years went on I began to realize that my breath units didn't require so long a line. By my middle period I was mainly working with tetrameters, which eliminated at least one adjective from every line. In my current phase I've stripped that down still more. I want the energy to be concentrated in my nouns and verbs, and I write mostly in trimeters, since my natural span of breath seems to be three beats.

It seems to me so natural now that I scarcely ever feel the need for a longer line. Sometimes I keep a little clock going when people talk to me and I notice they too are speaking in trimeters. Back in the Elizabethan Age I'd have heard pentameters.

CB: Does the increased accessibility of the poems in *The Testing-Tree* indicate a significant change in your aesthetic?

SK: At my age, after you're done—or ruefully think you're done— with the nagging anxieties and complications of your youth, what is there left for you to confront but the great simplicities? I never tire of birdsong and sky and weather. I want to write poems that are natural, luminous, deep, spare. I dream of an art so transparent that you can look through and see the world.

CB: Occasionally a poem of yours—"The War against the Trees"* is an example—will sound mock heroic on the page, and I am surprised that the tone in which I've heard you read it is not at all mock heroic.

SK: Irony is one of the ingredients there—but I shouldn't call it mock heroic.

CB: Take a line like this: ". . . the bulldozers, drunk with gasoline, / Tested the virtue of the soil." Or: "All day the hireling engines charged the trees . . . forcing the giants to their knees." It's the magnification of the event and the personification of the bulldozers and the trees.

SK: Well, I suppose that for me the rape of nature is an event of a certain magnitude. My feeling for the land is more than an abstraction. I've always been mad about gardening, and used to think, when I was strug- gling to survive, that I could end my days quite happily working as a gar- dener on some big estate. In Provincetown I tend my terraces flowering on the bay. I'm out there grubbing every summer morning. The man in one of my poems who "carries a bag of earth on his back" must be my double.

CB: One doesn't think of you as a pastoral poet, but you draw a good deal of your sustenance from the natural world. For most of your adult life you've chosen to live in the country.

SK: With the first five hundred dollars I saved after coming to New York I bought a hundred-acre farm on Wormwood Hill in Mansfield Cen- ter, Connecticut, and moved there with my first wife. That was in 1930. I loved the woods and fields and the grand old eighteenth-century house, with its gambrel roof. But we were poor, and living conditions were primitive, without electricity or central heating or even running water. Eventually I made the improvements that the house required—mostly with my own hands—but I couldn't save the marriage. Later, for the span of my second marriage, I lived in Bucks County, Pennsylvania—beautiful country. That's the locale of "River Road." I've always needed space around me, a piece of ground to cultivate, and the feel of living creatures. I'm never bored in the country. Very few of my poems deal with urban situations.

CB: What about the need for friendship and literary stimulation?

SK: I didn't realize what I was missing until one evening Ted Roethke drove down to New Hope from Lafayette and knocked at my door, unannounced, with a copy of *Intellectual Things* in his hand. It astonished me that this big, shambling stranger knew my poems by heart.

CB: Roethke at this time had published only a few poems?

SK: He had published practically nothing, but was working on the poems that eventually became *Open House*. That was a saving relationship for both of us. I sensed he needed me even more than I needed him.

CB: You were both lonely. But he sought somebody out.

SK: He was much more aggressive than I, more socially ambitious, and he soon had a world of literary friendships, of which I would hear when he came to see me. He would tell me about Louise Bogan and Léonie Adams and Rolfe Humphries and, a bit later, Auden and all the others that he sought out and gathered to him. But he did not bring us together. His policy was to keep his friends apart.

CB: Were you a loner on some principle or were you naturally shy?

SK: As a young man I was preternaturally shy. For years it was difficult for me to reach out to others. I'd lived such an inward life for so long. I think I'm more open with people now.

CB: In your early poems there are fairly frequent references to your youth as being a period of despair, as if you resented it. In one you say, "innocence betrayed me in a room of mocking elders."

SK: I've been through many dark nights, but the guilts I've expressed aren't meant to be interpreted confessionally. Somebody once asked me, quite bluntly, what it was I felt so guilty about. I replied, "For being fallible and mortal." Does that make me sound terribly glum? Believe me, I've had my share of joys. And I'm still ready for more.

CB: You had an unhappy period in the army during World War II. What were the circumstances?

SK: Briefly, I was drafted, just short of my thirty-eighth birthday, as a nonaffiliated pacifist, with moral scruples against bearing arms. My understanding with the draft board was that I would be assigned to a service unit, such as the Medical Corps. Instead the papers on my status got lost or were never delivered, and I was shuttled for three years from camp to camp, doing KP duty most of the time or digging latrines. A combination of pneumonia, scarlet fever, and just downright humiliation almost did me in. While I was still in uniform, *Passport to the War*, my bleakest book, was published, but I was scarcely aware of the event. It seemed to sink without a trace.

CB: In the period before you went into the army, what magazines were you publishing in?

SK: I was publishing very little then. Witty, elegant, Audenesque poems were in demand then, not mine. I was lucky to get my book published at all. Practically every major publishing firm rejected it before Holt took it. I had the same unflattering experience with my *Selected Poems*, fourteen years later, before Atlantic accepted them.

CB: Aside from Roethke, did you have any staunch supporters?

SK: I had more than I knew, but no lines of communication between us. Imagine my surprise to learn, on my discharge from the army in '45, that I had been awarded a Guggenheim fellowship, for which I had never applied. When I inquired how it could have happened, I was told that Marianne Moore, whom I wasn't to meet until years later, had been my intercessor.

CB: Your earlier poems have been accused—I should say that is the right word—of being overly intellectual . . .

SK: [Laughs] . . . which is nonsense.

CB: But when one dwells on the paradox that such work as you have produced is urbane only in its complexity, not in its concerns, then one begins to see that there is something real in your choice to live apart from the city. Perhaps there is something about much thought, small conversation, and the endless blue of country skies that stunts the smart aleck and develops one's mystical sense, as if one is left without a language adequate for wonder. In the language that one does find, there is both great strain and mystical attainment.

SK: One of my primary convictions is that I am not a reasonable poet.

CB: One of your poems—"The Science of the Night"—has a passage: "We are not souls but systems, and we move in clouds of our unknowing." Is that a direct reference to the text by the medieval religious mystic?

SK: Yes. *The Cloud of Unknowing*—haunting phrase. But, sure, I think that what we strive for is to move from the world of our immediate knowing, our limited range of information, into the unknown. My poems don't come easy—I have to fight for them. In my struggle I have the sense of swimming underwater toward some kind of light and open air that will be saving. Redemption is a theme that concerns me. We have to learn how to live with our frailties. The best people I know are inadequate and unashamed.

CB: Can you say something about how you manage to find "the language that saves"?

SK: The poem in the head is always perfect. Resistance starts when you try to convert it into language. Language itself is a kind of resistance to the pure flow of self. The solution is to become one's language. You cannot write a poem until you hit upon its rhythm. That rhythm not only belongs to the subject matter, it belongs to your interior world, and the moment they hook up there's a quantum leap of energy. You can ride on that rhythm, it will carry you somewhere strange. The next morning you look at the page and wonder how it all happened. You have to triumph over all your diurnal glibness and cheapness and defensiveness.

CB: One of my ideas about your poetry is that there are two voices, arguing with each other. One is the varied voice of personality, the voice that speaks in the context of a dramatic situation. The other is an internal voice, the voice that's rhythm. It governs a poem's movement the way the waves govern the movement of a boat—seldom do the two want to go in the same direction.

SK: The struggle is between incantation and sense. There's always a song lying under the surface of these poems. It's an incantation that wants to take over—it really doesn't need a language—all it needs is sounds. The sense has to struggle to assert itself, to mount the rhythm and become inseparable from it.

CB: Would you say that rhythm is feeling, in and of itself?

SK: Rhythm to me, I suppose, is essentially what Hopkins called the taste of self. I taste myself as rhythm.

CB: How wide a variety of rhythms do you feel?

SK: The psyche has one central rhythm—capable, of course, of variations, as in music. You must seek your central rhythm in order to find out who you are.

CB: So you would agree you could say about music that Bach's central rhythm is devotional and Mozart's is gay, sunny, and exuberant. How would you define your own rhythm in these terms?

SK: Mine, I think, is essentially dark and grieving—elegiac. Sometimes I counterpoint it, but the ground melody is what I mostly hear.

CB: With respect to rhythm, could you discuss your term "functional stressing"?

SK: Functional stressing is simply my way of coping with the problem of writing a musical line that isn't dependent on the convention of alternating slack and stressed syllables. What I usually hear these days is a line with three strong stresses in it—that's my basic measure. I don't make a point of counting stresses—the process is largely unconscious, determined by my ear. A line can have any number of syllables, and sometimes it will add or eliminate a stress. Rhythm depends on a degree of regularity, but the imagination requires an illusion of freedom. The system of stresses is the organizing principle of a poem. I tend to dwell on long vowels and to play them against the consonants; and I love to modulate the flow of a poem, to change the pace, so that it quickens and then slows, becomes alternately fluid and clotted. The language of a poem must do more than convey experience: it must embody it.

CB: Is this what you look for in the poems of others, that feeling of there it "happened" to him, that feeling of oneness with his subject? Take a writer like D. H. Lawrence, who's utterly unlike you.

SK: Nevertheless, he's a poet I admire. I think of "The Snake" or, better still, "The Ship of Death"—his ecstatic funeral song. He's a dying man, sailing out toward the unknown—a rocking, redundant movement—and you're on board with him, sharing his destiny, a passenger on the same ship, which is so real you feel the flow of the sunset and the coming of the night.

CB: And that transcends any literary consideration?

SK: It transcends it. You mustn't let the aesthetic of a period determine for you what's good or bad in poetry.

CB: That's why it must be so annoying for you to have critics praise you for your skillful craft.

SK: Oh, I hate that. I take it as a put-down. Unless craft is second nature, it means nothing. Craft can point the way, it can hone an instrument to a fine cutting edge, but it's not to be confused with an art of transformation, that magical performance.

CB: Frost talks about the poet, or himself rather, as a performer, as an athlete is a performer. In what sense do you mean that writing is a performance?

SK: A trapeze artist on his high wire is performing and defying death at the same time. He's doing more than showing off his skill: he's using his skill to stay alive. Art demands that sense of risk, of danger. But few artists in any period risk their lives. The truth is they're not on a high enough wire. This makes me think of an incident in my childhood. In the woods behind our house in Worcester was an abandoned quarry—you'll find mention of it in "The Testing-Tree."* This deep-cut quarry had a sheer granite face. I visited it almost every day, alone in the woods, and in my magic Keds I'd try to climb it, till the height made me dizzy. I was always testing myself. There was nobody to watch me. I was testing myself to see how high I could go. There was very little ledge, almost nothing to hold on to. Occasionally I'd find a plant or a few blades of tough grass in the crevices, but the surface was almost vertical, with only the most precarious toehold. One day I was out there and I climbed—oh, it was a triumph!—almost to the top. And then I couldn't get down. I couldn't go up or down. I just clung there that whole afternoon and through the long night. Next morning the police and fire departments found me. They put up a ladder and brought me down. I must say my mother didn't appreciate that I was inventing a metaphor for poetry.

CB: In "The Testing-Tree,"* when you threw the three stones against the oak, you don't mention how many hit. If you hit once, it was for love; twice, and you would be a poet; three times, and you would live forever.

SK: I got awfully efficient. In the end I almost never missed. I've always excelled at hand-and-eye coordination, any sort of ball game. That makes me think of a game I used to play with Roethke. I put a little wastebasket at one end of the room, and then we'd try to pitch tennis balls into it from the opposite corner. Each successful pitch was worth a dime. If I made ten shots in a row and he made three, he owed me seventy cents. Well, I was really phenomenal at this, and I made a small fortune from

Roethke. In fact, he refused to play with me ánymore because he said I was practicing during his absence. It's true enough. Sometimes I still play that game against myself.

CB: How did you get involved with teaching?

SK: When I was in the service I received a letter from Lewis Webster Jones, the president of Bennington, offering me a teaching job when I got out of the army. I was staggered. I had never taught before. I'd been free-lancing and editing for the H. W. Wilson Company, but I hadn't taught at all and I couldn't understand why I was being asked to come and teach at Bennington. It turned out that Roethke, who had been teaching there, had had a violent breakdown and had locked himself into his cottage, threatening anybody who came near him, especially the president. He was finally induced to carry on a conversation. He said he knew the jig was up—he'd have to leave. But he'd come out and be peaceful on one condition—that they invite me to take his place.

CB: Did you look forward to this?

SK: I'd always been hungry to teach, though I thought I never would after my initial rejection at Harvard.

CB: Could you go into that?

SK: At Harvard I stayed on for my master's with the thought of becoming a member of the faculty. It seemed to me a not unreasonable expectation, since I had graduated *summa cum laude* and won most of the important prizes, including the Garrison Medal for Poetry. When I inquired about it, the word came back from the English faculty that I couldn't hope to teach there because "Anglo-Saxons would resent being taught English by a Jew." I was humiliated and enraged. Even half a century later I have no great feeling of warmth for my alma mater. Of course that was in the dark ages of the American academy. A few years after I left, Jews were no longer considered to be pariahs. From this vantage point I'm glad I didn't stay and become an academician. All those years of struggle taught me a great deal about the vicissitudes of life. My scrambling for survival kept me from being insulated from common experience. It certainly fed my political passions.

CB: What did you do after you left Harvard?

SK: I went back to Worcester and became a staff reporter on the *Worcester Telegram*. I had been a summer reporter on the *Telegram* since my sophomore year, when I wrote an impertinent letter to the editor, saying that I thought the paper could use somebody who knew how to write. As proof of my literary prowess, I enclosed an impressionistic panegyric on James Joyce—this was in 1923. In a few days, much to my amazement, I received a letter from Captain Roland Andrews, editor in chief, saying that by God I *could* write and a job was mine for the asking. As a full-time member of the staff I became assistant Sunday editor and wrote a literary column and did some features. Then I was assigned to the Sacco-Vanzetti case. I soon saw that a terrible injustice was being perpetrated. My particular assignment was to cover the judge, Judge Webster Thayer, a mean little frightened man who hated the guts of these "anarchistic bastards." He could not conceivably give them a fair trial. I was so vehement about this miscarriage of justice, so filled with it, that around the newspaper office they used to call me "Sacco." After the executions, I became obsessed with the notion that Vanzetti's eloquent letters should be published and received permission to see what I could do about it. I gave up my job on the *Telegram* and went to New York alone. I had nothing, no money, no friends. I made the rounds of the publishing houses, but nobody would touch the book. The whole country was in the grip of one of its periodic Red scares. I was virtually penniless by the time I landed a job with the H. W. Wilson Company.

CB: You quit your job with the *Worcester Telegram* expressly to find publication for the letters?

SK: I sensed it was time for me to leave. Curiously, I was twenty-three when I came to New York, about the same age as my mother when she landed at the immigrant station on Castle Garden.

CB: Your career seems larger at both ends. You first published when you were quite young and now, as you have put it, you're threatening to become prolific.

SK: I like the verb "threatening."

CB: What sort of function or role are you trying to accomplish in your own criticism?

SK: I'm not programmatic. I suppose I try to establish the connections between language and action, aesthetics and moral values, the individual and society.

CB: Your pieces on other poets are invariably sympathetic at heart.

SK: I've made a point of not writing about poets with whom I am not sympathetic. There's plenty of negativism around about poets. I don't feel any need to contribute more. Of course I recognize differences. For example, my essay on Robinson Jeffers attacks his political insensibility about Hitler, but at the same time it is written with true respect for his achievement as a poet. If you understand a poet's key images, you have a clue to the understanding of his whole work. I wish criticism would spend more time in the intimate pursuit of those central images. That's a more productive concern than ratings and influences.

CB: What is the origin of your early imagery of spikes and cones and spheres?

SK: I don't know. It could be religious, or cubistic, or scientific. I haven't mentioned that I had an apprenticeship with Alfred North Whitehead during my last year at Harvard. He was giving an advanced course in the nature of the physical universe. I didn't have the prerequisites, but I wanted very much to be one of the handful permitted to study with him. I went to see Whitehead. He asked me why I wanted to be in his group. I said, "I'll give you two reasons. I admire you extravagantly and I hope to be a poet." He said, "You're in." I learned a lot from him.

CB: You also met the "Moon Man" in Worcester?

SK: Dr. Robert H. Goddard. Yes. This was in the spring of 1926 while I was on the *Telegram*. One day the city editor said to me, "There's a crazy man in town playing around with rockets. Why don't you go over and see him?" So I went over to Clark University, where Goddard was professor of physics. I may have been the first person ever to interview him. This was shortly after he had made the great experiment outside the city limits of Worcester—in an open field in Auburn he had fired the first liquid-fueled rocket. He told me about this with quiet intensity. I said, "How high did it go?" And he said, "One hundred eighty-four feet in two point five seconds." "Is that all?" I said. His voice turned a little shrill. "Young man, don't you see? It's all solved! We'll make it to the moon! Because the principle is right, don't you see, don't you see?" He went to his blackboard. A little man, very professorial looking, completely obsessed with his calculations and diagrams. I have an unpublished poem about this encounter. He made me feel somehow connected with him, as though both of us were shooting for the moon, in different ways.

CB: His story was your story?

SK: I suppose I made it mine. That's the way with the imagination.

CB: Not many poets writing during the early years of your career were attracted to science?

SK: And no wonder. After a quarter of a century I still have to explain to audiences what I am doing with the metaphor of the red shift in "The Science of the Night." Such terminology ought to be just as common knowledge as the myths were in ancient Greece. The vocabulary of modern science is fascinating—I read everything I can find about pulsars and black holes and charm and quarks—but, by and large, the vocabulary remains exclusive and specialized. The more we know about the universe, the less understandable it becomes. The classic world had more reality than ours. At least it thought it understood what reality was. In 1948, I recall, Niels Bohr visited Bennington and drew a neat picture of neutrons and protons on the blackboard. In the question period that followed I asked him, "Is this really the structure of the atom, or is it your metaphor for the present state of our information about it?" He preferred then not to accept that distinction. Today a diagram of the atom would look vastly different, more complicated, and I would not need to repeat the question.

CB: Scientists think their metaphors are not heuristic.

SK: The popular impression is that their metaphors are real and the poet's metaphors are unreal.

CB: Why do you suppose the metaphors of scientists are taken with much more seriousness than those of poets?

SK: Because we live in a pragmatic society, and the effects of science are evident, whereas the consequences of poetry are invisible. How many truly believe that if poetry were to be suppressed, the light of our civilization would go out?

CB: If there are few serious readers of poetry, how is its light disseminated?

SK: Largely it's disseminated among the young. A sizable fraction of the youth in our universities read poetry, hear poets and are excited by them. Any poet who travels across the country knows this to be true. Many of these students will go out into the world and never read another book of poems, but if only a fraction of them retain their interest, it will be a significant change for the better. It occurs to me that, though poets don't have a large readership, their product in diluted form comes down to the mass population—in popular music, popular song, in all the areas of commercialized art. Popular art in this country today is a reduced, somewhat degraded form of high art, in contrast to other epochs, when popular art fed high art. Writers of the ballads inspired the poets of the romantic movement. Nursery rhymes entered into the imagination of the poets in all centuries. Now we are getting the reverse process—high art, in its diluted state, touches everybody. Bob Dylan couldn't have existed if Dylan Thomas hadn't existed before him.

CB: Since the media occupy a paradoxical relationship to art as diluters, but also as disseminators, are they allies of art?

SK: They could be, but they aren't. Yet every once in a while something comes along to remind you of possibilities. Haley's *Roots* on TV, for example, which stirred a nation's conscience—at least for a few nights. It gave white masters an opportunity to redeem themselves through guilt. Incidentally, I was in Ghana and Senegal last spring. The curious thing that struck me was that young African poets are trying to forget their tribal and colonial past. The main collective effort is to move into high technology and to overleap centuries of industrial backwardness. The poets want to jump smack into the Western world and write like Westerners. They study and imitate us. One young Ghanaian told me he felt guilty about not writing in his tribal language, but he scarcely knew it and it was too difficult to master for literary purposes. In our culture, we have a counterphenomenon. Our poets are trying to rediscover our tribal past, the bonds that hold us together. The search back into the roots of our common life is an archetypal journey. We have to go back and reconstruct the foundation myths so they will live again for us. Poetry is tied to memory. As we grow older, our childhood returns to us out of the mists. I may be mistaken, but my impression is that early in the century—I'm speaking in general terms—a child had fewer advantages, but he was more innocent, more hopeful, more ambitious than his grandchildren today. We really believed then that society was on our side.

CB: You've lived most of your life outside the poetry establishment. Do you consider yourself to be a part of it now? Has your attitude toward it changed?

SK: I wish I knew what the poetry establishment is. It's curious that nobody speaks of the fiction establishment. Poets don't get their rewards in the marketplace, so maybe they tend to take honors and prizes and the illusion of power much too seriously. There's a heavy accumulation of bile in that famous Pierian spring. Some poets seem to think they have to kill off their predecessors in order to make room for themselves. If you live long enough and receive a bit of recognition, you're bound to become a target. The only advantage of celebrity I can think of is that it puts one in a position to be of help to others. The phrase "community of poets" still has a sweet ring to me.

CB: For sheer good company, you seem to prefer painters to poets.

SK: I count myself lucky to be married into their world. I envy them because there is so much physical satisfaction in the actual work of painting and sculpture. I'm a physical being and resent this sedentary business of sitting at one's desk and moving only one's wrists. I pace, I speak my poems, I get very kinetic when I'm working. Besides, I love the social and gregarious nature of painters. Poets tend to be nervous and competitive and introverted. My image of discomfort is three poets together in a room. My painter friends—among them Kline and de Kooning and Rothko and Guston and Motherwell—were enacting an art of gesture to which I responded. When I insist on poetry as a kind of action, I'm thinking very much in these terms—every achieved metaphor in a poem is a gesture of sorts, the equivalent of the slashing of a stroke on canvas.

CB: You have produced some sculpture—wire sculpture and assemblages.

SK: Sometimes I feel I'm a sculptor manqué. I love working with my hands. In my garden, my woodworking. My hands want to make forms. Though my poems often deal with the time sense, I'm inclined to translate that into metaphors of space. I like to define my perimeters. I want to know where a poem is happening, its ground, its footing, how much room I have to move in.

CB: You organize a poem spatially?

SK: It's one of the ways a poem of mine gets organized. I follow the track of the eye—it's a track through space.

CB: The Fine Arts Work Center in Provincetown, which you helped start, would seem to be a reflection of your concern with making a community of artists and writers.

SK: Art withers without fellowship. I recall how grievously I missed the sense of a community in my own youth. In a typical American city or town poets are strangers. If our society provided a more satisfying cultural climate, a more spontaneous and generous environment, we shouldn't need to install specialized writing workshops in the universities or endow places like Yaddo or MacDowell or Provincetown. In Provincetown we invite a number of young writers and visual artists from all parts of the country to live at the center for an extended period, working freely in association. Our policy is not to impose a pattern on them, but to let them create their own. In practice, instead of becoming competitive, they soon want to talk to one another about their work problems, they begin to share their manuscripts and paintings, they arrange their own group sessions, they meet visiting writers and artists and consult with them, if they are so inclined. Most who come for the seven-month term are loath to leave. Many of them stay on as residents of the town.

CB: Can you comment on the quality of the work of young poets?

SK: I hate to generalize, but I'll make a stab at offering a few broad conclusions. My first and main observation is that no earlier generation has written so well, or in such numbers. But it's a generation without masters: dozens of poets are writing at the same level of accomplishment. My explanation is that what we're experiencing is the democratization of genius. It's also clear that few poets have much of anything to say. Practically the only exceptions are the liberated women, who have the authentic passion of a cause. It's no accident that my first five Yale selections were men, my last three female. Another point is that few young poets have mastered traditional prosody. The result is that they don't really know how to make language sing or move for them. There's a modicum of music in most of what's being written today. They're not testing their poems against the ear. They're writing for the page, and the page, let me tell you, is a cold bed.

CB: Among your recent work, "Three Floors"* stands out for its musical effects.

SK: Studs Terkel, who interviewed me last fall in Chicago, told me it was one of his favorites. He had me read it while someone played *Warum* in the background—on tape, of course. A little corny, perhaps, but it was quite moving to hear that music, which I hadn't really heard since my childhood. I realized that I had actually written the poem to that melody. The poem goes back to more formal patterns. It's the only rhymed stanzaic poem in *The Testing-Tree*. And not because I planned it that way, but simply because it came to me that way. It would have been a lie to force it into a different mode. You have to trust the way a poem comes to you. I don't expect it to happen, but I don't negate the possibility of my returning to a more formal verse tradition.

CB: Literary tradition has accumulated suspicions about the sincerity of any poet's feelings toward conventional subjects. There are certain poems of yours that seem oblivious to this. A poem like "Robin Redbreast"*—until its ending—seems to strain sentimentally after the large problem of being a little bird, though its end is so powerful—when the robin is picked up, the poet sees the blue sky through a bullet hole in his head—that I am ashamed of my reaction to the earlier part of the poem.

SK: Maybe you're confusing pathos with sentimentality. My reverence for the chain of being is equivalent to a religious conviction. I don't apologize for my strong feelings about birds and beasts. Was Blake being sentimental when he wrote, "A robin redbreast in a cage / Puts all Heaven in a rage," or "A dog starv'd at his master's gate / Predicts the ruin of the state"?

CB: Often your poems deal with dreams.

SK: Often a poem *is* a dream, but I don't necessarily say it is.

CB: Are there any specific poems that come to mind?

SK: The one that first occurs to me is "Open the Gates."* It begins with a vision of the city of the burning cloud. Like Sodom and Gomorrah—cities of the plain. Those images of dragging my life behind me and knocking on the door and the rest of it are straight out of dream. I woke at the moment of revelation, just when the gates were opening. Another source of that poem my be the Doré illustrations to Dante's *Inferno*, one of the magic books of my childhood. My images usually have an experiential root. In "The Testing-Tree"* the image of my mother in the last section, the dream passage, goes back to a conversation with her in her eighties. She told me she had a proposal of marriage from a man of about the same age. He thought they should live out their lives together and take her off my hands; it was a practical thing. I asked her: "Do you really care for him?" She shook her head. "You know there are only two old men I have any use for. One's Bernard Shaw and the other is Bertrand Russell." She meant that. Another image in the same section is of a sputtering Model A that "unfurled a highway behind / where the tanks maneuver, / revolving their turrets." In '45, after my discharge from the army, I drove a Model A cross-country, stopping on the way at a little oasis in the middle of the desert called Silver Springs. A few days later I pushed on to the West Coast. Several years later I drove back from the University of Washington, where I'd been visiting poet. I took the route through Death Valley into Nevada to see my oasis. When I approached, armed guards appeared from every side and ordered me away. It turned out that the place was now Yucca Flats, the testing ground of the atom bomb. This is all curiously in the background of the poem, somewhat mysteriously translated. And the lines about "in a murderous time": I wrote those lines the night that Martin Luther King was assassinated. I had been working on the poem for weeks, but couldn't get the ending right. I was visiting Yale at that time, reading manuscripts for the Yale Series, and staying with R. W. B. Lewis, an old friend of mine. We were listening to the radio when we heard about the assassination of King, with whom I had been associated, raising money for the civil rights movement. Suddenly, as I sat listening to the announcement, the lines I needed came to me.

CB: What is the source for the imagery of depreciation toward the end of this poem, such as the "cardboard doorway"?

SK: I see a movie set, furnished with memories like studio props. Doorways figure largely throughout the poem—entrances into my past, into the woods, into truth itself. I had recently gone back to Worcester to receive an honorary degree from Clark University and had asked to be taken to the scenes of my childhood. The nettled field had changed into a housing development, the path into the woods had become an express highway, and the woods themselves were gone. That's where the poem began, with the thought that reality itself is dissolving all around us.

CB: You indicate that with images pasted together like a collage?

SK: A montage, I would say.

CB: Can you say something about the arrangement of the lines for this poem?

SK: I started working with flush margins, and had difficulty achieving any sort of linear tension. Furthermore, I found the look of the page uninteresting, that long poem with all those short lines. I didn't develop a triadic sense until I began tinkering with the lines, as I often do at the beginning of a poem, trying to find the formal structure. The moment I hit on the tercets, the poem began to move.

CB: I am impressed by your capacity to break the tone abruptly or to shift the voice in a poem. Sometimes it is only for a line, but these outbreaks seem to have an idiosyncratic dramatic function.

SK: It's something I may have learned from working with dramatic monologues. In an extended passage I sense the need for an interruption of the speech flow, another kind of voice breaking into the poem and altering its course. I recall one occasion when I was hunting for a phrase to do just that, so that I could push the poem one step further, beyond its natural climax. My inability to achieve the right tone infuriated me. I must have tried thirty different versions, none of which worked. I was ready to beat my head on the wall when I heard myself saying, "Let be! Let be!" And there it was, simple and perfect—I had my line. If you have a dialectical mind like mine and if a poem of yours is moving more or less compulsively toward its destination, you feel the need of a pistol shot to stop the action, so that it may resume on another track, in a different mood or tempo. One of the reasons I write poems is that they make revelation possible. I sometimes think I ought to spend the rest of my life writing a single poem whose action reaches an epiphany only at the point of exhaustion, in the combustion of the whole life, and continues and renews, until it blows away like a puff of milkweed. Anybody who remains a poet throughout a lifetime, who is still a poet let us say at sixty, has a terrible will to survive. He has already died a million times and at a certain age he faces this imperative need to be reborn. All the phenomena of his life, all the memories, all the stuff that makes him feel himself, is rematerialized and reblended. He's capable of perpetuation, he turns up again in new shapes. Any poem he writes could be a hundred poems. He could take a poem written at twenty or thirty and reexperience it and come out again with something absolutely different and probably richer. He can't excuse himself by saying he has written everything he has to write. That's a damn lie. He's swamped with material, it's overwhelming.

CB: What are your thoughts on the way you end a poem?

SK: I think of a beginning, a middle, and an end. I don't believe in open form. A poem may be open, but then it doesn't have form. Merely to stop a poem is not to end it. I don't want to suggest that I believe in neat little resolutions. To put a logical cap on a poem is to suffocate its original impulse. Just as the truly great piece of architecture moves beyond itself into its environment, into the landscape and the sky, so the kind of poetic closure that interests me bleeds out of its ending into the whole universe of feeling and thought. I like an ending that's both a door and a window.

CB: Your poems are packed; they have a weight. To me, it is a question of scale.

SK: Thanks. I've heard the opposite reaction, that my poems are too heavy. One critic wrote quite recently that my poems sounded as though they had been translated from the Hungarian. I don't know why, but somehow that made me feel quite lighthearted.

CB: Most of your poems are written in a high style.

SK: That used to be truer than it is today. I've tried to squeeze the water out of my poems.

CB: Mostly in your earlier poetry you have a stylistic habit of animating abstractions by hinging them to metaphors, as in the "bone of mercy" or the "lintel of my brain."

SK: There's some confusion about this type of prepositional construction. When it has weak specification, when it incorporates a loose abstraction, it is a stylistic vice, and I've grown increasingly wary of it. I resist phrases like "stars of glory." But when I say "the broad lintel of his brain," I am perceiving the brain as a house. The brain is not, in this usage, an abstraction. It's just as real as the lintel. Pound was the first, I think, to define this particular stylistic vice, and modern criticism has blindly followed suit, without bothering to make the necessary discriminations. In any event, I don't accept arbitrary rules about poetry. Do you want to try me with another example?

CB: Take a phrase like "the calcium snows of sleep."

SK: I like it, though I'm not the one who should be saying so. It's fresh and it happens to be true, scientifically true. During sleep the brain deposits calcium at a faster rate than when it's conscious. Besides, the "snows of sleep" have nothing in common with the "stars of glory." The construction is legitimately possessive, analogous to the "snows of the Russian plains." Sleep is where the snow is falling.

CB: Do you have a reading knowledge of Russian?

SK: I've described the method of these translations in the introduction to the Akhmatova volume. If I didn't have someone to help me with the Russian text, I would certainly be lost. I've worked mostly with Max Hayward. I not only want a word-by-word translation, in the exact word order, but any kind of gloss that would be helpful to me, such as the meanings of a word's roots. The root sense of a word may supplement, or even contradict, its current usage. Etymology is one of my passions. I like to use a word in a poem with its whole history dragging like a chain behind it. And then we go over the sound. We read the poems aloud. I translate only when I feel I have some affinity with the poet. Even with respect to a poet I don't feel particularly close to—Yevtushenko, for example—when I was asked to translate some of his poems, I fastened on to some of his early lyrics, which are among the best poems he's written.

CB: What is the affinity you feel with Voznesensky?

SK: It was Voznesensky who got me started with the Russians. Andrei came to this country in the sixties and we met and had a good feeling about each other. How can I explain these things? He wanted me to translate him and I felt I could do it—again, selecting the poems that I wanted to translate. I enjoyed doing it, and I learned something too. Every poet I've ever translated has taught me something. One of the perils of poetry is to be trapped in the skin of your own imagination and to remain there all your life. Translation lets you crack your own skin and enter the skin of another. You identify with somebody else's imagination and rhythm, and that makes it possible for you to become other. It's an opening toward transformation and renewal. I wish I could translate from all the languages. If I could live forever, I'd do that.

CB: Many of the Russian poets you've known personally. Do you feel different about Baudelaire, whom you know only through his work?

SK: I know Baudelaire too—he was dealing with exactly the kind of issues that concern me. Problems of good and evil, the sexual drama. As a young man I was attracted to the violence of his inner life, the force of his rhetoric, and the hard structure of his poems, the way they build and make such a solidity of thought and image and feeling. In a poem like "Rover" I am very aware of my debt to him. The life of a poet is crystallized in his work, that's how you know him. Akhmatova I never met. She died in '66 and I never encountered her, but she's an old friend of mine in spirit. She taught me something, taught me the possibility of dealing quite directly with the most painful experiences.

CB: You are referring to the execution of her husband and the imprisonment of her son, as well as the government repression of her poetry?

SK: "Requiem 1935–40" is a good example. The background of the poem was excruciating, and yet out of it she made a poem that is personal at its immediate level but universal in its ultimate form. It transcends the personal by viewing the historic occasion through the lens of individual suffering. Nothing is diminished in her poems: all her adversities and humiliations. She wrote with such burning and scrupulous intensity that she became part of the historic process itself—its conscience and its voice.

CB: Do you envy the disasters of other poets, even if those disasters lack the historical dimension of Akhmatova's?

SK: Sufficient unto each poet are his own disasters! The victims of history have a certain grandeur. One saves one's tears for those who fall victim to themselves. Their cries lacerate us. I'm thinking of Berryman, Sexton, Plath. . . . Perhaps it is in the nature of our age to be most moved by poems born of weakness rather than of strength. All the same, I yearn for an art capable of overriding the shames, the betrayals, the lies; capable of building something shining and great out of the ruins. The poets that seem most symptomatic of the modern world are poets without what Keats called negative capability. They do not flow into others. The flow of their pity is inward rather than outward. They are self-immersed and self-destroying. And when they kill themselves, we love them most. That says something about our age.

CB: The tragic sense no longer seems pertinent to our lives.

SK: The tragic sense cannot exist without tradition and structure, the communal bond. The big machines of industry and state are unaffected by our little fates. All the aggrandizement of the ego in the modern world seems a rather frivolous enterprise, unattached to anything larger than itself. Number 85374 on the assembly line may have a life important to himself and his family, but when he reaches sixty-five and is forced out of the line, another number steps in and takes his place—and it doesn't make any difference. The artist in the modern world is probably the only person, with a handful of exceptions, who keeps alive that sense of the sharing of his life with others. When he watches that leaf fall, it's falling for you. Or that sparrow . . .

CB: The most difficult thing is that the adversary does not inspire confrontation. Evil has lost its cape and sharp horns. Hitler was evil but he was not a satanic figure.

SK: The opportunity for confrontation with evil was greater in an earlier age. It becomes more and more difficult to intercede in behalf of one's own fate. The overwhelming technological superiority of the military apparatus protects the tyrant, as an emblem of evil, from his people. As Pastor Bonhoeffer learned, you cannot get at evil in the world. I've written about his moral dilemma when he joined the plot to assassinate Hitler. Evil has become a product of manufacture; it is built into our whole industrial and political system, it is being manufactured every day, it is rolling off the assembly lines, it is being sold in the stores, it pollutes the air. And it's not a person!

Perhaps the way to cope with the adversary is to confront him in ourselves. We have to fight for our little bit of health. We have to make our living and dying important again. And the living and dying of others. Isn't that what poetry is about?

New York /1977

Living the Layers of Time

by Richard Jackson

Richard Jackson: In her book, *Wordsworth: Language as Counter-Spirit*, Margaret Ferguson talks about the inherent link between discourse and themes in Wordsworth's arrangement of his poems. She calls the progress of his classification a "metaphoric journey through life." Could you comment on the relation of theme and language in the light of your own development from more traditional to more functional or intuitive ones?

Stanley Kunitz: My method of working is such that I don't predetermine the form. The form is what emerges in the actual writing, or—more accurately—"saying," since my writing develops out of a process of incantation. I am very fond of a dramatic structure, which isn't always evident on the surface, an image or episode that carries the action of the poem and gives it momentum. Once I launch into that action it more or less moves by itself because it has an end in view, an end that I can't see but which the poem does. There is another kind of poem to which I was particularly devoted in my younger days. It is a dialectical poem, in which I explore the contradictions of the self, the argument within. The poem unfolds in terms of that argument, which then proceeds to some sort of truce at the end. My meditative poems are an outgrowth of that dialectical approach.

RJ: The poems often have aphoristic endings, whether it's an aphoristic line like "The souls of numbers kiss the perfect stars" or an aphoristic event like the end of "Journal for My Daughter." The aphoristic ending sends the reader off into richly connotative regions, and the endings seem to be even more open in the late poems.

SK: Perhaps I'm less positive about the meanings of things than when I was younger. I like the enigma of an ending that is both a door and a window. It's a release of tension to arrive at a point of clearing where one is able to affirm something, even if that affirmation contains a principle of negation within it.

RJ: That moment is sometimes like a meeting place of eternity and time, permanence and change, being and becoming. This concept seems very crucial for you. In "Change," for example, you talk about the mind's powers to move; man can adapt to change "because the mind moves everywhere." Later in the poem you say how man progresses in order to define himself—"Becoming, never being, till / Becoming is a being still." Another example would be "The Mound Builders," where several different periods lend their perspectives against the speaker at the end.

SK: I read Plato in my youth and never stopped meditating on the relationship between the worlds of being and becoming. In "Change," one of my earliest poems, the words "being still" can be read two ways—as suggesting endurance in time and as indicating a certain "stillness" beyond time. One of the things that has always fascinated me is the persistence of the psyche through all the changes of the body, all the phases of one's history. There is that self which is indestructible, at the kernel of everything one is and does. In my own case, I've been following its traces all this year [1978], as I've been putting together the poems of a lifetime for publication—my first such comprehensive collection. I've been writing poems for half a century now—a staggering thought—and I've been through many transformations. Of course, my style has changed quite radically, maybe even become its antiself, but from first to last I can detect the presence of that same old vulnerable blob of protoplasm that has my name attached to it.

You mentioned "The Mound Builders." I'm glad you did, for it's a poem that doesn't seem to have attracted much critical attention. I wrote it in 1962, following a reading tour down South, in the course of which I had paid a visit to the Ocmulgee National Monument in Georgia. There I read the inscription, "Macon is the seventh layer of civilization on this spot," which somehow struck me as a rather depressing bit of information. Back in my motel room I heard, on the TV news broadcast, that President Kennedy had announced the resumption of nuclear testing—which made me wonder about the imminence of an eighth layer. In my poem I attempted to cut through time layers, expose them to view as aspects of the eternal present. History isn't a series of dots in a moving line, but a manifold tissue of events, connected with different epochs. In certain of my poems, particularly the longer ones, I seem to want to fold back these layers, to give a spatial extension to time. One lives in the present, but also in other times, past and future. I feel that I am not only living now, but also in other times, past and future. Now is one of the locations of my life, but so is my childhood and, beyond that, the childhood of the race. Even my own death is part of my occupation. That density of feeling, when it saturates a poem, is what I describe as psychic texture.

RJ: That sense of spatial extension is related to Coleridge's organic form and to that sense you described of the gradual emergence of the poem, isn't it? His poems spatialize time, too.

SK: Particularly in his free-flowing odes. Coleridge describes two kinds of form, mechanistic and organic. Mechanistic form is predetermined, filled in by language. Organic form develops from the materials inherent in the poem. He uses the working of clay as his metaphor. The most appropriate image for the process may be that of a living thing growing, coming alive and sending out its antennae one way and another, as it searches out new areas of feeling or meaning. The concept of organic form leads one to try to arrive at some sort of satisfaction of an impulse by engaging it in an action which ultimately leads to its exhaustion. In that sense Valéry was right when he said that poems were not so much finished as abandoned.

RJ: Another way of presenting things is through the apostrophe or invocation, devices you use more than many other poets. Apostrophe resists narrative, sequential time, and yet it allows the poem to send out its antennae, as you say.

SK: True, but one has to guard against letting the apostrophe become a merely rhetorical trick, a mechanistic shifting of gears. I'm not sure that I'm more addicted to it than other poets. If I am, it may be because I'm so aware of the divided self. Sometimes the person you address in a poem is your other self, that Other who is also you. At other times you have to call on an outside agent, human or divine, to spring you from your self-made trap. Another consideration is the monotony of simple declarative sentences in flat succession. Few contemporary poets, I'm grieved to say, seem to understand the importance of syntax as a means of modifying the vibrations of a line, or of propelling it forward. You need to change the pitch of your voice to keep your poem from going dead on you. You want it to open up, to rove free. This is something that Hopkins, above all, understood. He was a supreme master of invocation. And, of course, a great prosodist.

RJ: As a poem of yours opens up, it seems to confront a threshold. There is a whole section in *Selected Poems* called "The Terrible Threshold." In "The Flight of Apollo,"* it is a threshold between our world and infinity. In "Robin Redbreast,"* the speaker looks through the bird's skull to a blue, eternal sky. There is always this sense of being caught at, but looking beyond, the threshold. For example, in "Open the Gates,"* the end becomes a new beginning—"I stand on the terrible threshold, and I see / the end and the beginning in each other's arms."

SK: Yeats wrote, in a late quatrain, "It is myself that I remake." He was referring to revisions, but his observation is true in a larger context. The poet is forever making and remaking himself in an effort to surpass himself. I think of poetry as, above all, an art of transformation and transcendence. At every important stage in his journey the poet has to "cross over."

RJ: A number of your poems involve a kind of Jungian movement into and out of a mire, a mortality. In "Green Ways,"* you talk about the "self's prehistory." In "King of the River,"* you describe an evolution going from a salmonlike self to "the threshold / of the last mystery, at the brute absolute hour." You have the sense of inheriting a higher life and being always banished from it—an ambivalent endurance.

SK: A lot of reasoning goes into the making of a poem, but the great leap is from memory and awareness to the rapture of the unknown. That can't be a wholly logical procedure. Reason can play all sorts of clever and even beautiful word games—that's what Coleridge meant by Fancy—but the imagination is a deep-sea diver that rakes the bottom of the poet's mind and dredges up sleeping images. The visionaries teach us that we have to become ignorant before we can become wise. Jung's special insight was that we need to go back and confront our past before we can become strong enough to move forward. The athlete who wants to jump over a high crossbar first retreats several yards, so that he can gain momentum for his leap. Poetry is our most sophisticated use of language, but it is also our most primitive. It has its source, deep under the layers of a life, in the primordial self. If we go deep enough, we may discover the secret place where our key images have been stored since childhood. There are chains of other images attached to them, the accretions of the years. A single touch activates the whole cluster.

RJ: Freud visualized a knot, an impenetrable tangle of images, leading in a number of directions.

SK: His theory of neurosis led him to see these images as traumatic and repressed. No doubt many of them are, but an artist's key images can include some that relate to experiences of joy or ecstasy, images that give him his first glimpse of Eden. If you could plot all these images, as you do the stars in a constellation, you would have a reasonably accurate representation of the creative identity.

RJ: One of these image clusters, at least in the poems from your middle years, includes words like "stain," "defilement," "contagion," "corruption," "vileness," "waste," "infection"—the list could go on. In "Single Vision," you talk about the "stain of life," for example. The notion often seems to carry moral or theological overtones, too, like Blake's vocabulary in *Songs of Experience*.

SK: To set the record straight, "Single Vision" appeared in my first book, *Intellectual Things*, published in 1930, so that I was in my early twenties when I wrote it. Of course I owed a lot to Blake, including the title of this particular poem and of the book as a whole. Even then I had a perception of evil, which wasn't based on much experience of it. It's true, as you point out, that in my middle years my vision really darkened. I went through a bad time. "My bones are angry with me," I wrote in a poem I called "The Guilty Man." In the catastrophic period that culminated in World War II and my four years of military service, I felt politically helpless and personally defeated. My "guilt" took on existential dimensions. I did not know how to live anymore with myself or the world around me. The original flaw, I perceived, was to be born mortal and fallible. We have all been expelled from the Garden, but the ones who suffer most in exile are those who are still permitted to dream of perfection.

RJ: The poet in your work often speaks "the serpent's word." As in "The Science of the Night," he fails to make contact with others. The self dredged up out of the unconscious in "The Approach to Thebes" turns out to be a monster. Do these images have a general application?

SK: They derive from the predicament of the artist in Western society. In the dominion of the arts nobody is more insecure than the poet, who has neither a community to address nor a commodity to sell. If he has a political function, it must be in an adversary role. With few exceptions, poets live separate existences, outside the mainstream, less a part of our culture than of our counterculture, of which they are an unorganized segment. So it is that, in a defensive reaction, their temptation is to become completely self-preoccupied, to lose the human touch, to devote all their energies to the cultivation of ego and sensibility. Paranoia is the vocational disease of artists. That's what I mean by the transformation into monster.

RJ: This tendency seems more pronounced from the romantics on.

SK: It isn't an accident that the beginnings of romanticism coincided with the advent of the Industrial Revolution. We all know that the romantics defended nature against the incursions of the "Satanic mills." What isn't so clear is that they were defending the craftsman and artist, the whole man making the whole thing, against the theory of the division of labor and the new technology of mass production. It's a rare artist today in whose work we perceive, above all, the emanations of humanity rather than the pride of the specialized ego.

RJ: In your later poems, the threshold, the self, seems less "terrible." The perspective seems to have become more ironic, perhaps more stoical, certainly less "angry."

SK: That rage of my middle years almost consumed me. I suppose that I have made my peace with at least some portions of myself. This has modified my voice. Age hasn't made me more conservative—I still think of myself as a radical intelligence—but I have learned how to be less impatient with failure, including my own. I have chucked a lot of baggage and am stripping down, however reluctantly, for the last few miles of my journey. The immediately important things are to keep on living, to keep on working, to keep on building a world of affections.

RJ: The sense of being a father, say, in "Journal for My Daughter," deals with this, doesn't it? The image of the father is widespread in your poems, referring to your own father and to yourself.

SK: In the constellation of my images I suppose that the quest for the lost father, the one I never knew, is pivotal. To find the father is to find oneself. And to become a father is to reenact an archetypal mystery. That's to become part of a majestic drama. At the same time, in another perspective, it's a curious and humbling phenomenon to step into one's place as an insignificant link in the infinite chain of being.

RJ: That finding of the self is often put in Wordsworthian or Blakean terms. "Poem" describes an experience that is "a dream . . . or not a dream" in which the speaker moves in a cyclic way between dream and reality, the outer world and the inner self, until they seem to coalesce. And "Geometry of Moods" talks about the coincidence of circles of self and world that never quite coincide, as in Wordsworth.

SK: These early poems often announced themes that continue to haunt me to this day. I read Wordsworth during my school years, as I read Blake, and shared his excitement about the reciprocity between nature and self. I think, too, of Coleridge's exclamation: "O Wordsworth! we receive but what we give / And in our life alone does Nature live." Let me add that the natural world has been the most sustaining of all the forces in my life through the worst, the darkest, periods. The fact that I have an abiding sense of joy and participation in the natural world is fortifying; it compensates for much human failure.

RJ: There's a sense of intensity not only about your feelings for the natural world but for the world at large. Talking about the flowers, but also the whole world and his own ability to love and imagine, Coleridge confesses his dejection that "I see, not feel, how beautiful they are." Feeling is crucial, not knowledge.

SK: Agreed. I keep on accumulating information because I was born curious and don't know how to stop. But I realize that my knowledge is worth little to me, or to anybody else, unless I can incorporate it into a world of feeling. I suppose that's one of the reasons why I continue to write poems.

Provincetown / August 1978
[*Acts of Mind: Conversations with
Contemporary Poets*, ed. Richard Jackson,
University of Alabama Press, 1983]

Translating Anna Akhmatova

by Daniel Weissbort

Daniel Weissbort: How did the project originate, the cooperation with Max Hayward, because I know you worked on other projects with him?

Stanley Kunitz: I had worked previously with Max on the Voznesensky translations. In '64 Arthur Gregor, who was poetry editor of Macmillan at that time, approached me, asking whether I would be interested in doing a translation of Akhmatova, and offered a contract. I got in touch with Max and he was agreeable and we signed. . . . It took us eight years to complete the project, because we had to wait for Max's visits to this country to go over the material, and both of us had other commitments, and finally there was a changing of the guard at Macmillan and Arthur no longer was with the firm. Since nobody remaining at Macmillan seemed particularly interested in the project, I secured a release from the contract and switched over to my own publisher, Atlantic Monthly Press. That's the history . . . It wasn't till '72 that we turned in the final manuscript. The book was published in '73 and there's still a lively demand for it.

DW: Could you say something about your work procedure?

SK: Max went over all the available poems of Akhmatova and made very precise transliterations . . .

DW: The entire œuvre?

SK: The ones that he thought would be of any interest. And these transliterations were word for word, with no literary pretensions, but adequate for letting me choose the texts I wanted to translate. In the end I came across a few poems by myself that I felt were needed to complete the book, and these I added to the table of contents.

Along with the transliterations, which were accompanied by a phonetic approximation of the Cyrillic text and indication of the stresses, Max sent me another version in readable English prose. During our sessions together he would read the poems aloud to me in Russian. This was of the utmost importance, for the soul of a poem, I have always felt, is in its sound. When I read my versions back to him, above all I wanted them to *sound* right.

In general, whatever I did with the text was acceptable to Max. He did not claim to be a poet and he certainly did not want to be a critic of my poems. Only in a few cases did he feel that I had misconstrued the sense or the tone. He did not leave me much room for error, since his prose renderings were meticulously accurate and his marginal glosses on difficult passages examined ambiguities or supplied relevant biographical or historical information. Sometimes he would say of a word, "This is truly untranslatable, but here are some of the possibilities."

DW: He was an ideal collaborator, in that he didn't interfere with your own inspiration or insights.

SK: Right! He was not defending the territory of Slavic linguistics! [Laughter.] And he was happy if what I gave back to him came out sounding like a poem!

DW: Had you read, before the proposal was made for a collection of Akhmatova, much of her work in translation?

SK: I had seen several translations. Not, I think, a full text, but isolated poems. And I felt most of them were not very promising. [Laughter.] But I sensed that behind these poems there was a tone of voice, an urgency, a moral and political passion that excited me. And I also felt that the more I read her poems, the more I understood that in a curious way, in the fulfillment of her destiny, she had become an allegorical figure. She was the history of Russia of her time.

DW: To what extent was Max able to convey more impalpable aspects, I mean the tone, the general feeling of what kind of poet she is, how it all works in Russian?

SK: We had very little conversation in that area. Max's introduction was not written until after we were through with the work. So I didn't have the benefit of his insights to begin with. I did read whatever I could about her and the other poets of that era. The rest was largely intuition. I might add that though I gave a lot of myself to her, she more than paid me back. I learned something from her about transparency of diction, directness of approach to a theme, the possibility of equating personal emotion with historical passion.

DW: That was what I was going to ask you, what you felt you had gained . . .

SK: And actually, by the time I had finished those translations, I felt that I had been profoundly affected in my own life. Not that I think my work sounds anything like Akhmatova.

DW: No, not something one would immediately discern stylistically.

SK: But it did modify me a few millimeters!

DW: Do you, in fact, know any Russian?

SK: So little that I might as well say no.

DW: This method, one might say, is the standard method of translating in Russia itself. You have a scholar or linguist, working with a poet.

SK: Akhmatova herself did that.

DW: Some people have expressed doubts about a method where the final translator, the poet, has no immediate contact with the original language, but did you feel any doubts about this?

SK: I trusted Max implicitly. And I knew that if I had any doubts about a reading, he would be able to help me. I also felt that if I'd had an ordinary, rudimentary grasp of Russian—equivalent, let's say, to my grasp of French or German—it might have been more of a hindrance than a help. Because I had the benefit in this case of sharing the erudition, the linguistic brilliance, of one of the great Slavists. That's the work of a lifetime, and I doubt that most poets in English are going to spend a lifetime acquiring that much command of another language.

DW: Yes, that's quite true. It sometimes happens by chance, or historical accident, where bilingualism occurs.

SK: Max had the notion that since I do have East European ancestry, my genes knew more Russian than I did. He'd say, "Oh, you really caught that. How did you do it?"

DW: You said you were attracted to the way Akhmatova linked the personal and the political. She also worked, in her early days, in very classical form . . .

SK: And wrote very feminine, domestic poetry.

DW: Yes. But I wonder whether the constrictions of that very formal classical meter and rhyme scheme, in particular, run somewhat contrary to your own . . .

SK: To a degree, but I too had started as a formal, metrical poet. Of course, I went through a radical change. Akhmatova remained more of a formalist, but her late poems are certainly more open stylistically than her early work. Actually, I sensed a certain correspondence in our development.

DW: There has been a view, much put around lately, that translators of formal poetry, especially formal Russian poetry, have tended to ignore the formal side. It seems to me that your Akhmatova translations represent a very nice balance between formal demands and semantic accuracy, even if not of the literal, verbal kind. Verbal accuracy, literal accuracy is, in any case, often a contradiction in terms. Strictly speaking, it is impossible!

SK: The genius of each language is unique. Each poem is also unique, with its individual inflection, rhythm, pitch, pacing, auditory pattern, etc. So much of it can only be implied in translation. What is most readily translatable is the matter of a poem, its substantive ground, which there is no excuse for betraying, even in the absence of equivalents. All the rest—its music, its spirit, its complex verbal and psychic tissue—one tries to suggest as best as one can. It's foolish to argue for the exact reconstruction of a poem in another language when the building blocks at one's disposal bear no resemblance to those of the original.

DW: Do you think the absolutist demand for the "exact reconstruction of a poem" as you say, expresses the unrealistic, idealistic ambition to somehow transform English into a kind of Russian—in this case a Russified English, which is somehow, magically, both English and Russian and therefore is not obliged to compromise between them?

SK: There's a kind of purism in literature that is just as destructive as fanaticism in religion. I equate the two.

DW: To return to Akhmatova herself, I am often struck by her very precise sense, for a lyric poet, of time and locale—place.

SK: Her awareness of time and place is consistent with her exercise of the dramatic imagination. Among modern poets she vies with Yeats in her mastery of the dramatic lyric.

DW: She brings an enormous amount of her life into the poetry.

SK: I admire her ability to capture a scene, to introduce a dramatic confrontation, and with such economy of means. Her poems hardly ever sprawl. She has a fierce attention to her destination.

DW: Were these aspects that you found . . .

SK: Yes, congenial . . .

DW: Can you trace influences, if I might put it that way, in your own work, subsequent to translating Akhmatova, of her example? I guess what I'm trying to say is this: there are, on the one hand, your actual translations of Akhmatova and, on the other hand, there is something which occasionally happens when a poet translates another poet, or perhaps which always happens, if it is a real meeting, in other words, a kind of translation through the translator's own work, a kind of transcendence . . .

SK: Mainly what my work with Akhmatova did for me was to . . . keep me alive to the possibility of translating human situations, conflicts, disturbances into poems that go beyond the personal, that can be read as existential metaphors. She confirmed my image of the poet as a witness to history, particularly to the crimes of history.

DW: Let me, perhaps, stress a slightly different aspect of that same question. Supposing you were another poet reading your, Stanley Kunitz's, translations of Akhmatova, having a similar congeniality for Akhmatova; would merely reading the poems, in someone else's translation, have as potent an effect as translating them yourself? In other words, does translation imply a higher degree of assimilation? Obviously we both believe it does, but I would be interested in your comments.

SK: Yes, I'm sure this happens in any extended work of translation. Not so much if you translate individual poems, but if you take on the whole body of a poet's work and move, as one tries to do, into the dominion of that poet's imagination. To do that is to extend the boundaries of one's own imagination, to become, in a way, magnified. .

DW: I was wondering also, because the point has sometimes been made about Lowell's translations for instance (at least his *Imitations*), that rather than opening himself to another poet, he somehow . . .

SK: . . . used the poet as a springboard.

DW: Yes. Would you say that's fair criticism?

SK: Fair enough. But you have to understand that this is what he set out to do. He did not demand of himself any great fidelity to the original text. He thought it was more important to produce a poem by Lowell. And that's what he did. My intention is quite different. I insist on the premise of affection for the original text and loyalty to it, *insofar as it is compatible with the production of a new poem in English*. Sometimes these are quite incompatible directives. Sometimes you have to sacrifice a grain of fidelity, simply because it sounds rotten in English.

If you study Max's transliterations of Akhmatova, you can see that certain lines, taken literally, sound preposterous or silly. Every language reflects a set of social conventions and has its roots in the character and history of a people. In a poem that deals with human affections, it is the culture that determines how much expressiveness is tolerable in an exchange between persons. What sounds genuine and moving in one language may strike the reader in another language as bombastic or insincere. I found such instances in Akhmatova's poems. There were also opposite cases, where the literal English version of a line came through as so flat and unevocative that the intensity had to be stepped up one notch in order to save the poem from collapsing. Occasionally a closure that Max assured me was quite grand and resonant in the Russian tongue had so thin a sound in English that I felt obliged to modify the text in order to get the vibrations right. These were not easy or wilful choices.

DW: Perhaps we might now turn to an actual translation. You mention one of these poems as being particularly problematical. Might we perhaps look at that one? I believe it was the poem "We're all drunkards here . . ."

SK: Oh yes, a famous one, the poem used against her by the establishment, because its opening line indicates how immoral, how corrupt the whole society of bohemian poets was: "We're all drunkards here, and harlots."

DW: It's also, I suppose, a particularly striking example of dramatic writing.

SK: Yes, she captures a scene. She has what Henry James called a scenic imagination, which he believed to be the secret of the novelistic art. What he learned to do was to select a few crucial encounters or conflicts which required elaboration in great detail, and then to bridge them with summaries. Poetry dispenses with the bridges, but the gift of the scenic imagination is indispensable for the writer of dramatic lyrics.

DW: Yes. Her life is the bridge. You said that this poem was, perhaps, one of the few poems where there was some controversy between you and Max.

SK: That's too strong a word. But I think it was the only poem where we had some debate about the interpretation. And if we can go over it, I'll point out where. I may be able to locate the letter in which he comments on that.

DW: He has something in his Introduction explaining the circumstances of "The stray dog" and so on. The poem is on page 51 of the book.

SK: Yes. here it is: "When it was first published in the journal *Apollon* in 1913, this poem was titled 'Cabaret Artistique.' " Max discusses it in the Introduction on pages 13 to 14. . . . Maybe I should comment on what happens in my version of the poem, as compared with the original. Well, maybe I should read Max's version, stanza by stanza, and then comment on what I've done with it.

This is Max's rendering into English. [Reads Max Hayward's literate, stanza 1: see Appendix 1.] My version reads . . . [reads final version, stanza 1]. "Wretched," I think, is stronger than "unhappy." "Unhappy" is a dead word. He says "flowers and birds / Yearn for the clouds." Well, in English it's too short a line and too vague in its feeling. I want to suggest the tight metrics of the original, the concentrated power of the stanzaic structure, without becoming a slave to the prosody. My use of off-rhyme, as in "to-gether / gather," gives me a measure of freedom.

Max's version. [Reads MH's literate, stanza 2.] The trouble here is that the English paraphrase doesn't sound like Akhmatova. It's overly naive, even ingenuous.

DW: Yes, that's right. In Akhmatova it seems lucid and simple, but not ingenuous.

SK: In fact, she is confiding her sexual motivation for wearing so narrow a skirt. In 1913, to say that in a poem took a bit of courage, no doubt. [Reads final version, stanza 2.] I want those lines to sound mature and bold and feminine all at once—qualities I associate with Akhmatova.

DW: It's curious, because in the second line, where Max translates it quite literally, "The smoke above it is so strange," that's exactly what the Russian says and it is so beautiful, so expressive, and yet so dead when literally translated.

SK: Which is why I change it to "strange shapes above you swim." For the sake of a little metaphorical life.

Next stanza. [Reads MH's literate, stanza 3.] My version, "The windows are tightly sealed," ties in with the preceding skirt image and has the advantage of economy and energy, linear tension, in contrast to the literal rendering, "The windows are blocked up for ever:/What's outside? Sleet or thunderstorm?" Each language has its own natural order. The acceptable locution in English is "thunder or sleet." "What's outside?" is awkwardly sibilant. I prefer "What brews?" because it harmonizes with "your eyes" in the second line following and because it has an appropriately ominous inflection.

DW: Which I think may be in the Russian, because it uses the word *tam*, meaning literally, rather indeterminately, "there," in this case "outside," rather than some more precise expression for that.

SK: It could be argued, I suppose, that the line "How well I know your look," preceding "your eyes like a cautious cat," is an arbitrary insert lacking textual justification. The truth is that, since Max's paraphrase in this passage was considerably more economical than the Russian, I had to invent something to meet the demands of the given stanzaic structure. My interpolation, hinting at the intimacy of the male-female relationship, is quite unintrusive. Indeed it is implicit in Akhmatova's text. The important consideration for the translator in this case is to present the poem as an aesthetic whole, conveying the sense of its formal order in the midst of great emotional agitation. I have seen a free-verse translation of this very poem relying on word-for-word correspondence with the original that missed this point entirely.

To turn to the last stanza—here is Max's translation. [Reads MH's literate, stanza 4.] No doubt it works beautifully in the Russian, but in English paraphrase it's a letdown. This is what I did with it. [Reads final version, stanza 4.]

In my reading of the poem it's the kind that seethes with violence from the start and needs to erupt violently at the last. Poetry in English rests on the power of its verbs. Hence the strong verb "rots" in the final line. My original version was even stronger: "But that one dancing there, / I hope she'll rot in hell." An expression of jealous rage seemed to me to be the gist of the conclusion. But Max demurred, complaining in a letter, which I have here, that this was carrying things too far. [Laughter.] He wrote: " I am a little unhappy about 'I hope she'll rot in hell.' I believe that we discussed this before. Her feelings about Glebova-Sudeikina were obviously mixed, but basically she was very friendly. There are other poems in which she more or less absolves her from blame over Knyazev (who was killed, as you remember, in a brawl) and takes it on herself. The same is true of her dedication to O.S. in the poem. I think, therefore, it would be best not to put this so strongly, particularly as there is no warrant for it in the original. Literally: 'That one dancing there will surely be in hell.' In other words, just a plain statement, not a wish or hope." Max almost convinced me. I changed the line to the version as published.

DW: He just felt this was not the kind of thing that Akhmatova would say?

SK: In her later poems, which were darkened by her sense of political betrayal, she was perfectly capable of denunciation. But this was an early poem, personal and ambivalent, so that the corrected version is probably truer to the original.

I think we should go back now and comment on Max's notes to the poem [see MH's transliteration]. For example, in stanza 2, end of the stanza, the word *stroinyey* is rendered as "graceful," but the gloss tells more: "This word refers to elegance of figure. It suggests tall, graceful, slim, wellbuilt, etc." It was the gloss that led me to the adjective "trim."

DW: The photographs one has seen of her seem to bear out that impression.

SK: In the next stanza his note on the second line, "for ever blocked up are the windows," reads: "This has a rather more concrete sense than in English, since Russians seal up their windows in a most elaborate way against the cold in winter." Without that explanation I doubt I would have arrived at "The windows are tightly sealed."

DW: Ah, yes, so it came from the note, rather than from the literal translation.

SK: We can see another example in the opening line of the last stanza, literally "Oh how my heart longs!" Max comments, "The verb [*toskuyet*] means to be full of misery, apprehension, foreboding, etc." My solution was to distribute those connotations through the line: "O heavy heart; how long. . . ."

DW: Yes, *toskuyet* is one of those highly problematical words which all languages, to the despair of translators, contain. It cannot be translated literally!

SK: Shall we talk about the poem that pays homage to Pasternak? It's one of my favorites. What it intimates about the role of the poet in the modern world needs to be understood and reinforced. The temptation is to regard poetry as primarily a verbal skill. In her view of poetic genius Akhmatova stressed the importance of character in relation to history. In this poem to her friend, written in the time of the Stalin terror, Akhmatova pays what I would suppose to be the ultimate tribute to a fellow poet, in that her images are drawn from Pasternak himself. There's a delicacy about that gift, that gift of reciprocity, that touches me infinitely.

So now, to get back to the translation. I wanted to infuse it with a lyrical tenderness, but that was hard to manage, given the amount of information that needs to be conveyed. To include all that information and yet to ride the wave of a melodic line—this was the challenge that had to be met.

Take the literal version, for example, of the opening stanza. [Reads MH's transliteration: see Appendix 2.] It is out of Max's gloss again that I get my direction. The paraphrase itself won't do. [Reads MH's literate, stanza 1.] I have to fight for a rhythm. [Reads final version, stanza 1, pausing after line 2.] See, I like those heavy stresses, that jamming effect. [Reads on.] I think it was "ice frets," Max's phrase, that gave me the clue to the music I wanted to hear. Then the next stanza. [Reads MH's literate, stanza 2.] Out of that I get . . . [reads final version, stanza 2]. I've kept the images almost exactly, but the rhythm has been transformed. It's back into the lyric mode.

And then the next stanza. [Reads MH's literate, stanza 3.] Some of that comes through. [Reads final version, stanza 3.] Consider the phrase given to me: ". . .he/Is timidly making his way over pine-needles." I give it back as "it means he is tiptoeing over pine needles." The difference is in the lightfootedness. Poetry is always trying to embody gesture in language.

And the next stanza. [Reads MH's literate version, stanza 4.] When Max wrote the note he wasn't sure about the reference to the "Daryal Stone." He noted, "This probably means the Caucasus, but I'll have to check." Well, it does. As I discovered for myself, Pasternak had a lodge in the Caucasus, in the Daryal Gorge. [Reads final version, stanza 4.] Again, I tried to establish the rhythmic base. My ear rejects "Accursed and black, from some funeral or other," but accepts "from another funeral." Somehow, the whole meaning is changed.

And then the next stanza. [Reads MH's literate, stanza 5.] Again one senses that something quite noble in the original has suffered a diminishing. How to restore its luster? [Reads final version, stanza 5.] Here I'm working with the complex of feelings behind the language, as given, rather than with the literal sense. Since we know that a literal translation of poetry is a delusion, is it permissible to substitute on occasion an equivalent for what one believes to be the true intention of the poet? I think so, but it's a risky procedure, and arguable.

DW: Yes, it comes up again and again. Whereas a poet-translator will often have the audacity to do that, someone else lacking that confidence will not.

SK: Oh, yes. But poets are born to dare. [Laughter.] Who would complain if I had kept to the rendering, stanza 6, "Of verse reflected in new space"? Yet I am sure that "reverberating" is the right verb in that line. At least in English it's right. And then the blessing: "He has been rewarded by a kind of eternal childhood," in the last stanza. That's a good line as it stands. But "With the generosity and sharpsightedness of stars"; what a mouthful! "And he has inherited the whole of the earth / And he has shared it with everybody." I couldn't let this poem die like that. So . . . [reads final version]. I know I've taken chances, but not with the spirit behind the text, and so I believe that I've been faithful, in my fashion, to Akhmatova.

DW: Well, finally, I was wondering whether you had any other translation projects, or whether you had done any translations since the ones we have been discussing.

SK: No . . . Oh, I've done a few random translations, but I'm going on seventy-seven now, which is hard for me to believe [laughter], and I still have poems of my own to write, which is also hard to believe. So I can't afford to spread myself thin.

DW: Did you do much translation in the past, before your work with Max?

SK: Not intensively, though very early I translated from the Spanish and French, some Baudelaire in particular. And in recent years I've done a few Mandelstam poems, and a rich poem of Ungaretti's, which I include in my collected volume. And I've done a few things of Bella Akhmadulina, some of which are still in my files. Incidentally, I've always felt that I should do more with Mandelstam, and maybe one of these days, despite my reservations, I might try my hand at it.

DW: Well, of the many versions there have been, perhaps the closest to coming into poems in English are Merwin's, which are among the earliest.

SK: I feel about Merwin's that they have a grace and something magical too about them, but that maybe they are more elusive than they ought to be. I might be wrong. One wants to strike at the terrible crystal, but in Mandelstam's case the difficulty is in finding where the crystal is.

New York /1982
[*Translating Poetry: The Double Labyrinth*
ed. Daniel Weissbort. MacMillan, 1987]

APPENDIX ONE: WE'RE ALL DRUNKARDS HERE

MH's transliteration

A *Fsye mi brázhniki zdés, bludnítsi,**
　　All we-are tipplers here. harlots,
B *Kak nevéselo vméste nám!*

* A somewhat unusual word since it is used in the Biblical Great *Whore* of Babylon. *Harlot* just about gets the old-fashioned flavor.

How cheerless together we-are!*
A *Na stenákh tsvetí i ptítsi*
On the-walls flowers and birds
B *Tomyátsa po oblakám.*
Long for clouds.
A *Ti kúrish chórnuyu trúbku,*
You smoke black pipe,*
B *Tak stránen dimók nad nyéy.*
So strange-is smoke above it.
A *Ya nadéla úskuyu yúbku,*
I-have put-on narrow skirt,
B *Shtob kazátsa yeshchó stroinyéy.*
So-as to-appear even-more
graceful.

A *Natsegdá zabíti okóshki:*
For-ever blocked up / are / the
windows:*
B *Shto tám, iźmoros il grosá?*
What's there, sleet or
thunderstorm?*
A *Na glazá ostorózhnoy kóshkif*
To eyes of-careful cat*
B *Pokhózhi tvoyí glazá.*
/Are/ like your eyes.

A *O, kak sértse moyó toskúyet!*
O, how heart my longs!*
B *Nye smértnovo-l chasá zhdú?*
Am-I deathly hour awaiting?
A *A tá, shto seychás tantsúyet,*
But she, who just-now
is-dancing.

B *Nepreménno búdet v-adú.*
Certainly will-be in-hell.   [January 1, 1913]

This is a simple colloquial phrase meaning quite simply: "What a miserable time we're having."

You is in "thou" form and she must be addressing Gumilyov, as in most of these early lyrics.

This word refers to elegance of figure. It suggests tall, graceful, slim, well built, etc.

This has a rather more concrete sense than in English, since Russians seal up their windows in a most elaborate way against the cold in winter.
Izmoros can mean either sleet or hoarfrost.
There means "outside."
"Careful" here means wary, prudent.

The verb means to be full of misery, apprehension, foreboding, etc.

MH's literate

We're all drunkards here, and harlots,
How unhappy we are together!

On the wall flowers and birds
Yearn for the clouds.

You puff on a black pipe,
The smoke above it is so strange,
I have put on a narrow skirt,
{ To set off my figure even better. }
{ To seem even slimmer yet. }

The windows are blocked up for ever:
What's outside? Sleet or thunderstorm?
Your eyes are like
The eyes of a cautious cat.

Oh, how my heart is heavy!
Can I be waiting for the hour of death?
But she who is dancing here now
Will certainly go to hell.

Final version

We're all drunkards here, and harlots:
how wretched we are together!
On the walls, flowers and birds
wait for the clouds to gather.

You puff on your burnished pipe,
strange shapes above you swim,
I have put on a narrow skirt
to show my lines are trim.

The windows are tightly sealed.
What brews? Thunder or sleet?
How well I know your look,
your eyes like a cautious cat.

O heavy heart; how long
before the tolling bell?
But that one dancing there,
will surely rot in hell!

APPENDIX TWO: BORIS PASTERNAK

MH's transliteration

*Ón, sam sebia sravńivshi s konskim
  glázom.*
He (who) himself himself compared
  to horse's eye,
Kosítsa, smótrit, vídit, uznayót,
Squints, looks, sees, recognizes,
I vót uzhé rasplávlenim almázom
And then already a-molten diamond
Siyáyut lúzhi, izniváyet liód.
Shine puddles, frets ice.*

Ice frets (eats its heart out—example of P's fondness for the pathetic fallacy, using colloquial, homely images. Or, on the contrary, raising the ordinary to a higher level: puddles shine like molten diamonds.

V lilóvoi mglé pokóyatsa zadvórki,
In lilac haze repose backyards,
Platfórmi, bróvna, listia, oblaká
Platforms, logs, leaves, clouds.
Svíst parovóza, khrúst arbúznoi kórki,
Whistle of-locomotive, crunch
  of-watermelon rind,
V dushístoi láike róbkaya ruká,
In perfumed kid-glove timid hand.

*Zvenít, gremít, skrezhéshchet, biót
  pribóyem—*
Ringing, roaring, grinding, crash of
  breakers—
I vdrúg pritíkhnet,—éto znáchit, on
And suddenly there-is-silence,—
  this means he
Publívo probiráyetsa po khvóyam
Timidly is-making-his-way over
  pine-needles,
Shtób ne spugnút prostránstva chútki són.
So-as not to-startle space / out of its /
  light sleep.

Light in sense of easily awakened from.

I éto znáchit, on schitáyet zórna
And it means he is-counting grains
V pustíkh kolósiakh,—éto znáchit, on

In empty ears,—it means he
K plité daríalskoi, próklatoi i chórnoi,
To slab of-Darial, accursed and black,
Opiát prishól s kakíkh-to pokhorón.
Again has-come from some funeral.
I snóva zhót moskóvskaya istóma
And again he-is-racked
    by-Moscow's fever,
Zvenít vdalí smertélni bubenéts—
Rings in-distance deadly sleighbell—
Kto zabludílsa v dvúkh shagákh ot dóma,
Someone has-got-lost two paces
    from home,
Gde snég po póyas i vsemú konéts . . .
Where snow / is / up-to waist and
    everything is-finished . . .

Fever translates *istoma*, a difficult word meaning vaguely discomfort of the spirit caused by the excessive demands of the environment, or life in general—as a result one is uneasy, bored, fretful, etc.

Za tó shto dím sravníl s Laokoónom,
For his having smoke compared
    with Laocoon,
Kladbíshchenski vospél chertopolókh,
(For having) sung-of graveyard
    thistles,
Za tó shto mír napólnil nóvim zvónom
For his having world filled
    with-new sound
V prostránstve nóvom otrazhónikh stróf
In space new reflected of-verses.

On nagrazhdión kakím-to véchnim
    détstvom,
He-is rewarded with-kind-of eternal
    childhood,
Tói schchédrostiu i zórkostiu svetíl
With-the generosity and
    sharpsightedness of-stars,
I vsiá zemliá bilá yevó naslédstvom,
And all-of earth has-become his
    heritage,
A ón yeyó so vsémi razdelíl.
And he it with all has-shared. [January
    19, 1936]

MH's literate

He, who has compared himself to
    the eye of a horse,
Peers, looks, sees and identifies,
And, at once, like molten diamonds
Puddles shine, ice eats its heart out.
    / broods, pines, frets /

In lilac mists repose backyards,
Platforms, logs, leaves, clouds.
The whistle of a locomotive, the
    crunch of a watermelon's rind,
A timid hand in a perfumed kid
    glove.
{   breakers crash   }
{ Ringing, roaring, grinding, the crash of breakers— }
And suddenly silence,—that means   And silence all at once,
    that he   release,
Is timidly making his way over   It means he is tiptoeing
    pine-needles,   over pine-needles
So as not to startle the light sleep of
    space.
And it means, he's counting the
    grains
In empty ears,—it means that he
Has come again to the Daryal   This probably means
    Stone,   the Caucasus, but
Accursed and black, from some   I'll have to check.
    funeral or other.

And again Moscow, sweltering,
    burns,
The deadly sleighbell rings in the
    distance—
Some one's lost two steps away
    from home,
Where snow's up to the waist and
    all is finished . . .
For having compared smoke with
    the Laocoon,
For singing of graveyard thistles,

For filling the world with a new
    sound
Of verse reflected in new space,

He has been rewarded by a kind of
    eternal childhood,
With the generosity and
    sharpsightedness of stars,
And he has inherited the whole of
    the earth
And he has shared it with
    everybody.

Final version

He who has compared himself to the eye of a horse
peers, looks, sees, identifies,
and instantly like molten diamonds
puddles shine, ice grieves and liquefies.

In lilac mists the backyards drowse,
and depots, logs, leaves, clouds above;
that hooting train, that crunch of watermelon rind,
that timid hand in a perfumed kid glove . . .

All's ringing, roaring, grinding, breakers' crash—
and silence all at once, release:
it means he is tiptoeing over pine needles.
so as not to startle the light sleep of space.

And it means he is counting the grains
in the blasted ears; it means
he has come again to the Daryal Gorge,
accursed and black, from another funeral.

And again Moscow, where the heart's fever burns.
Far off the deadly sleighbell chimes,
someone is lost two steps from home
in waist-high snow. The worst of times . . .

For spying Laocoön in a puff of smoke,
for making a song out of graveyard thistles,

for filling the world with a new sound
of verse reverberating in new space,

he has been rewarded by a kind of eternal childhood,
with the generosity and brilliance of the stars;
the whole of the earth was his to inherit,
and his to share with every human spirit.

The Poet in His Garden

by Christopher Busa

"How does a poet garden?" I asked Stanley Kunitz, a lifelong gardener who has received a Pulitzer Prize for poetry, among other honors and recognitions that have earned him a reputation as one of America's most distinguished poets. At eighty, he remains vigorous, claiming to have subdued ("through willpower") the arthritis in his lower back. He gardens every summer day at his Cape Cod house, within view of Long Point Light, the beacon at the very end of the spiraling Cape. Here the atmosphere is fabled for its clarity. The light, refracted off the water, has attracted artists since the beginning of the century, when they discovered its power to intensify color. Blues are bluer and greens are greener. Kunitz, a gardener naturally alert to fragrance, notices that this air is "brine-spiked."

Kunitz does most of his writing at night, occasionally working until dawn. His study seems buried in the bottom of the house, a basement cell, spare and tidy and sometimes damp. There is one window; three heaps of compost are the only thing in its view. Beneath the window, out of view, is a narrow area for propagating cuttings. "Imagination," Kunitz says, "implies a surplus energy beyond what is needed for simple survival. When I come to the desk and the poetry, it's after I've used my body up in the day. Then I can move into that interior realm, which is still intact. Working in the garden, I'm always thinking, but often I feel my mind free-floating. I'm concentrating on what I am doing, but there is another level, another tier of the self that is whole and moving in its own secret way."

Although Kunitz lives the greater part of the year in New York City, his favorite writing season is the autumn he spends on the Lower Cape, as his garden is dying out. It is this garden he describes in a recent poem, "The Snakes of September"*:

> All summer I heard them
> rustling in the shrubbery
> outracing me from tier
> to tier in my garden,
> a whisper among the viburnums,
> a signal flashed from the hedgerow,
> a shadow pulsing
> in the barberry thicket.
> Now that the nights are chill
> and the annuals spent

117

I should have thought them gone,
in a torpor of blood
slipped to the nether world
before the sickle frost.
Not so. In the deceptive balm
of noon, as if defiant of the curse
that spoiled another garden,
these two appear on show
through a narrow slit
in the dense green brocade
of a north-country spruce,
dangling head-down, entwined
in a brazen love-knot.
I put out my hand and stroke
the fine, dry grit of their skins.
After all,
we are partners in this land,
co-signers of a covenant.
At my touch the wild
braid of creation
trembles.

The "north-country" spruce that figures in this poem is one of four Alberta spruces, roughly placed in the corners of the rectangular garden. They provide an unobtrusive axis that is for the garden's design what a line of association is for a poet: something usually not noticed until it is pointed to. These treelike shrubs are quiet presences a little taller than a man, in the shape of a cone. They seem manicured with a military ceremony, the very embodiment of social order, like a Swiss guard. ("You think they are male?" Kunitz enlightens me, "You have not seen them at dusk, when they are female.")

The most important organizational feature of the garden is a series of terraces that squiggle longitudinally from the street to the house. These terraces (the "tiers" in the poem) are built from low brick walls, the serpentine curve of each terrace echoing another as they rise up from the very definite slope of the garden. Of course, the brick structure is always half-hidden while the garden blooms—the immediate impression is one of cresting energy, like a giant wave rolling through a beam of sunlight, folding color within color. There are five terraces of varying width, each with drifts of its own colors, whose moments of display are staggered through the season. The central terrace is exclusively blue or blue-purple flowers.

Among them: *Veronica, Statice, Salvia, Stokesia, Lisianthus, Campanula, Platycodon, Aster x frikartii*. Kunitz is enchanted by blue, "the most difficult of all garden colors," he says.

He notices the color deepen while the afternoon deepens, "blue-fair and serene," in the words of one poem about Indian summer, which Kunitz also associates with blue. "Yes," he agrees, "blue is a religious color, the color of the spiritual life. I use it as a color stress, for the contrast it provides to the prevailing yellows, pinks, and reds, the most common of garden colors."

Kunitz bought this house almost thirty years ago, when the front yard was something less than a garden—it was a barren sand dune. A few wisps of witch grass, but nothing more, grew. The whole area—about two thousand square feet—was unstable. Later, Kunitz would build the soil using his formula for perfection: one-third sand, one-third peat moss, one-third compost, plus plenty of seaweed and cord grass collected off the sea bottom at low tide. But first he realized that the only solution for the steep grade of sand was to terrace it. "Then everything fell into place: The garden became like a poem in stanzas. Each terrace is a stanza, or perhaps a section of a poem." Poems are the productions of artists, not engineers, so it is only to be expected that Kunitz, who labored for two summers to prepare his space, struggled like a lord of creation with Formless Matter: "Have you ever worked with live, dry, loose sand?" he asks. "It's like shoveling water."

Over the years his garden has grown elaborate. Each terrace is edged with *Heuchera sanguinea, Dianthus, Astilbe, Lobelia, Potentilla,* or *Ajuga*. I walked on a meandering pine-bark path over the crest, past *Hibiscus syriacus* (Bluebird), the cluster of fragrant roses, the variegated hydrangea, past the *Cotinus coggygria* (purple smoke tree) that glows uncannily in the suppressed light of twilight and brushes an adjacent late-blooming Indian-spice (*Vitex agnuscastus*). Then around the corner of one of the "north-country" spruces, down past the *Euonymus* hedge that shields the garden from the street, arriving now at the front gate where a visitor would enter, taking the flower-lined walk across worn railroad ties to arrive at the front porch, where I would begin again the walk just completed. One could circle endlessly and see new things each time. The height of the shrubs and flowers is varied, designed to obscure one view while it reveals another: "A Japanese idea of never being able to see the whole at once," says Kunitz.

A lyric poet is concerned with ways to concentrate experience within a small space. Thus, when Kunitz speaks about the art of poetry, he speaks also about the aesthetic of his garden: "The work of the imagination is not only in achieving magnification of experience by enlarging it, but also in achieving intensification of experience by reducing it in scale, so it becomes almost like a microscopic field." Because Kunitz's garden is small, every inch of space is used. No part can look bare or unkempt. "Keats's desire to 'load every rift with ore' comes to mind," he says. "I even move plants when they stop contributing. Often I pot them and replace them with others. Later, I replant them. But temporarily, they've lost their rental space."

Kunitz inherited one scarecrow of a tree, a chokecherry, which was afflicted with numerous ills. It was the only tree on his property. It stood pathetically in a low depression just beyond the boundary of the garden. He recalls, "The tree was ugly. It attracted bugs. It blocked my view." He wanted to chop it down, but did not want the stump. He recalled Martha Graham admonishing her students at Bennington, where Kunitz also taught: "Self-consciousness is ugly!" The sad gesture in the scrawny, gnarled trunk suggested a Graham dance, "The Lamentation."

What to do with the tree? Kunitz says, "I thought I would transform it into something I loved." Somewhat astonished at the confident way he can sound cruel, he explains how he choked the chokecherry by training Baltic ivy to sheath it. He had pruned the branches. The gesture evolved into "an oxymoron," says Kunitz, "both an artifact and something organic." He calls the tree his "Lamentation Tree."

It is the first thing he looks at each morning, he says. The tree is charismatic because it embodies death. "Like us," says Kunitz, "it lives and dies at once." It enacts with upraised, amputated arms the image of the suffering it undergoes. This is a pervasive theme in Kunitz's poetry. A beached whale dying on the beach is magnificent when its parched skin becomes parchment for teenagers to carve their initials on: The whale becomes "like us, / disgraced and mortal."

Searching Kunitz's poetry, I have found a song that his Lamentation Tree sings. It is called, "An Old Cracked Tune"*:

> My name is Solomon Levi,
> the desert is my home,
> my mother's breast was thorny,
> and father I had none.
>
> The sands whispered, *Be separate,*
> the stones taught me, *Be hard.*
> I dance, for the joy of surviving,
> on the edge of the road.

Gardening is an aspect of Kunitz's meditative life. "Many of my poems come to me while I'm working in the garden. And I feel a direct flow of energy from the earth itself. When I garden, I'm deep in physical sensations and nourished by a storm of images. I need these day-by-day satisfactions."

The poet's garden occupies a semipublic space. A glimpse is available from the street. The garden itself borrows a view of the bay, across the street. In this bay—Provincetown Harbor—the Pilgrims signed the Mayflower Compact upon their arrival in the New World (to simplify history, one might say the Pilgrims left Provincetown and settled in Plymouth because the soil in Provincetown was so poor, so sandy, so like the desert of Solomon Levi). Today, Provincetown is gregarious, but not puritan. More like a Mediterranean fishing village, with the eave of one house tucked under the wing of another, the town is closely packed and gets along as an extended family. Portuguese emigrants from the Azores work a large fleet of fishing vessels, painted festively in places where the paint is not worn to bare wood.

Another local, democratizing influence is the swelling population of artists and writers who have colonized the town (notable are Robert Motherwell and Norman Mailer). "Is the essence of a private garden privacy?" Kunitz answers, "My garden is shaped by circumstances. Sure, it's a highly personal garden, but it's public space. I do control it. The hedge obliges people to observe from the wrought iron gate. I control their angle of vision. I have thought about shutting off the garden from public view with a more solid barrier at the entrance. No doubt that would make me happier; it would also make me guilty. I am part of this community. To a degree I enjoy sharing it. People stop and go 'Ooh' and 'Ah' and I say 'Thank you, thank you,' but I do not talk. I often tell them I am the hired hand."

Like poetry, gardening can be a technique for enlarging the ego through modesty. "A tendency more and more apparent in modern life is for the artist to cease to be common, to share general concerns. Now he is becoming a specialist, or a technician at an advanced level, really a machine for converting the life into poetry or fiction or painting. One is thinking, 'How am I going to make a little poem out of my knowledge of flowers?' I reject that attitude." Kunitz believes that too many artists today have a tendency to distance themselves from ordinary experience, such as cooking, eating, gardening. "When I was a child in Worcester, Massachusetts, where the woods had spongy paths and were still Indian-haunted, I had a little garden. This, because I wanted to. Nobody told me, do this, do that. I called my first garden a Victory Garden, though I was not old enough yet to know what that meant. I just thought if anything grew, it was a victory."

How does a poet garden? Mostly by caring. "Gardening for me is a passionate effort to organize a little corner of the earth, which I want to redeem. The wish is to achieve control over your little plot so that it appears beautiful, distinguished—an equivalent of your signature in the natural world."

Provincetown /1984
[*Garden Design*, Winter 1984-85]

The Buried Life

by Caroline Sutton

When most of us are settling down for the night, Pulitzer Prize–winning poet Stanley Kunitz is just beginning to work. He writes between midnight and dawn, has never taken a nap in his life, and manages still, at the venerable age of eighty, to get by on about four hours of sleep. Will he ever slow down? "No," scoffs the poet with a glint in his eye. "That's my circadian rhythm. And you must never break your rhythm."

Kunitz's resonant and rhythmical poems are full of allusion and metaphor. Some are metaphysical, most are rich in details of the natural world. Above all, Kunitz's voice is his own and difficult to categorize. "There's always a kind of poetry that is in fashion in each decade," he says, "and I never have fitted into any of those categories." Despite the vagaries of poetic fashion, the long list of honors crediting Kunitz include a fellowship from the National Endowment for the Arts, the Amy Lowell Poetry Traveling Fellowship, a Guggenheim grant, and *Poetry*'s Levinson Prize. Atlantic Monthly Press has just published his new book, *Next-to-Last Things: New Poems and Essays*. It contains thirteen highly polished poems and nine prose pieces on subjects ranging from his friend Robert Lowell to his mother's childhood in Lithuania and her emigration to New York.

Dressed casually in an olive sports jacket and plaid shirt, Kunitz greets us in his elegant Greenwich Village apartment. The living room houses an array of art objects collected on his travels; the walls are blanketed with art. "I was very close to all the chief painters of the so-called abstract expressionist work," notes Kunitz, gazing at a Robert Motherwell dedicated to the poet on his sixty-first birthday. Among others, he points out a Philip Guston drawing based on a Kunitz poem and several vibrant paintings by Kunitz's third wife, Elise Asher. Smiling warmly, the balding, mustached poet settles into a velvet armchair to talk about his life, his art, and his new book.

The poems in *Next-to-Last Things* draw on Kunitz's love of rural life. He has spent much of his life in the country and now divides his time between New York and Cape Cod. "Many of my poems come to me while I'm digging in the garden on the Cape, pruning or doing the chores every gardener must do," he says. "But I'm not content with merely being a reporter of the scene. My poems are always looking for something beyond that stretch of land. What I'm looking for is to somehow come in touch with the mystery of existence itself. And it becomes even more mysterious with the years."

Talking specifically about his new poem, "The Snakes of September,"* Kunitz adds, "The local particulars lead you into universals. You see a pair of snakes in your garden twining, and suddenly you think of the whole principle of creation of which this is an emblem. But if you didn't care for those two snakes hanging out of that Alberta spruce and if you didn't have some tenderness of feeling about them, you would never arrive at the conclusion of the poem, or the universal thought that it has led to."

To our query about what process occurs from the moment an idea for a poem germinates to the time it appears on the paper, Kunitz answers: "A lot depends on where the poem starts. Sometimes it starts from an idea. That isn't usually the way it works with me. Sometimes it starts with an image and sometimes it starts with nothing but a rhythm and then you have to find your poem. You have to go deep into your buried life in order really to bring to the surface that cluster of images that will hold in balance the elements that have excited you and which awake memories. I like to think of a poem as being written in layers. That's what I look for in a poem, a poem that's woven. Just as a tapestry cannot be woven out of a single set of threads because you need another set of threads as a counterweave, so too I think of a poem as consisting of these crossweavings of thought and image and feeling."

For Kunitz, writing an essay is much the same as creating a poem. "I spend as much time, just as much care on a prose essay as I do on a poem," he says. The poems and the essays [in *Next-to-Last Things*] seem to me to be of a piece and I hope they will be read as such." Among his new prose is an enlightening exposition on the "physicality" of poetry. "Poetry originated in song and dance," insists Kunitz. "I don't separate the language of the poem from the language of the body." Like many poets, Kunitz paces in his study while at work.

Acknowledging that he has never been a prolific poet, Kunitz adds, "I think that explains why I am able to continue as a poet into my late years. If I hadn't had an urgent impulse, if the poem didn't seem to me terribly important, I never wanted to write it and didn't. And that's persisted. I suppose my conditioning has been not for the sprints but for the long-distance races. I think the imagination remains young, it's only the body that wears out. My imaginative life is just as intense and glowing as it's ever been. And I hope to continue to write poems."

Kunitz can hardly remember a time when he wasn't writing poems. As a young boy growing up in Worcester, Massachusetts, writing and reading were passions from the third grade on. Kunitz's father committed suicide just before he was born, and his mother, a dress designer and manufacturer, was away all day, but his teachers actively encouraged him to write. "I founded a literary magazine in high school," says Kunitz with a twinkle in his eye, "and of course immediately became editor, which gave me an opportunity to publish my stuff from the beginning."

After graduating *summa cum laude* from Harvard, with his first collection of poems in progress, Kunitz headed for New York in 1928 to try his fortune. "I knew nobody in the literary world and I felt very much a stranger in the city. Early in 1929 I stuffed my poems into an envelope and sent them off to Doubleday Doran, which was then the biggest publishing house in Manhattan. I thought I might as well start with a big one. And to my amazement, about two weeks later, there was a phone call and a voice said, 'This is Ogden Nash. I'm the poetry editor at Doubleday. I've just been reading your manuscript. We very much want to publish it.' I thought, my God, it's so easy, life is going to be very simple. But it wasn't."

The first book was *Intellectual Things*, published in 1930. By the time a second book was completed, Kunitz was ready for a change. He submitted the work to a number of publishers and, after some refusals, arrived at Holt. *Passport to the War* was published while Kunitz was in the army "and it sort of fell dead without even a thump. This kind of book was certainly not one to stir up patriotic feelings," remarks Kunitz. "I don't think it was published at the right time; but that didn't discourage me, obviously.

"When the time came for me to publish a selected volume, I put it together and showed it to at least seven publishers, all of whom turned it down. It just didn't seem to be the kind of poetry that was in fashion at that time. I think they were looking for Audenesque poems during that period."

At length, through his friend Richard Wilbur, Kunitz came to Atlantic, where editors Seymour Lawrence and Emily Morison Beck issued *Selected Poems: 1928–1958*. Later, Peter Davison became Kunitz's longtime editor. "I have been very happy publishing there," says Kunitz, "because of a mutual feeling of loyalty and confidence and respect. It's a great advantage to have a publisher who is waiting for your next book, instead of having to peddle it."

Despite Kunitz's luck at finding publishers, making a living writing poetry has been hard. To make ends meet in the thirties and early forties, Kunitz worked for the H. W. Wilson Company editing literary reference books. After the war, he got his first teaching job at Bennington College and has since taught at the New School, the University of Washington, Queens College, Brandeis, and Columbia. In the coming year, he will give seminars in creative writing at various colleges around the country.

"Teaching is replenishing," says Kunitz. "I enjoy working with the young and sharing with them in that whole process of the creative act. I feel I've learned a great deal from my students, as I hope they've learned from me. It's an act of reciprocity, and I think it's one of the things that has kept me alive as a writer."

The change in Kunitz's work over the course of his career points to his continued growth and vitality. "My early poems were very intricate, dense and formal," he recalls. "They were written in conventional metrics and stanzaic patterns. My primary influences were the metaphysical poets, particularly Herbert and Donne, along with Blake and Hopkins. I was drawn toward a more open and less involuted style as my subject matter began to change, became more connected with exploring the psyche—getting down to the roots of the imaginative life—and involved with the events of an epoch. So the poems were turning both inward and outward at the same time. Eventually I began to seek a much simpler, more available and more accessible speech pattern. And certainly in my late poems I've learned to depend on a simplicity that seems almost nonpoetic on the surface, but has reverberations within that keep it intense and alive. I like to think of it as being a transparency of language through which one can see the world. I think that as a young poet I looked for what Keats called 'a fine excess,' but as an old poet I look for spareness and rigor and a world of compassion."

In a voice that is deep, rolling, and unhurried, the poet continues, "I suppose another impulse that dominates my whole activity as a poet is the urgent need to transmit what it means to be alive at this given moment in history. This is one of the great functions of poetry through the ages. To me that's one of the responsibilities of the poet. And above all one has to be determined never to lie, because that's the unforgivable sin against poetry itself."

Kunitz does not believe that it is the poet's responsibility to try to change the social or political climate of his day. "You can't make that your function," he says. "If you write a poem to persuade others to believe or not to believe or to act in such and such a way, if you're trying to convert them to a political cause, you're using poetry as a tool and poetry resents being so employed. What one tries to do always is to convey the intensity and the truth of one's passions and one's thoughts. Some will listen and perhaps it will be of help to them in changing their own lives and their own hearts, but the poem cannot deliberately set out to do that."

In light of the tremendous value Kunitz places on poetry and his high standards for it, we ask his opinion of the poetry being written today. "I don't believe," he states emphatically, "there ever was a society in the history of humankind that had more poets of quality than we have now in the United States. The difficulty is that so many of them are alike and do not have a distinctive voice. It's the poetry of a generation. And since it's taught in the creative writing programs, it tends to have a certain stamp of workmanship on it and less idiosyncratic genius than in previous epochs when poets were self-taught.

"Poetry, like everything else, tends to become a highly specialized production," Kunitz continues. "All our society is moving toward greater and greater specialization. The poet originally was the myth maker. The poet knew everything that could be known about what was going on in the tribe or in the society that fostered him because the amount of knowledge that was available could be embraced by a single mind. But society becomes more and more complicated and compartmentalized. The poet today tends to develop narrowly as a technician of the word cultivating a rarefied linguistic skill, not as the great generalist defined by Wordsworth, that is to say, a representative person speaking to other persons in the common language of their shared concerns."

Is Kunitz hopeful that the readership of poetry in this country will grow? "I doubt that poetry in the foreseeable future will have vast audiences," he replies, "given the degree of specialization in our society and the nature of our money-driven, power-driven culture. Nevertheless, as I travel around the country reading and lecturing on various campuses, I am struck by the level of understanding and responsiveness, the presence of so much compassionate idealism, among the young people who care about poetry and who actually seem to hunger for it. There are more of them than one might reasonably expect. Many more. And that gives me hope for the day when they will step into the mainstream of American life."

We walk down a hallway lined with photographs to his study, where Kunitz proudly shows us programs from the five-day Stanley Kunitz Festival held in Worcester this October in honor of the poet's eightieth birthday. "While there is no community at large in the United States for the poet, there are small oases," smiles Kunitz. "It was such a rare phenomenon to have the sense of a whole community participating in welcoming someone for writing poems. I have to count it as one of the miracles of the age."

New York / 1985
[*Publishers Weekly*, December 1985]

Life between Scylla and Charybdis
by Michael Ryan

The life of a poet is crystallized in his work, that's how you know him.
                                                    —Stanley Kunitz

This is one of the poems by Stanley Kunitz I love the most:

MY SISTERS

Who whispered, souls have shapes?
So has the wind, I say.
But I don't know,
I only feel things blow.

I had two sisters once
with long black hair
who walked apart from me
and wrote the history of tears.
Their story's faded with their names,
but the candlelight they carried,
like dancers in a dream,
still flickers on their gowns
as they bend over me
to comfort my night-fears.

Let nothing grieve you,
Sarah and Sophia.
Shush, shush, my dears,
now and forever.

The poem is beyond comment, or underneath it, at least in the language of criticism, which is "a kind of translation," as Eudora Welty says, "like a headphone we can clamp on at the U.N. when they are speaking the Arabian tongue." "My Sisters" resists this translation exceptionally well because its Arabic is silence—the silences of the past, of lost time, death, and eternity. These are different silences, I think, and one of the accomplish-

128

ments of the poem is that it differentiates them, it makes them distinct and present and felt as such, and then gathers them into that tender, heart-breaking final sentence—"Shush, shush," a comforting gesture, a wish for silence as relief from sadness or grief or a child's night-fears (and so calling back to stanza two), a wish for silence as relief from frailty and mortality. Just as the past becomes present (through the agency of "the candlelight they carried" that "still flickers"), and the comforted finally becomes the comforter (and vice versa), that last gesture transforms the preceding silences into one silence that includes not only the poem's characters but also its readers. At least this reader. It makes me feel the intimate texture of the simple, inexhaustible fact that—as Kunitz put it in an interview—"we are living and dying at the same time."

The way it does this is primarily nondiscursive, through structure, movement, music, and drama. "The best part" of a poem, Frost said, is "the unspoken part." Almost all of "My Sisters" is unspoken in this sense, like Hardy's "During Wind and Rain," which so exceeds its commonplace idea, that human beings are mortal, by embodying its emotional truth in structure and rhythm, refrain and variation, in the voice that begins each stanza and begins the poem, "They sing their dearest songs," and the voice that invariably answers and closes the poem, "Down their carved names the rain-drop plows."

"My Sisters" has two voices, too, but their function and relationship are very different from those of Hardy's poem. The voice of the first stanza frames the rest of "My Sisters" like one of Vermeer's half-opened windows that filter and admit the light in which everything appears at once palpable and numinous. It strikes me as a voice out of nowhere, from the wilderness of inner space, not the same "I" that speaks the second and third stanzas but given terrestrial life by the second "I." "There is an aspect of one's existence that has nothing to do with personal identity, but that falls away from self, blends into the natural universe," Kunitz wrote in *A Kind of Order, A Kind of Folly*. This, I believe, is the first "I" of "My Sisters," appropriately distinguished by italics from the personal "I" who has memories and affections and a life in time; one of the dramatic undercurrents of the poem is probably *their* blending together "into the natural universe" of silence.

In any case, the first line—"*Who whispered, souls have shapes?*"—sets the tone. It echoes in my ear "Who said, 'Peacock Pie'?"—the beginning of a strange, wonderful poem by a strange, sometimes wonderful poet, Walter de la Mare, who is much loved in England and mostly unread in the United States. De la Mare's is another poem in two voices, one that questions and one that replies, a mechanical arrangement meant to go nowhere, unlike

"My Sisters," which moves great distances gracefully "like dancers in a dream." "My Sisters" is, in fact, a miracle of movement, traveling from the impersonal undervoice of the opening to the intimate direct address of the ending, invariably immediate and increasingly dramatic. Is it this movement over the fluid three-beat lines marked by irregular rhymes and half-rhymes which makes the form feel like a membrane that can barely contain an overwhelming grief and sweetness? The way the three-beat line is used is a joy to look at closely. The second sentence of the second stanza, besides being a wonder syntactically and lodging in the dramatic image so it won't be forgotten, is cut into lines of extraordinary rhythmical beauty and function. "Like dancers in a dream" is the pivotal line of the six-line sentence. The return to the strict iambic trimeter after the rhythmical variation of the previous three lines physiologically and psychologically brings the line home. The satisfaction of the rhythmical expectation mounting since the last strict iambic trimeter ("who walked apart from me") is bonded to content, and the image of the "dancers in a dream" acquires the authority of that satisfaction. "Like dancers in a dream" also immediately reestablishes the ground beat, the rhythmical context for the lines following it. "Still flickers on their gowns"—another iambic trimeter—reinforces this, but unlike the previous three lines it isn't end-stopped, a subtle variation, but enough with the line's slightly increased duration to echo the ground beat yet still keep the rhythm fluid. Now, in the next line, when the second beat occurs before it "should"—"as they *bend* over me"—that moment takes on terrific emphasis, even if, especially if, this emphasis is registered subconsciously while we are attending to the drama, the meaning of the words. The gesture of bending becomes palpable beneath its description or representation.

Also, the subconscious rhythmical effect is so powerful at that moment, it keeps us locked in the remembered scene to a degree that makes the astonishing move into direct address after the stanza-break feel simple and natural. This kind of pivot or "turn"—what Petrarch called the "volta" between the octave and sestet of the sonnet—seems inherent to poetic form, and there are all sorts of turns in all sorts of poems, but this one, because of its marriage of solidity and wildness, seems to me inspired: "Let nothing grieve you, / Sarah and Sophia." And, by saying the names, the story that had "faded with their names" is restored; the sisters are given life, as in a ritual of the dead, at least for the ritualistic, rhythmic time of the poem. Their silence is shaped and, in the poem's last gesture, accepted and honored.

A great deal could be written about how the last stanza uses the established iambic trimeter to depart from it, but I want to look at only two lines, both examples of foreshortening but of different kinds. The first line—"Let nothing grieve you"—has three beats but a syllable missing in a strategic position. The unexpected silence extends the long vowel of "grieve"; because of the metrical pattern, the word literally must be given more time than it normally takes to say it, just as the syllable "you" acquires a stronger stress than it would have in conversation. If there were an unstressed syllable between "grieve" and "you," for example, "Let nothing grieve for you," the glide of the long ē—Emily Dickinson's favorite vowel, like a scream—wouldn't require extension because the sound would be encased in the iambic trimeter. As it is, the held note makes a very affecting music.

And the last line of the poem, working within and against the metrical grid, is even more effective and affecting: "Now and forever." Period. Two stresses and a feminine ending. In the ensuing silence after the last, unstressed syllable, after all those three-beat lines, the final beat never comes. Its absence is palpable, as if the silence itself were stressed, an endless incompletion, a longing for something missing, something lost.

The wealth of mystery in the poem, a good part of which is acquired through its rhythm and music, is not obscured by the slightest mystification. Its depths are discovered and displayed in a language absolutely simple and clear, words, as Wittgenstein said, "like film on deep water." Kunitz himself said in *The Paris Review* interview: "I dream of an art so transparent you can look through and see the world." He surely has already accomplished this, and much more, in "My Sisters."

Stanley Kunitz was eighty last July. As much as a young poet could learn about writing poetry from his poems, he or she could learn about the vocation of poetry from his prose. The book to mark his birthday appropriately includes poems and essays. But his life with poetry has not been confined to writing. For Kunitz, poetry is a spiritual discipline, a way of being and knowing oneself and the world, and he has purposefully presented himself as an example in a century when it has probably never been harder to live a poet's vocation and never been easier to cultivate a poet's "career," pathetic as such a "career" is next to those valued by corporate society.

In this regard, though his style was initially suffused with Hopkins and the Metaphysical Poets, the figure of John Keats in his "vale of Soul-making" has been Kunitz's main spiritual guide. In "The Modernity of Keats," first published in 1964, he wrote that Keats's "technique was not an aggregate of mechanical skills, but a form of spiritual testimony." And this observation is recast as Kunitz's central assumption a decade later in the foreword to *A Kind of Order, A Kind of Folly*: "One of my unshakeable convictions has been that poetry is more than a craft, important as the craft may be: it is a vocation, a passionate enterprise, rooted in human sympathies and aspirations."

Theoretically, it may appear that this vocation could be a private affair between the poet and his or her own soul, as it surely was for Emily Dickinson and for Hopkins, though even in the latter case this was not necessarily by choice. Hopkins wrote to his friend Dixon in 1878: "What I do regret is the loss of recognition belonging to the work itself. For as to every moral act, being right or wrong, there belongs, of the nature of things, reward or punishment, so to every form perceived by the mind belongs, of the nature of things, admiration or the reverse." And, later in the same letter, more from the gut than from the Jesuit: "Disappointment and humiliation embitter the heart and make an aching in the very bones."

How many poets have sooner or later been poisoned by this bitterness? It's clearly from the desire and need for an audience that disappointment and humiliation and worse have inevitably come. Yet even if this desire and need were eliminated in the poet's heart, "Art is social in origin" (as Jane Ellen Harrison says bluntly in *Ancient Art and Ritual*), and poetry still retains its fundamental social character, even when the difference between the sale of five thousand copies of a volume of poems, which is unusual, and fifty thousand copies, which is almost unheard of, is the difference between minute fractions of one percent of the population. In response, poetry can and sometimes has become hermetic, opaque, precious, and prosaic; it can become difficult—as Eliot said it *must* be in this century—like a child suffering from lack of attention and love. It can refuse to give pleasure, even to the poet who writes it. And the figure of the poet may become the *poète maudit*, Gérard de Nerval walking his lobster on a leash and hanging himself with a shoelace, dandified, flippant—or doomed, as in the sad incarnation of Delmore Schwartz in an essay entitled "The Vocation of the Poet in the Modern World":

> In the unpredictable and fearful future that awaits civilization, the poet must be prepared to be alienated and indestructible. He must dedicate himself to poetry, although no one else seems likely to read what he writes; he must be indestructible as a poet until he is destroyed as a human being.

In the absence of an audience, are the available choices either killing the poetry or killing the poet? It's interesting and moving to watch how poets have tried to negotiate this Scylla and Charybdis in their lives and ideas and work. In his "Preface to *Lyrical Ballads* (1800)," Wordsworth internalizes the conflict between the poet and a culture which has abandoned him because his original social function is served by more efficient institutions and technology. Wordsworth tries to rescue the poet's social role by asserting that "the Poet binds together by passion and knowledge the vast empire of human society, as it is spread over the whole earth, and over all time." Yet, in the same essay, having imagined this grand audience out of the thinnest air, he admits that, in fact, the Poet's "own feelings are his stay and support."

For poets since the Industrial Revolution, Wordsworth articulates the predicament, but his solution is a formula for solipsism or, as Keats charitably called it, the "Wordsworthian or egotistical sublime." Grandiosity ("the vast empire," etc.) and isolation ("his own feelings are his stay and support") can only feed and increase each other, and, if their marriage is insular, can only breed bombast. They can kill the poet's soul and consequently his art, and can even become—as in the case of Delmore Schwartz and the dominant figures of Kunitz's generation—a risk to his life.

This danger is exactly what Whitman is addressing in this great passage from his "Preface" to the 1855 edition of *Leaves of Grass*:

> The soul has that measureless pride which consists in never acknowledging any lessons but its own. But it has sympathy as measureless as its pride and the one balances the other and neither can stretch too far while it stretches in company with the other. The inmost secrets of art sleep with the twain.

The poet's "own feelings are his stay and support" for Whitman, too, but his "measureless pride," essential to enduring the lack of an audience and its economic and psychological implications, is offset by a "sympathy as measureless" for other people and even for other things outside of the self. This is the crucial counterweight to the solipsism that is Whitman's explicit currency, and from the tension between them he makes his poetry: "The inmost secrets of art sleep with the twain." Tested by poverty and loneliness to the degree that, as Kunitz quotes him in "At the Tomb of Walt Whitman," he sometimes felt his poems "in a pecuniary and worldly sense, have certainly wrecked the life of their author," the balance of "measureless" pride and sympathy is nonetheless the key to Whitman's spiritual discipline and probably to his survival.

It is also a remarkably accurate description of Stanley Kunitz. His poetry, his character, and his ideas are born of these polarities. From his new book, *Next-to-Last Things*:

> If it were not for [the poet's] dream of perfection, which is the emblem of his life-enhancing art, and which he longs to share with others, generations of men and women would gradually sink into passivity, accepting as their lot

second-rate or third-rate destinies, or worse. If one is to be taught submission, in the name of progress or national security, it is redemptive to recall the pride of one [Keats] who averred that his only humility was toward "the eternal Being, the Principle of Beauty, and the Memory of great Men."

The paradox, of course, is that a "life-enhancing art" which the poet "longs to share with others" isn't subject to the modification, opinion, or response of any other human being—"the eternal Being, the Principle of Beauty, and the Memory of great Men" being ideas—much less of any audience at large. And if the idea of the poet's preventing "generations" from sinking "into passivity" sounds like Wordsworth, in an earlier essay and somewhat different mood, Kunitz shows himself to be fully aware of the hazards of such "measureless pride":

> One of the dangers of poetry, certainly, is grandiosity. Let us not deceive ourselves: a poet isn't going to change the world with even the most powerful of his poems. The best he can hope for is to conquer a piece of himself.

In Kunitz's view, the spiritual discipline of poetry implies and incorporates the poet's social function. The poet is "an embodiment of resistance":

> resistance against universal apathy, mediocrity, conformity, against institutional pressures to make everything look and become alike. This is why he is so involved with contraries.

He is "the representative free man of our time":

> The poet, in the experience of his art, is a whole person, or he is nothing. . . . He is uniquely equipped to defend the worth and power and responsibility of individuals in a world of institutions.

Consequently, and most pointedly:

> The poet speaks to others not only through what he says but through what he is, his symbolic presence, as though he carried a set of flags reading Have a Heart, Let Nothing Get By, Live at the Center of Your Being. His life instructs us that it is not necessary, or even desirable, for everyone to join the crowds streaming onto the professional or business highway, pursuing the bitch goddess.

In other words (though a paraphrase is hardly needed), the poet's vocation has an important social function even if his poetry is drowned out by the noise of TV, movies, commercials, and factories spuming forth new products. It's a vocation inherently subversive to corporate ideology, spoken symbolically and by example:

> Poets are subversive, but they are not really revolutionaries, for revolutionaries are concerned with changing others, while poets want first of all to change themselves.

If those dedicated to social change through civil disobedience spend a lot of time in jail, the poet's dedication to changing himself implies a life of internal exile in a society built for profit, in—as Ronald Reagan calls it— "the age of the entrepreneur." Kunitz's most recent statement, in *The Paris Review* interview, is also his most urgent:

> Evil has become a product of manufacture, it is built into our whole industrial and political system, it is being manufactured every day, it is rolling off the assembly line, it is being sold in the stores, it pollutes the air. . . .
> Perhaps the way to cope with the adversary is to confront him in ourselves. We have to fight for our little bit of health. We have to make our living and dying important again. And the living and dying of others. Isn't this what poetry is about?

In this light, a poem as apparently apolitical as "My Sisters" takes on political content and becomes a political gesture, ineffective as it may be against the million movies and TV programs in which life is sentimentalized and death is trivialized. The political nature of poetry has no more to do with subject than with its rendering, in making us feel living and dying are more important than property and "the national interest," in using language clearly and accountably, unlike the way politicians and commercials use it. Insofar as the poet's vocation is a public act, it can be an act of conscience with a social function, though the border between public and publicity in this media culture needs constant checking. If the vocation of poetry Kunitz describes were arranged in a line, it would look like his characterization of "the power of the mind": "to transform, to connect, to communicate"—the first ("to transform") being the poet's relation to himself in his spiritual discipline, the second ("to connect") his relation to the world and to others, and the third ("to communicate") his social function, both through his poetry and his "symbolic presence." Of course, it isn't a line. It's all these at once.

This outline of Kunitz's ideas really is "a kind of translation" from "the Arabian tongue" of his prose. He certainly never presents them this systematically. They have more vitality and nuance combined with his many other convictions, concerns, and affections. Reading his essays, I get a transfusion of his indomitable spirit, his "fierce hold on life," which is much more important to me than my agreement. There are excellent reasons, for the sake of the poetry itself, to try to rescue its social function, even when from all appearances it has none. Poets from Horace to Sidney to Eliot have tried to do so, finding themselves at the edge of exile within the versions of civilization in which they lived. For Kunitz, poetry is a manifestation of hope and life, for the culture as well as for the individual— this is the source of its power and poignance. He argues for the essential seriousness of poetry, and for clarity and depth and music at a time when intelligent critics, perhaps unconsciously reflecting the political atmosphere, indulge triviality and obscurity and praise superficial linguistic invention.

> In the best poetry of our time—but only the best—one is aware of a moral pressure being exerted on the medium in the very act of creation. By "moral" I mean a testing of existence at its highest pitch—what does it feel like to be totally oneself?; an awareness of others beyond the self; a concern with values and meaning rather than with effects; an effort to tap the spontaneity that hides in the depths rather than what forms on the surface; a conviction about the possibility of making right and wrong choices. Lacking this pressure, we are left with nothing but a vacuum occupied by technique.

In exactly this sense, Kunitz's example to poets of my generation is a moral example, put forward consciously with an awareness of the hazards of doing so. He has said, "The poet's first obligation is survival," by which he means spiritual as well as literal, knowing from experience the conflicts between the two for a poet in this culture: "No bolder challenge confronts the modern artist than to stay healthy in a sick world."

Visiting Stanley Kunitz a few years ago, during a difficult period, I made the standard complaints about the poet's life that anyone who has been around poets has heard a thousand times. That means he had heard them a hundred thousand times, and maybe even voiced them once or twice when he was living in absolute obscurity on almost nothing, as he did for over twenty years. But he listened until I was finished, and then replied, "But, Michael, poetry is something you give to the world." If I'm ever able, as Chekhov said, "to squeeze the slave's blood out of my veins," this is the type of blood I would replace it with.

[*American Poetry Review*, Sept./Oct. 1985]

To My Teacher

by Louise Glück

About a year ago, in a classroom, I was asked to comment on my training as a writer. So I talked about my remarkable teachers, first Léonie Adams, then Stanley Kunitz. In fact, I was being drawn out to confirm a theory, a parable meant to connect the person presented, the fierce poet in the display case, with the obliging, malleable girl I must once have been, the diligent student who, after cautious apprenticeship, boldly cast off authority in order to write the true poems, the poems of experience, not written to please. This is the formula: a young girl is rescued by good fortune or energetic labor from the coffin of gender, meaning supervision by men. That myth arose to explain a perceived reality. But no one myth can explain all reality. What I found interesting in that classroom was the efficiency with which the teacher, also a woman, rejected nuance in favor of clean categories and individual testimony in favor of a cherished conception. In any case, those years didn't feel like that. What they were, what they meant, what I would have been without them, is hard to say, as the relation of teacher and student is hard to summarize. When it goes well, something passes between these figures, a species of love, one of the very few whose limitations do not impose suffering.

I met Stanley Kunitz when I was nineteen, having studied for two years with Léonie Adams. Both taught at Columbia, at the School of General Studies. They were in some ways alike, or what I took from them was similar. Teaching is not a series of opinions to be annexed: both Adams and Kunitz taught habits of thought, severe, strenuous, passionate—the giddiness of great discipline and great ambition. I had stopped taking class with Adams over a difference in taste, not directly regarding my own work. One evening, she'd read what seemed to her a shockingly bad poem, then being much praised. That poem was, for me, an epiphany; it told me how I wanted to sound. And, obviously, Adams was not the person to help me sound like that.

I don't know if, at nineteen, I seemed malleable. Like all people with a powerful sense of vocation, I was concerned with what I could use; by some absolute rule I recognized those minds I needed. I was less concerned, being self-absorbed, with the degree to which, by exposing myself to other wills, I might myself be changed. That is, I felt it necessary that I change; I wanted to be more than I was. At what point is the self, the voice, so wholly realized as to make its every project sacred? Obsession with authority as a principle of annihilation preserves the individual at the expense of growth. Even twenty-five years ago, it seemed clear to me that if my talent were so fragile, so precarious, as to require insulation from the world, it would never produce what I dreamed of anyway. So I made a sort of contract: I was prepared to be changed, but only by instruments of my own choosing. In that choice, I was meticulous.

Kunitz was my teacher for five years. But "teacher" seems the wrong noun, or maybe "teach" is the wrong verb. It seems simultaneously limited and coercive, as though its end product were to be a treaty of perpetual accord. For five years I overheard a splendid mind engaged with words, with what was the most crucial involvement in my life. I saw a kind of rigor in practice, and thought the sacrifice of contentment (which I didn't have anyway) was well worth such serious joy.

As the myth contends, I wrote to please him. In this, he was one in a series of projections, beginning with my mother. But the advantage in trying to please Kunitz was immense: what he wanted was to be surprised. This meant that lines like the lines he admired in January would not interest him in March. His voice became that part of my own mind that has been, since childhood, the tireless drill sergeant saying *move, move*, but in his voice concrete criticism substituted for mortification: where my own mind says *you are a fool to have hoped*, which produced anguish and justified laziness, Kunitz's voice would comment on the weak line, the dull word, the specific opacity. Where I damned and abandoned, he exhorted and compelled in the way only an outside voice can, because it can be excused praise. I felt, much of the time, doomed and exhilarated, or, in practical terms, always very tired, like a salmon swimming against the current. I had, in Kunitz, not only a persuasive argument for stamina but a companion spirit, someone my poems could talk to. Because what was clear from the first was that nothing in them was lost on him. I owe a great debt to Léonie Adams, but in the most profound sense Kunitz was the first human being by whom I felt entirely heard and this fact was a source of endless happiness. It couldn't have been, the sensation couldn't have lasted, if it translated into blanket approval. I wanted approval, but more than that I wanted to be heard, which is, I think, a more convincing proof of existence. One scene in particular haunts me. And if it is, in fact, an image of rescue, what I would stress are the means of rescue.

Several years have passed. The classes at General Studies have ended; Kunitz has not yet begun to teach at the School of the Arts. The School of the Arts doesn't exist. But I am to send him poems, keep him informed about the progress of my manuscript, which has for some time been moving from bored hand to bored hand. It is, for me, a very bad year. All my life there have been periods of painful silence: this is something different.

I am writing with unusual fluency, writing one poem after another, but each poem in turn fills me with terror. They are that bad—not badly written, but empty, forced, accumulating, as a group, into a devastating verdict. This verdict is bad enough as I think it; I cannot face hearing it spoken. So seeing Kunitz at some reading causes wild anxiety. I am chastised: Why have I sent him no poems? I must promise to send him poems.

My next problem is that promise: the problem is I have to keep it. And part of me, the stoic who was once so ready to let the fragile gift wither, thinks maybe this is just as well, that sooner or later the worst has to be encountered. The other part of me counsels flight. But I send the work. And then, amazingly, I am invited to Twelfth Street to discuss it. A most interesting turn. Because this is a man of honor: having read the poems, he still wants to talk to me. For the next week, I feel very strange, feel as I felt years later when a poem was praised for what seemed to me its weakness. I feel a superficial calm and deeper agitation. It appears that either Kunitz will tell me, kindly, gently, that I am not a poet, or that Kunitz has read the poems wrong, has made a dreadful error, and I am not sure which turn is the more painful.

The house, which I get to see under these black circumstances is wonderful, filled with all kinds of fascinating objects, so that exclamation can legitimately postpone the inevitable conversation. We drink martinis. We talk about this and that. And I begin to think that perhaps I am the one who is wrong, that perhaps the poems are somehow eloquent and interesting, that perhaps they mark some advance I can't as yet take in. This is the only explanation for such extended amiability: Kunitz is not a person to refuse the difficult task, neither would he sadistically prolong it. I begin to feel a liquid well-being; I feel, actually, better than I have in about a year.

The poems were spread across his desk. I was standing in the doorway, from which distance they seemed quite impressive, unquestionably numerous, definitely printed with actual words. What Kunitz said was, "Of course, they're awful." And then, "But you know that." I referred this information immediately to God. I told Him that if He existed I wouldn't cry. That was about all that could be asked, since it was clear that I was, finally, really in the nightmare.

The turn was this, that Kunitz remarked, quite casually, that this didn't matter, that I was a poet. What he meant, I think, was something more precise, conservative and liberating, a concept wholly new to me. Not that the poems were of any worth, but that they did not constitute, despite their number, a prophecy.

We spent several minutes going through the work. Maybe we would save a few lines. We saved nothing; in relief and joy, I used all the daring words—trash, junk, fraud. Which seemed no longer an admission but a victory, heady in the way writing was heady. It was immeasurably important to do this in Kunitz's presence. He had done two things: paid me the compliment of speaking the truth, and afforded me the opportunity to follow suit. To learn through experience. Or, more accurately, to affirm a lost perception—what I had felt writing, and in psychoanalysis. That whatever the truth is, to speak it is a great adventure.

[*American Poetry Review*, Sept./Oct. 1985]

Lighting the Lamp

by Francine Ringold

Francine Ringold: One of the poems ("Lamplighter: 1914") in your newest volume *Next-to-Last Things*, which was published recently [1985] by Atlantic Monthly Press, ends with these splendid lines:

> I stood on the rim of the buggy wheel
> and raised my enchanter's wand,
> with its tip of orange flame
> to the gas mantles in their cages,
> touching them one by one,
> till the whole countryside bloomed.

There are many people who refer to you as a wizard, or an enchanter, if you will.

Stanley Kunitz: Well, it's damn hard work! [Laughter.] As for this poem, it goes back to an experience in my childhood when I was living on a farm, in a little village with the Indian name of Quinnapoxet, outside of Worcester, Massachusetts. The village has long since disappeared from the map. I guess I can claim to be the only living poet who was once a lamplighter on a country road.

FR: And you really did this?

SK: Yes . . . went round in a horse-drawn buggy from one lantern to another, lighting them at dusk.

FR: You know that reminds me, of course, that you are eighty . . .

SK: Eighty-one. I hate to tell you another birthday slipped by.

FR: It's hard to guess your age, talking to you, watching you move, your mind just as active as ever. Only this lamplighter now gives you away!

SK: I even remember the first automobile to come down the Quinnapoxet road. That's in the poem too. It was a Stanley Steamer—unfortunately not named after me. My horse bolted when that fuming contraption came chugging around the bend.

FR: When you say in the last line, "till the whole countryside bloomed," that reminds me you were featured in the magazine *House Beautiful*, in an article and photo essay on "A Poet's Garden." Which

141

leads me to the inevitable question: What is the relationship, if any, between poetry and gardening?

SK: In one of my poems I say, "He loved the earth so much he wanted to stay forever." Maybe I'll buy that for an epitaph! One is always trying to penetrate the mysteries of existence, and the things that grow are little allegories—every one! They speak of the terrible will to survive and the struggle toward the light. And the rewards are great: just the simple joy of bringing something to life and seeing it bloom in the midst of so much that's ugly in the world. And then again, I think every garden represents something of a personal triumph over ugliness and disorder, over nonexistence. It's like conquering a piece of yourself.

FR: An act of shaping, as we do in a poem.

SK: This vast chaotic planet and then this little plot of land you've made your own, given it your mark, your copyright signature.

FR: It's wonderful to see you in a garden and to see the bloom of words and flowers emerging as if they were inseparable. I can't help thinking, too, that gardening has been good for you—physically, I mean.

SK: Well, of course, poetry—this sedentary trade—is notorious for torturing the back and neck muscles. After sitting long hours at a desk I'm desperate to do something that will involve the whole body, restore my pleasure in its mobility and expressiveness. The soul suffers otherwise. Language that has no roots in the physical being is a dead language.

FR: I once heard you say that the garden is a lesson in being.

SK: Did I say that?

FR: I'm pretty sure you did. Certainly a garden reminds us of the seasons of our life, the stages of our passage.

SK: Yes, but it goes beyond memento mori. Gardeners watch the calendar and the weather, and they change with the seasons. They whistle at their work, even when the lilies wither. They won't pretend that a compost heap is beautiful, but they know that it serves a purpose. And they welcome the spring, because that's when they feel born again. Poets are supposed to die young, whereas gardeners are famous for their longevity. Now there's a paradox I won't try to resolve. The elegiac and the ecstatic modes must simply learn how to live together. I like to think that even at the submicroscopic level, day in and day out, whether I wake or sleep, my cells are going through their prescribed gyrations, their dance of division and subtraction, subject to the same law that rules the entire pulsing universe. There's a kind of rapture in that awareness, mixed with awe. Some lines I wrote once come back to me:

> Let me not say it, let me not reveal
> How like a god my heart begins to climb
> The trellis of the crystal
> In the rose-green moon;
> Let me not say it, let me leave untold
> This legend, while the nights snow emerald.
>
> Let me not say it, let me not confess
> How in the leaflight of my green-celled world
> In self's pre-history
> The blind moulds kiss;
> Let me not say it, let me but endure
> This ritual like feather and like star.

FR: "A poem without secrets," says Stanley Kunitz, "lies dead on the page." These secrets, his garden, the body of his thought and feeling, are his gift to us—a legacy of poetry—from 1928 to the present.

October 16, 1986 radio broadcast
KWGS-FM, Tulsa, Oklahoma
[*Nimrod* April, 1991]

A Visit to the Poet's Studio

by Susan Mitchell

A couple of months ago during a long night of insomnia that seemed the price paid for my recent dislocation from New England to South Florida, I reread Dante's *Vita Nuova* and Stanley Kunitz's *Next-to-Last Things* (The Atlantic Monthly Press, 1985). It was not only the fact that, once again, I was starting my life over that returned me to Dante and, for that matter, to Kunitz whose poems bear witness to his own powerful drive for spiritual renewal and transformation. I chose these writers because I had read them so often I knew they would give me an alternative to geographic place: they were a familiar intellectual soil I was already rooted in and a soil made all the more hospitable by my own numerous underlinings, asterisks, personal jottings penciled in margins. Here, said each marking, was a place I had stopped and thought and dreamed before. As I settled into that long reading, first one, then the other book spread open in my lap, the night itself opened up around me. Nights in South Florida, I was to learn that night, are not really dark, but different shades of blue. When I glanced up from my reading, there was the swimming pool, clearly visible, an eerie pale blue in the artificial light of the courtyard; and beyond the swimming pool and the rustling date palms, a deep water canal, sometimes navy, sometimes a muddy violet—colors not so much seen as sensed whenever a rhythmic slap of waves against the dock signaled the passing of a boat on its way to the Intracoastal. My move to Florida has coincided with the start of the rainy season, and at intervals during that night, torrents of rain would suddenly gush, plummet, and pour in columns so thick it was hard to tell whether the rain was falling or growing up from the earth, stalactite or stalagmite?—and then as abruptly as it had begun, the rain would stop. Sometimes a bird let fall long plumes of song, though with the source of the singing invisible, it seemed as if the air had become saturated with music, as well as with water, and at intervals had to spill down in trills and rivulets of song. Other times, birdsong arced, then dropped like a flare, the music momentarily illuminating the farthest reaches of the night: I was seeing all the way to the Keys where Florida trails off into dots and dashes—the geographic impulse tapering into archipelagoes, into the Dry Tortugas where the state finally dives into wild waters of the Atlantic or else lifts on a sudden updraft, soaring with the black frigate birds above the last malarial outpost, Fort Jefferson, where Dr. Samuel Mudd, guilty of setting the broken leg of Lincoln's assassin, wrote long letters home to Maryland and his wife.

During that night I felt lost within the enormous flatness of Florida, a terrain so filled with water—lakes, swamps, inlets, rivers, irrigation canals—that from the air, much of the state appears in continual motion; and at the same time, I felt the proud possessor of a geography that seemed to contract as easily as it could expand: the state suddenly reduced to that hand-sized piece I loved to snap into the jigsaw puzzle map of the United States I was given for my ninth birthday—Florida, an exciting Benadryl pink against the deep wooden blue of the Atlantic. It was within this shifting terrain that I read *Next-to-Last Things*, a book which is itself unusually concerned with shape shifting. "I will try to speak of the beauty of shapes," says Socrates in a passage from Plato's *Philebus* that provides the epigraph for the book's first section of thirteen poems. The shapes Socrates has in mind are the primal lineaments of the natural world and geometry: "straight lines and curves and the shapes made from them by the lathe, ruler or square." With this passage, we are close to the Platonic notion of ideal forms, those primordial figures from which the concrete, sensuous world is copied. And with ideal forms, we are in the the studio where creation begins.

What Henry James called "the sacred mystery of structure" has always been of crucial importance for Kunitz. Accumulative, circular, dialectical—these, he told his poetry workshop students at Columbia University, are the three basic patterns that shape meaning in poems. As Kunitz explained each fundamental pattern, I felt as if the keys to the universe had just been handed over to me. And, in a way, they had. For these structures inform not only works of art, but also the natural world, and are probably a part of the human brain in the way that the dark spot that draws the bee deep inside the flower is probably a part of the bee's eye. In *Next-to-Last Things*, shapes abound, sometimes as dimly felt presences—

> Out there is childhood country,
> bleached faces peering in
> with coals for eyes.
> ("The Abduction"*)

other times as distinct, recognizable forms—

> On the back door screen
> a heavy furpiece hangs,
> spreadeagled, breathing hard,
> hooked by prehensile fingers,
> with its pointed snout pressing in,

> and the dark agates of its bandit eyes
> furiously blazing. Behind,
> where shadows deepen, burly forms
> lumber from side to side
> ("Raccoon Journal")

But it is not the shapes of living figures, or even the shapes of phantasms, that preoccupy Kunitz in this book. What fascinates him is the shape of human consciousness, the shifting shapes of the poet's mind at work, its "rush of forms"—that place of becoming I think of as the poet's studio.

As early as his first book, *Intellectual Things* (1930), Kunitz was concerned with mind, and in a tightly packed sonnet, entitled "Organic Bloom,"* he expressed three ideas which were to turn up again and again in his work, though it is only now in *Next-to-Last Things* that these ideas are fully explored. Listen, first, to the early sonnet:

> The brain constructs its systems to enclose
> The steady paradox of thought and sense;
> Momentously its tissued meaning grows
> To solve and integrate experience.
> But life escapes closed reason. We explain
> Our chaos into cosmos, cell by cell,
> Only to learn of some insidious pain
> Beyond the limits of our charted hell,
> A guilt not mentioned in our prayers, a sin
> Conceived against the self. So, vast and vaster
> The plasmic circles of gray discipline
> Spread outward to include each new disaster.
> Enormous floats the brain's organic bloom
> Till, bursting like a fruit, it scatters doom.

To begin with, this sonnet shows Kunitz attempting to find visual shapes for mental processes. In another poem from the same book, "This Very Tree," Kunitz speaks of "the candelabrum of pure thought," and in still another, "Mens Creatrix," he writes, "Brain, be ice, / A frozen bowl of thought." Second, "Organic Bloom" shows Kunitz connecting processes of thought with organic processes that work in cycles: like fruit, the thinking processes appear to ripen—then burst. In another poem from *Intellectual Things*, "Motion of Wish," the wish, which is "sprung from the brain," goes "through evolutions of the seed." Like the Creation of the Lurianic Kabbalah which works on a triple rhythm of contracting, bursting apart, and healing, the creative process for Kunitz is combustive, culminating in explosion. And there is another important connection with Kabbalistic tradition. In Lurianic thought, the vessels of Creation break because what God has to say, His name, is too strong for His words; in "Organic Bloom," the brain bursts because, like the vessels of Creation, it is unable to contain its own thinking processes. Which brings me to my third point. "Organic Bloom" pictures the mind continually evading and escaping itself, paradoxically extending beyond its own contours. While in this early poem the mind's expansiveness takes a Freudian form, with forgotten—or repressed—guilt and sin relegated to regions of mind still uncharted, nearly fifty years later, Kunitz's fascination with inclusiveness turns up again, this time stripped of all psychoanalytic thinking. In a conversation with Chris Busa, reprinted in this volume, Kunitz says: "I sometimes think I ought to spend the rest of my life writing a single poem whose action reaches an epiphany only at the point of exhaustion, in the combustion of the whole life, and continues and renews, until it blows away like a puff of milkweed." When I read this passage, I immediately thought of "Organic Bloom." As in that early poem, the thinking process, for Kunitz, is still organic, its rhythms comparable to the cycles of plant life. There is even the same combustive energy, the thinking process exploding, blowing away "like a puff of milkweed." And finally, there is the same desire for inclusiveness, a need to record the mental processes of a lifetime in a single poem. Kunitz himself has observed: "Occasionally, I am astonished to find, through all the devious windings of a poem, that my destination is something I've written months or years before, embedded in a notebook or recorded on a crumpled scrap of paper, perhaps the back of an envelope. That is what the poem, in its blind intuitive way, has been seeking out. The mind's stuff is wonderfully patient" (*A Kind of Order, A Kind of Folly*).

But while the model Kunitz proposes for a single poem is reminiscent of "Organic Bloom" in some ways, in other respects it is very different. Where the sonnet stressed the compactness of the brain, the more recent model emphasizes the vast realms of space human consciousness contains—and not only because this single poem would follow the action of the whole life. Kunitz has replaced the image of fruit with the image of the milkweed pod. When milkweed explodes, the seed-bearing puffs do not blow away all at once; they lift into the air at rhythmic intervals, blowing away gradually, fitfully. And the journey they trace in the air includes not only the puffballs but the spaces between their eruptions; just as in passages of music where there are many rests, the pauses are meant to be heard and the listener must feel the musicians playing the silences as well as the notes. When, in his conversation with Busa, Kunitz talks of organizing his poems spatially—"I follow the track of the eye—it's a track through space"—I see those puffs of milkweed, the intervals between them. Poets' models, the blueprints or maps for poems they hope to write, are peculiar because they tend to combine qualities that are essentially incompatible. In a poem that has always impressed me as Elizabeth Bishop's own aesthetic model, she describes a monument that would certainly never stand, but that brings together through its architectural peculiarities contradictory elements in her own style, which combines the exotic with the domestic, the highly ornate with the plain:

> Then on the topmost cube is set
> a sort of fleur-de-lys of weathered wood,
> long petals of board, pierced with odd holes,
> four-sided, stiff ecclesiastical.
>
> ("The Monument")

And there is a poem by A. R. Ammons, "The Arc Inside and Out," which reconciles in the image of "periphery enclosing our system with / its bright dot," Ammons's own opposing needs: the minimalist need for "the impoverished diamond" and the "heap shoveler's" need for sheer "plenitude." Kunitz's model implies a need to give form to consciousness itself—to stand somehow outside the workings of his own mind so that he can discover the shape of what is essentially elusive because it is in a continual state of becoming; or, as Kunitz succinctly stated the paradox in an early poem, "Change"—"Becoming, never being, till / Becoming is a being still." Combustive, agitated, explosive—Kunitz's model is primarily kinesthetic, the whole life danced out, with the image of the milkweed giving visual form to a process that is at first felt inside the body as rhythm. "Even before it is ready to change into language," Kunitz says, "a poem may begin to assert its buried life in the mind with wordless surges of rhythm and counterrhythm. Gradually the rhythms attach themselves to objects and feelings" (*A Kind of Order, A Kind of Folly*). To discover the rhythms by which the mind beats out its thoughts, to find the pattern in what is continually moving, dying and renewing—all this is implied by Kunitz's model for a poem that would record the combustion of the whole life. Unlike other models of artistic inclusiveness—Marcel Duchamp's *Box in a Valise* (1941), for example, which contains miniature reproductions of nearly all his works—Kunitz's model is not stationary, but in motion: it pulses with thought.

As I read Kunitz's *Next-to-Last Things* during my long night of insomnia, it seemed to me that the single poem whose action continues and renews until it blows away like a puff of milkweed was quite possibly this book. For one thing, *Next-to-Last Things* has "world enough, and time" to be that poem, more world and time than any of Kunitz's previous books. Though its first section is made up of only thirteen poems, that section alone enacts a drama that moves simultaneously through three different levels of time—personal, mythical, and creative. With the first poem, "The Snakes of September,"* the speaker is in a garden that could be Kunitz's own garden at 32 Commercial Street, but we are also reminded of that other mythical Garden by two snakes entwined "in a brazen love-knot," as if defiant of the Fall. With the last poem, "The Wellfleet Whale,"* there is again a personal experience drawn from Kunitz's own life, his encounter with a finback whale, foundered and dying on Wellfleet beach, an encounter which appears to be a manifestation of a greater mythical event. Because many phrases in the poem—phrases like "news of your advent," "keepers of the nightfall watch," "hour of desolation," and "huge lingering passion"—allude to Christ's Passion and because the tourists and souvenir hunters who crowd around the whale, carving initials in its flanks and peeling strips of its skin, recall the crowds of Christs's tormentors depicted in the great Renaissance paintings by Brueghel and Bosch, this poem, like the first in this section, enacts a mythical as well as a personal drama: a drama that takes in the grand sweep of Christian time from the Creation to the Passion—and also redefines one aspect of that drama, the Fall. For Kunitz, the Fall does not seem to be caused either by human pride or human yearning for more knowledge (Kunitz is too fearless a transgressor of limits to accept such interpretations). Rather, the Fall is displaced from the Garden, which remains defiantly innocent, to the scene of Christ's death on the cross; that is, the Fall coincides with the loss of our greatest human ideals, with the loss of those figures that, like the whale—"pure energy incarnate / as nobility of form"—embody beauty, majesty, grace, with the loss of those ideal forms that thrill us, stirring our wonder and awe. When the speaker of "The Wellfleet Whale" expresses his sense of loss—"You have become like us, / disgraced and mortal"—I feel as if a curtain has suddenly been ripped, as if the very fabric of life has been torn. Whatever the reader is going to do with this profoundly disturbing revelation will require time, and therefore the book wisely provides no more poems. Instead of comfort, it offers the reader another mode of thinking entirely: the second half of the book consists of a rich variety of prose genres—essay, memoir, conversation, and journal entry—all sustaining a kind of fugal dialogue with one another, as well as with the poems in the opening section. While several memoirs extend the poet's personal history with rich remembrances of close friends, the poet Robert Lowell and the artist Philip Guston, and even take the reader back to Kunitz's childhood with the story of his mother, Yetta Helen Dine, the major thrust of the prose, it seems to me, is toward an exploration of the creative process, as particularized in Kunitz's own experiences. Not only do several of the essays explore the origins of some of Kunitz's poems, but through the inclusion of so many different prose forms, this section seems to embody the creative impetus of the thinking process itself, as mind continually finds new shapes to renew itself. From the more intuitive thinking of the earlier poems, this section shifts to the more cognitive, more rational thinking of the essay. From the more extroverted thinking of conversation and interview, to the more introspective thinking of the journal. These forms of thinking even vary as to how much silence—or space—they include, with the more fragmented journal entries awash in silence, a veritable archipelago of thoughts where mind trails off into the wild waters just beyond the limits of rational thinking, into what Kunitz might call "clouds of our unknowing." As in this journal entry: "When the Tzartkover Rabbi, celebrated in Hasidic lore, was asked his reason for failing to preach Torah for a long time, he gave as his answer: 'There are seventy ways of reciting Torah. One of them is through silence.' " By contrast, the conversation with Busa, which incidentally provides the best interview of Kunitz that I know of, is tightly packed, the voices of poet and interviewer spiraling around one another, braiding into intricate patterns of thought which suddenly unravel into a new design.

Because the book's second section not only explores the creative process as a discussable subject, but also embodies that process through its own shape shifting, certain poems in the first section, which themselves are concerned with poetic composition, are suddenly reactivated by the prose pieces. The reader goes back to "The Round," a poem which dramatizes through its own circular structure the poet's cyclic activity, his daily round, with its deep immersions in writing; as the poem closes, the speaker is scribbling on the blotted page the very words that began the poem— "Light splashed." What Kunitz envisioned in an early poem—"The end and the beginning in each other's arms" ("Open the Gates"*)—is now fulfilled through the form of "The Round," which, like the mythical uroborus, that circular snake which grasps its own tail in its mouth, wraps around itself. "The Wellfleet Whale" provides another look at the creative process. The poem begins with a journal entry, not a simulated journal entry, but a real excerpt which can be found in an earlier collection of Kunitz's prose pieces, *A Kind of Order, A Kind of Folly*. Beginning with the journal account allows Kunitz to overcome certain technical problems: for example, it frees him to plunge immediately into a lyrical address to the whale because he can count on the journal notation to ground the reader in all the necessary narrative information. But the journal-entry beginning also accomplishes something else. It allows the reader to discover those places where the poem has changed and transformed the original anecdote. As the reader compares the journal's account of Kunitz's encounter with the whale with the poem's account, reading re-creates the process of poetic composition, that wonderful period of indeterminancy where even the poem's structure is in a state of flux. To discover that the poem has substituted a *we* for the first person singular point of view of the journal is to reach that place in the creative process where a decision was made, where the possibility of a crowd scene suggestive of the crowds that milled around the dying Christ may first have occurred to the poet. Where the journal entry is anecdotal, verging on insight, the poem is interpretative, and the world it presents charged with meaning.

I suspect that it is the way in which the second section of *Next-to-Last Things* returns us to the poems of the first section, inviting us to read those poems through its own interest in the creative process, that finally provides the comfort which "The Wellfleet Whale" at first denies. As Yeats wisely understood, "All things fall and are built again, / And those that build them again are gay." The second section invites us to enter into the history of the poems in the first section, to explore the layers of experience they shape and transform: to reread "The Abduction," this time knowing something about its origins in Kunitz's reading on UFO adventures; to return even to a poem from an earlier book, "Green Ways,"* this time with the knowledge of Keats's influence on Kunitz's imagination. To read the poems in this way is to unsettle them, to return them to that place of pure becoming, that "terrible threshold" where the poet hears "a rush of forms" ("Open The Gates"). *Next-to-Last Things* is more filled with process, with the action of the mind, with poems caught in the act of becoming than any other Kunitz book, which is my other reason for thinking that this book is the combustion of a whole life. Most poets feel regret over what gets left out of their poems, and Kunitz, I think, is no exception. "Language overwhelms the poet in a shapeless rush," he writes. "It's a montage, an overlapping of imagery, feelings, thoughts, sounds, sensations, which have not yet submitted to regimentation" (*A Kind of Order, A Kind of Folly*). The shapeless rush has energy, excitement, vigor: the mouth filled with the poem in all its rich simultaneity, none of the wild feathers plucked. Some of the greatest poets have tried to preserve in their poems the shifting shapes of pure becoming when the poem dazzles with kaleidoscopic possibilities. Chaucer's dream poems, for example, appear to simulate early, rougher stages of their own composition, thus recording, or seeming to record, a series of broken-off attempts: they grow around these earlier versions the way a tree grows around its own rings. But it was especially

Dante who sought to preserve the emotional state that accompanied the writing of those poems addressed to Beatrice. That strange book, the *Vita Nuova*, alternates between sections of poetry and sections of prose, with the prose sections describing the circumstances of poetic composition. Since these circumstances often place a feverish, love-sick Dante at celebrations, banquets, and funerals where he is surrounded by shifting crowds of young women, Beatrice's friends, finally, those crowds which keep reforming, flowing into new shapes, become a metaphor for Dante's state of creative flux and seem as much a part of the poet's visionary experience, his own teeming mind, as a part of his quotidian experience. So imperceptibly do vision and reality shade into one another in the *Vita Nuova* that at times it is impossible to tell them apart. Dante keeps the reader positioned at that edge where the creative impulse keeps surging up, an edge so fine it is like an imaginary number, the square root of minus one, that symbol i which Leibniz called "an amphibian between being and nonbeing."

Perhaps it was my reading the *Vita Nuova* during the same night that I read Kunitz's book that made me especially sensitive to what I had missed on previous readings: the way so many of the poems in *Next-to-Last Things* seem to catch the very moment when they were first heard or glimpsed or sensed. The poems straddle that edge where the nonverbal rush of forms is first translated into words. Listen to the beginnings of two of the poems, "The Snakes of September,"

> All summer I heard them
> rustling in the shrubbery
> outracing me from tier
> to tier in my garden,
> a whisper among the viburnums,
> a signal flashed from the hedgerow,
> a shadow pulsing
> in the barberry thicket.

and now "The Image-Maker,"

> A wind passed over my mind,
> insidious and cold.
> It is a thought, I thought,
> but it was only its shadow.
> Words came,
> or the breath of my sisters,
> with a black rustle of wings.

The poems begin at the threshold of perception where seeing and hearing scorn the sense organs. Such poems upset the reader's orientation, for there is always more *out there*, they suggest, than the reader at first supposed. To a great extent, it is the forms and shapes that keep looking in at the poems' speakers, like the "heavy furpiece" pressed to the screen door in "Raccoon Journal" and "the bleached faces peering in / with coals for eyes" in "The Abduction," that make the reader so keenly aware of realms of space that keep growing vast and vaster, realms that elude human knowledge. But another, perhaps more important factor, is the way the poems' speakers keep pressing for a knowledge of their world that continually escapes them:

> Some things I do not profess
> To understand, perhaps
> not wanting to, including
> whatever it was they did
> with you or you with them
> that timeless summer day
> when you stumbled out of the wood,
> distracted, with your white blouse torn
> and a bloodstain on your skirt.

The woman described in the opening lines of "The Abduction" now lies beside the poem's speaker, as mysterious, as unknowable as the UFOs that perhaps abducted her into outer space—or the men, "a dumbshow retinue / in leather shrouds" who, more probably, gang-raped her. All the speaker has to offer the reader—and himself—are what the woman he loves has pieced together with him over the years; that is to say, what he has to offer are interpretations of an event that may itself be a fiction. "What do we know," the speaker concludes, "beyond the rapture and the dread?" What do we know, in other words, beyond the emotions stirred up by our own versions of the world, our own myths? With the concluding question, inner space becomes as vast and unknowable as outer space. And like the man depicted in "The Long Boat," whose "boat has snapped loose / from its moorings," the reader is also set adrift, "rocked by the Infinite!"

When I started to read *Next-to-Last Things*, I had expected to hear a voice I already knew, the generic Kunitz made familiar by all the particular encounters I have had with him—as his student at Columbia University, as a fellow at the Fine Arts Work Center, as audience at many of his poetry readings. Instead, I heard someone or something else, a thrilling presence, disembodied as the birdsong that kept erupting into my long night of insomnia. In a fascinating exchange that is preserved in Busa's interview of Kunitz, poet and interviewer distinguish between "the varied voice of personality, the voice that speaks in the context of a dramatic situation," and the voice of incantation, made up of sound and rhythm. The voice I heard that night was neither the voice of personality nor the incantatory voice, but a more impersonal, universal presence that seemed to sound from the beauty of shapes, from the primordial structures of the thinking process itself. I call this the ecstatic voice, and by ecstatic, I do not mean what I think many people mean when they use that word incorrectly as a synonym for euphoric. I am using ecstatic in its root sense to mean standing outside of or apart from or beyond one's usual self or one's usual sense of the world. The ecstatic voice articulates the shifting shapes of pure becoming, of mind exceeding itself, and is kin to the grand, protean structures of the natural world; those thunderheads that pile up on the horizon during Florida's rainy season, cumulonimbus balanced on cumulonimbus, mountainous altars to abundance, altars so affluent they can afford to spend themselves in further expansions, puffing up into anvil-shaped towers, until suddenly the altar topples, itself the sacrifice, spilling down as rain. While I sensed the ecstatic voice everywhere in *Next-to-Last Things*, I heard it especially in "The Image-Maker," a poem that seems miraculous to me in the way it moves at the very limits of consciousness, and in its closing lines, even extends a little beyond those limits through the sheer effort of envisioning them:

> I listen, but I avert my ears
> from Meister Eckhart's warning:
> *All things must be forsaken.*
> *God scorns*
> *to show Himself among images.*

Though the image-maker averts his ears from the master's warning, the reader of the poem, who now conceives of an imageless form of thinking, who probes its possibility, feels as if some boundary has just been transgressed. Perhaps the poem has led the reader to imagine life after death, a realm of shapes so pure they scorn particulars. Wherever the reader has been led, it is not a place visited before. The brain has just advanced into its own uncharted territory, paradoxically exceeding its own limits.

[*Provincetown Arts*, 1988]

Dancing on the Edge of the Road

A Conversation with Bill Moyers

This text is adapted from the raw tapes of interviews in New York City and Provincetown, Massachusetts, March 1 and July 28, 1989. The film version, with the same title, in Bill Moyers' six-part series, "The Power of the Word," was first presented on the Public Broadcasting System on October 13, 1989.

Bill Moyers: Do you remember the first time you truly experienced words, somehow, as part of your being?

Stanley Kunitz: I used to go out into the woods behind our house in Worcester, Massachusetts, and shout words, any words that came to me, preferably long ones, just because the sound of them excited me. "Eleemosynary," I recall, was one of my favorites. "Phantasmagoria" was another.

BM: I grew up in the South where Lincoln was not as revered as he was elsewhere. I remember the sound of that language, even to this moment:

> George Washington was a great big boss.
> He rode himself around on a big white horse.
> Abraham Lincoln was a goddamn fool,
> he rode around on a skinny old mule.

SK: When I was in the fourth grade, my teacher, Miss McGillicuddy, had assigned us a composition on George Washington to celebrate his birthday. I still remember my sensational beginning: "George Washington was a tall, petite, handsome man." Whether or not I suspected what "petite" meant, I found it too elegant to resist. Miss McGillicuddy, whose French vocabulary may have been no better than mine, thought my composition was fabulous, and every year from that point on into the next generation she used to read it to her new classes as a literary model. I spent a good part of my childhood exploring language, trying to find a new word every day in the unabridged Century Dictionary that was one of our household's prized possessions. And I haunted the public library. The librarian said sternly, "Five books. That's the limit you can take, Stanley. Five for the week." When I came back in a couple of days, she insisted I couldn't read that much so fast. I convinced her I had, and wangled permission to haul away five more. She was really a kind soul.

BM: Were these books of poetry?

SK: Some were. Of course, my taste in poetry was indiscriminate. Tennyson and Whittier and Longfellow and James Whitcomb Riley and Robert Service all seemed to offer equal enchantments. I knew Service's "The Cremation of Sam McGee" by heart and loved to declaim it:

> The Northern Lights have seen queer sights,
> But the queerest they ever did see
> Was that night on the marge of Lake Lebarge
> I cremated Sam McGee.

When I was graduated from elementary school as class valedictorian, the poem I chose to recite for the occasion was Kipling's "Recessional":

> Lord God of Hosts, be with us yet,
> Lest we forget—lest we forget!

By then I knew that language was tremendously important to me. I already felt drawn to the community of poets.

BM: Once in East Africa on the shore of an ancient lake, I sat alone and suddenly it struck me what community is: it's gathering around the fire and listening to somebody tell a story.

SK: That's probably how poetry began, in some such setting. Wherever I've traveled in the world, I've never felt alone. Language is no barrier to people who love the word. I think of poets as solitaries with a heightened sense of community.

BM: But, Stanley, is your community limited to other poets?

SK: I should be sad if that were true.

BM: Have you ever changed a poem you wrote long ago?

SK: There are a few old poems I've tinkered with, correcting a word here or a phrase there that was obviously wrong, but I think it's foolhardy to attempt radical revisions of early work. You are no longer the poet who wrote those lines in his troubled youth. Time itself is stitched into the fabric of the text.

BM: What has happened to the music of poetry? Why does poetry now simply lie there on the printed page, which you have called "a very cold bed"?

SK: One of the problems with poetry in the modern age is that it's become separated from the spoken word. When you ask students to read a poem aloud, you find they have no idea of the rhythm of the language, its flow, inflection, and pitch. They do not understand that stress and tonality are instruments of meaning. Is the fault wholly theirs? Poetry has strayed far from its origins in song and dance. With its gradual retreat into print and, currently, into the academy, it is in danger of becoming a highly technical and specialized linguistic skill. It has already lost most of its general listening audience.

BM: Is it possible that the rock musician is the poet of our day?

SK: It's a commentary on the state of our culture that the vast audience for rock and other varieties of pop seems to be quite satisfied at that level of communication. It doesn't feel a need for poetry. That disturbs me because poetry explores depths of thought and feeling that civilization requires for its survival. What does it signify that the mass of our adult population cares as little for the poets of the great tradition as it does for the moderns? The consoling thought is that children are still impressionable and ready to receive poetry, ready to make it part of their lives. But that's before they are spoiled. Our educational system has failed us in that respect, among others.

BM: I think back on the poems I read in high school—Shelley, Keats, and Byron. They rhymed. They had meter. That's not true any more.

SK: Certainly it's easier to remember verse that has a fixed rhyme scheme, a regular beat, and a standard length of line. Much of the pleasure we derive from the poetry of the past, regardless of its quality, is due to the fulfillment of expectations. But that's precisely the kind of aesthetic satisfaction that the most representative and seminal imaginations of this century taught us to question. Right now we seem to be entering a more conservative phase, but I'm not ready to greet the dawn of a neoclassical age.

BM: Do people quote your poems?

SK: Not by the tens of thousands, but I've heard of some who do. Perhaps it's relevant to note that I was trained in the metrical tradition— or, rather, I trained myself, since there were no creative writing programs in those days. At a later stage I became a lapsed formalist, choosing to write by and for the ear, without preimposed conditions. I trust the ear to let my rhythms go where they need to go. The ear is the best of prosodists.

BM: These lines of yours come to mind—I wish you'd comment on them:

> I dance for the joy of surviving,
> on the edge of the road.

SK: That's the ending of "An Old Cracked Tune,"* a poem that had its origin in a scurrilous street song remembered from my youth. The butt of the song's mockery was a stereotypically avaricious and conniving Jewish tailor. The very first line—the one I appropriated—went: "My name is Solomon Levi." It didn't occur to me until later that Solomon was my father's given name and that he was a Levite, a descendant of the priestly house of Levi. When the line from that odious song popped into my head, I wondered, "Can I redeem it?" And so I wrote the poem.

BM: Because it was anti-Semitic?

SK: Poems don't tell you why you need to write them. Perhaps you write them in order to find out why. Despite what I've said about the source, I didn't sit down to compose a poem about bigotry. My driving impulse was to embrace a wounded name.

BM: Why did you call the poem "An Old Cracked Tune"?

SK: I've never thought about it—the title came with the poem. "Old tune" must allude to the source of the poem, as well as to its being a sort of ancestral song. "Cracked" tells something about the speaker's age and voice and maybe about his state of mind.

BM: Do you remember the original lyrics?

SK: No. Only the first line and "zip-zip-zip" out of the refrain. The one person on earth, to my knowledge, who remembers that song is Richard Wilbur.

BM: The poet.

SK: Yes, and he can sing several stanzas of it—more, I guess, than I've ever wanted to remember. He may have heard it at Harvard years after I did.

BM: What did you mean when you said you wanted to "redeem" the man in the poem?

SK: I hoped to restore his dignity by identifying with him. Like him, the poet in our society is a marginal character, dancing on the edge of the road.

BM: Outside the mainstream. Yet the poem is not bitter.

SK: Poetry has a great digestive system. It can consume anything and recycle it. In another aspect, the recycling of the self is a condition of the creative life. We must continue to reinvent our lives until we arrive at the self we can bear to die with.

BM: I have no idea how one would begin to write a poem, and certainly I would not understand how to create a self. But poetry does seem to me to have an erotic quality, deeply sexual, and therefore creative and re-creative. But how do you do it? Is it with the word? Do you make love to the word?

SK: Every new poem is like finding a new bride. Words are so erotic they never tire of their coupling. How do they renew themselves? By their inexhaustible desire for combinations and recombinations.

BM: I know it's hard to invent a self, so we'll come back to that in a minute. I want to ask if it's hard to write a poem.

SK: Hard!

BM: What makes it such a struggle?

SK: Because in our daily lives we enslave words, use them and abuse them, until they are fit for only menial tasks and small errands.

BM: You have to kill a lot of clichés, don't you?

SK: You have to remove the top of your head and plunge deep into the unconscious life in order to come up with words that are fresh and sparkling. Poetry isn't written on schedule. A poem that occupies less than a page may take days, weeks, months—and still want more attention to set it right. You know, that's not very practical in the world's terms.

BM: The world is so meagerly supportive of the poet. How do you keep going?

SK: By outwitting the marketplace. Poets who flunk their lessons in the art of survival either drop out or die young. Above all, we need to buy time, meditation-time, but not at the world's price. One of the strategies I've learned is to stay alive when the rest of the world is asleep. When I shut the door of my study, the clocks stop ticking. A few minutes seem to pass, and suddenly it's dawn.

BM: On what are you meditating?

SK: You don't choose the subject of meditation, it chooses you. But you have to put yourself into a state of readiness.

BM: Are you meditating on memories, memories you're not aware of?

SK: Your buried life. The secret chambers of your heart.

BM: You have said that certain images are "key images." Are these memories of childhood?

SK: Usually so. I believe that at the center of every poetic imagination is a cluster of images associated with pivotal moments. That cluster is the key to one's identity, the purest concentration of the self. Poetry happens when new images or sensations are drawn into the gravitational field of the old life.

BM: In "Three Floors,"* which is one of my favorite poems, you are remembering your childhood.

SK: That poem is one of several stemming from the suicide of my father a few weeks before I was born. My mother kept just a few of his relics in a trunk in the attic, including a red Masonic hat and a walking stick, which figure in the poem. The time was World War I, when I was about ten. Another poem, "The Portrait,"* returns me to that attic, discovering a portrait of my father. When I brought it down to show to my mother, she tore it up.

BM: And your mother slapped you for finding it, as the poem says?

SK: Yes.

BM: Do you think she slapped you because you found the portrait or because she held you responsible for your father's death?

SK: Her rage was directed at him, not at me. She wanted to expunge his memory. I had discovered the only portrait of him in existence. She had destroyed all the others. No mention of him ever crossed her lips.

BM: For a long time you did not write about it.

SK: In "Father and Son,"* written in my mid-thirties, I pursue and ultimately confront his image. It was an act of liberation for me.

BM: Of whom is the portrait a portrait? Your father, your mother, yourself? Or the portrait of an experience that is an active memory?

SK: You are perfectly right to imply that it is more than my father's portrait.

BM: One of the poems you read the other night, "The Abduction,"* has these puzzling lines:

> Out there is childhood country,
> bleached faces peering in
> with coals for eyes.

SK: That memory goes back to the house on Providence Street in Worcester when I was eight or nine. There was a willow outside the window and the branches used to rub against the glass. In the middle of the night I would look out and see faces peering in. Night fears. Something I couldn't reveal to another soul.

BM: How do dreams play a role in the creating of poetry?

SK: In their fluidity and illogic dream images readily translate into poetry. Everything in "Quinnapoxet,"* for example, came to me in a dream, not the words, but all the images.

BM: Two people come into view, and a woman says, "Why don't you write?" The other is wearing a burial suit. Is he your father?

SK: That's the image.

BM: You salute him. That is a reconciliation?

SK: The recognition of a bond.

BM: And you dreamed this?

SK: From beginning to end. Then I began exploring what I had dreamed. In an illustrated article on sign language for the deaf I found the hand gesture I had made in my dream. It is the most reverential of all the signs for father.

BM: Do you sometimes think you're carrying on a conversation with ancestors you never knew?

SK: The arts, by their nature, are our means of conducting that dialogue. Where is the history of the race inscribed, if not in the human imagination? One of my strongest convictions is that poetry is ultimately mythology, the telling of the stories of the soul. We keep asking Gauguin's famous question, "Where do we come from, Who are we, Where are we going?" The echo that mocks us comes from the Stone Age caves. The poem on the page is only a shadow of the poem in the mind. And the poem in the mind is only a shadow of the poetry and mystery of the things of this world. So we must try again, for the work is never finished. I don't think it's absurd to believe that the chain of being, our indelible genetic code, holds memories of the ancient world that are passed down from generation to generation. Heraclitus speaks of "mortals and immortals living in their death, dying into each other's lives."

BM: The other night, at your reading, young people were applauding, and they had very special applause for "End of Summer."*

SK: That poem came to me in mid-life when I was living in Bucks County, Pennsylvania. The occasion is still vivid in my mind. I was out in the field, hoeing an old stand of corn under. Suddenly I heard a commotion overhead. A flock of wild geese, streaking down from the north, rattled the sky with their honking. I stood in the field, gazing upward with a sense of tumult and wonder, for something had been revealed to me: the story of migration had become my story. At that moment I made one of the most important decisions of my life. I dropped my hoe and ran into the house and started to write this poem. It began as a celebration of the wild geese. Eventually the geese flew out of the poem, but I like to think they left behind the sound of their beating wings.

BM: They brought a divine message.

SK: So it would seem. Don't forget that there were soothsayers in ancient times who practiced divination by studying the flight of birds.

BM: Why did you use the word "perturbation" in the second line, "A perturbation of the light"? Why not "commotion" or "disturbance" or "flurry"?

SK: There's more wingbeat in "perturbation." I might add that the rhythm is intentionally persistent, relying largely on the interplay between open and closed vowels. Listen:

> An agitation of the air,
> A perturbation of the light

Admonished me the unloved year
Would turn on its hinge that night

BM: Not everything you write comes from childhood country or night country. I remember seeing your poem about the moonwalk, "The Flight of Apollo,"* in *the New York Times*.

SK: You have a long memory, for that was in 1969. The *Times* had asked me for a poem in tribute to man's first landing on the moon, and fortunately I had one at hand, having written it in the days before Apollo II was launched. When I saw the actual landing on TV, I felt I had already been there. There was no need to change a word. I've always been fascinated by space exploration, so that it seemed quite natural for me to imagine myself a stranger on earth seeking a new home in the skies. Eventually, I suppose, the human race will have to move from this planet and settle elsewhere in the galaxy, for this planet will die.

BM: Beyond this planet, as you say in the poem, is "the intelligence of the stars."

SK: Simply on the basis of probability. I cannot believe that planet Earth is the only blob of dirt in the firmament that supports life.

BM: There is a man in one of your poems who "carries a bag of earth on his back," and it reminds me that you are a gardener who likes to work with his hands.

SK: I am enchanted with every step in the process of making things grow. In the grand view, I see gardening as a ritual drama, in which the whole cycle of death and rebirth is enacted annually. But that doesn't prevent me from undertaking the most lowly tasks and truly enjoying them, even weeding and grubbing. It strikes me that gardens and poems are equally unpredictable, given the vagaries of weather and imagination. A plant behaves beautifully one summer. The next summer it grows gigantic and predatory. Or languishes in the heat, disfigured and splotchy with mildew; or succumbs to the voracious appetites of cutworms and beetles and slugs. In the civilization of the garden such specimens must be treated as outlaws. Out with them! The poet in the garden cannot afford to be tenderhearted.

BM: In your later poems you write with much more simplicity and economy. Why?

SK: In a curious way, age is simpler than youth, for it has fewer options. In the beginning, life seems to offer us infinite choices, a bewilderment of opportunities. We have no certainties about our destination, or a path that will lead us there. We might become a scientist, or a theologian, or a farmer, or a poet. Who knows? Every time we make a significant choice—affecting, let's say, our education, or career, or involvement with others—we reduce, exponentially, the number of choices left to us. Finally, we arrive at the realization that the only remaining choice of any consequence, if it can be considered a choice at all, is between living and dying. This simplifies, as it purifies, the operation of the mind. What could be more natural than for the mature imagination at sunset to move toward economy of style and gravity of tone? When I read the late work of Hardy or Yeats, I get the distinct impression that the life of the poet is already passing into his poems.

New York and Provincetown /1989

Roots and Place

by Jonathan Blunk and Fran Quinn

At the western end of Commercial Street, apart from the cramped circles of boutiques and tourists that most know as Provincetown, Massachusetts, there is a remarkable, many-tiered garden. The house is largely hidden from view, but the garden, fronting on the street and the bays, enchants people passing by, most of them unaware that they are also passing one of the world's masters of poetry.

Stanley Kunitz sees little distinction between his gardening and those other activities for which he is more widely acknowledged: his writing, teaching, translating, and editorial work. All of this he continues to pursue vigorously at the age of eighty-five, with no signs of slowing down, as Fran Quinn and I discovered when we caught up with him in September of 1989. We spent more than three hours in his company, talking with him about his life, his work, and his views on the current state of American poetry.

Jonathan Blunk: You've said that at the center of every poetic imagination is a cluster of key images that go back to the poet's childhood. Does that continue to ring true for you?

Stanley Kunitz: Very much so. The sacred baggage of a life is a handful of images out of our private history that tell us more about ourselves than anybody else could ever know. I think of Akhmatova, in a testamentary vein, writing toward the end, "Herewith I solemnly renounce my hoard / of earthly goods, whatever counts as chattel. / The genius and guardian angel of this place / has changed to an old tree-stump in the water." That tree-stump image, out of the mists of memory, is what she would carry to the grave.

JB: I am curious how a sense of place enters into your work. It seems in recent years that you have become closer to Worcester than you were as a young man. How did that happen?

SK: I was damn anxious to get out of Worcester. I felt imprisoned in a parochial society and I wanted a bigger world. My strongest feelings were of rejection and denial. The early poems I published have almost no sense of place at all. They are essentially metaphysical and placeless. It is only as I grew older that I began to feel a need to explore my roots—the sources of my life and art. Over the years I was able to reconstruct my background and the formative events, some of them extremely painful, that set me on the track of poetry. Time has enhanced my sense of place and deepened my love for the natural world.

Fran Quinn: You have been associated with New York for many years.

SK: Associated, yes. But I don't have that deep feeling for Manhattan that I have for, let's say, Provincetown, or that I had for Bucks County, Pennsylvania, or for my first country place in Connecticut at Wormwood Hill. I'm not really an urban creature: I need to be working the land to come fully alive. When Elise and I lived in a brownstone on Twelfth Street, I had a small gem of a garden there.

FQ: When I think of Providence Street and that whole area in Worcester where you grew up on Vernon Hill, I don't see much open space there. When did you start to get that sense of the soil? Do you think that goes back as far as Worcester?

SK: Oh yes, My mother had a real feeling for the land, and the house she built when I was around thirteen, on Woodford Street—the setting for "The Testing-Tree"*—that was virtually the last house in town, with acres of woods behind us. I claimed territorial rights to those woods and the abandoned quarry at the end of one of its trails. We had a garden, with fruit trees, on Woodford Street, and I tended my own little plot. Much of my feeling for the natural world can be traced back to the long summers I spent in Quinnapoxet, just outside Worcester, on a farm that belonged to the Buteaus, a French-Canadian family.

FQ: I have associated you with very strong political convictions, as in World War II when you were a conscientious objector. It seems that you were always involved in a kind of different vision of what politics was than the mainstream of politics, let's say, in Worcester. Would you like to comment a little about those early political views and where they came from— how they helped to develop your vision?

SK: In the beginning I didn't know enough about the political structure to have clearly defined political convictions. I did know that the main struggle was to become a free person and that anything that impeded the assertion of one's individuality and independence was to be fought. Gradually I became interested in the idea of socialism, less as a practical instrument for change than as a philosophic base for my thinking about society. I followed world politics more than I did local politics, which seemed to me almost like a comedy—it was, I thought, inept and corrupt, so that I had no use for it. But I was fascinated by the world stage. I followed what was happening in Europe and then the World War—the First World

War—and its aftermath. I followed it with passionate attention. I was one of those who thought at first that the Russian Revolution signified the birth of a new society based on freedom and justice and equality. When I discovered the ugly truth, I was disenchanted. It frightens me that modern technology and weaponry and control of the mass media have given the world's governers dangerous increments of power, ready for use against their own people as well as against their enemies.

FQ: Where did you even come into contact with socialism in Worcester? Was there a little pocket of it somewhere?

SK: The public library is a great place for the dissemination of ideas. Actually my own mother—though she was a pioneer businesswoman, as a dress designer and manufacturer of children's dresses—was a socialist at heart. I shared her admiration for Norman Thomas, the perennial Socialist candidate for President, though I had even greater admiration for Eugene Debs. I had no party affiliation but my natural sympathies moved me left of center. As I grew older, I was influenced by philosophical anarchism, with its insistence on the primacy of the individual as opposed to institutions. That seems to me inherent in all my thinking—a fear and distrust of institutions, and the more powerful they become, as in the modern super-state, the more I distrust them.

FQ: That sense of individualism also seems to show up in your poetic career. I don't associate you, for example, with any "school" of poetry.

SK: If you write out of the center of your own being, how can you belong to a school of poetry? You are your own school.

JB: Can a younger poet find his or her way to that center through the help of a master? I am curious about the modern academic approach, but I am more interested in a personally styled pursuit of someone you would recognize as a master, whether they be living or dead, someone whose poetry you truly admire and call yourself a student of. Is that one way to get to that center of your own beliefs?

SK: When I was in my teens and thinking a lot about poetry, how to write it and how to survive as a poet, there was nobody to turn to, certainly not in my hometown. That was one of the reasons why I had to leave Worcester. There was nobody I could talk to about the things that mattered most to me, and I felt I had to test myself in the big league—I had to go to New York to find what stuff I was made of. Maybe I could find persons to communicate with, persons who shared my passions and convictions. That search for a community has been one of the dominant drives of my life, and the places I've lived in have for the most part been places where other artists and writers have found a congenial setting, an interactive workplace. My search for the right community is not inconsistent with my distrust of institutions, because a community is not an institution. The Fine Arts Work Center in Provincetown, for example, with which I have been closely involved since its founding, is designed to function as an enclave of new writers and artists at the beginning of their careers. Twenty of them are selected annually to come here for an extended period to live at the Center, to work independently, and to enjoy the company of their peers. The Center is often referred to as an arts colony, but that's somewhat misleading, and we're certainly not a school, being without faculty or curriculum. "Community" seems to me the best descriptive term.

JB: Did you choose a mentor as you started writing?

SK: I had no real mentors in the flesh. My spiritual mentor was William Blake, who scorned the ruling institutions of his time, including organized religion, and who believed that the true church is in the heart of one who believes that everything that lives is holy. Others yearn for the sacred, but Blake makes it his parish. He feels perfectly comfortable dining with the prophets Isaiah and Ezekiel, and does not doubt that his lines are dictated to him by heavenly messengers. Such blessings are not in the cards for those of us who are still in exile, but I consider any poet who believes in the evidence of things not seen and who aligns himself not with the powers of this earth but with the weak, the oppressed, the humiliated, to be somehow connected with Blake.

FQ: When I think of the poets in your generation, those born between 1898 and 1910 or so, they seem—more than almost any other generation—to be massively isolated and separated from each other.

SK: That's true enough. We were a smaller company then, a scattered few, with no common meeting-ground. As for the older poets, like Robinson or Frost or Stevens or Eliot or Pound, they were remote and inaccessible, or so they seemed to me. I felt they were so far out of my world that there was no reason for a connection.

FQ: Williams?

SK: He wasn't an early influence. I didn't meet him till late in his life, after his stroke, when I had begun to realize the magnitude of his achievement. It was an uneventful encounter, but I was glad it happened. In '63, when I become a judge for the Pulitzer Prize Committee, I seized the opportunity to vote for him to receive the award in poetry for his *Pictures from Brueghel*, but he did not live to accept the honor. It occurs to me, going back to your previous question, that if I had stayed in New York I might have had a quite different story to tell about my literary associations. But I fled as soon as I could and moved to the country in 1930. Two years after arriving in New York I was living on Wormwood Hill in Connecticut, where I was completely isolated. My next move was to Bucks County, Pennsylvania.

FQ: Wasn't there a pretty active literary circle in New Hope when you were there?

SK: That was still in the thirties, before the big influx. Some of the Algonquin crowd were there: Moss Hart, George S. Kaufman, Dorothy Parker. But I had nothing to do with them. They had big country estates outside of New Hope.

JB: That's where Ted Roethke sought you out?

SK: Yes. He came down from Lafayette College, where he was teaching, to see me.

JB: I discovered his writing by way of James Wright's work. In my studies in English at Cornell, I had to seek these people out on my own; in fact, I was discouraged from doing my thesis work on James Wright.

SK: That doesn't surprise me. He wasn't an academic favorite. I don't really trust academic taste in the arts. At Harvard in the twenties nobody taught me Hopkins and Yeats and Eliot and Joyce—I discovered them in the stacks and, like you, was discouraged from writing about them. As for Jim Wright, he audited my class at the University of Washington in the mid-fifties. He was a graduate student and had come to Seattle because of Ted. Ted was off on sabbatical, and I was poet in residence during his absence. Others in attendance that miraculous year, aside from Jim, included Carolyn Kizer, David Wagoner, and Jack Gilbert. We had a wonderful time.

FQ: Did you sense that the group was going to be really productive, even at that early stage, or were they still floundering around?

SK: It was obviously a superior group. The level of discussion and production was fantastically high. I expected them to shine and they did.

JB: Did you follow Jim Wright's work throughout his career?

SK: Our meetings were infrequent, but I kept close track of his work.

Incidentally, this coming spring [1990] will mark the tenth anniversary of the James Wright festival at Martins Ferry, Ohio, and I plan to be there.

FQ: Who are the poets of your generation that you felt any kind of camaraderie with?

SK: My closest friendships were with Roethke and Lowell. Ted was three years younger than I, and Robert (Cal to his friends) was twelve years younger. They were the companions with whose work and lives I was most deeply involved. Now that they are gone, my comradeship is largely with much younger writers—poets in their thirties and forties. Many of them were my students; some I met in my editorial capacity, especially for the Yale Series of Younger Poets; others just came my way. There are painters and sculptors too among my intimates. Age, in fact, has brought me more friends than I ever had. When I was young, I felt quite isolated; but now, except for the metaphysical loneliness, I don't feel lonely at all.

JB: I am curious about what connections can be drawn between Charles Olson's experience and your own. Both of you disowned Worcester for most of your lives. You were equally resentful of its parochialism and racist tendencies. And you shared a passionate love of Keats. Do you have an appreciation of his work? Did you know him at the time?

SK: I didn't really know Olson. We had only one encounter, which I'll tell you about. What you say about certain correspondences in our background is undoubtedly true. Both of us left Worcester in early manhood, though I preceded him by a few years; spent time at Harvard, and eventually set out on a journey, a journey largely of finding ourselves, making a world out of our mythologies. Partly because of our alienation from our birthplace, both of us, I think, were strongly motivated for the rest of our lives by the need for a community. Charles found it at Black Mountain and became in a way a cult figure, a sort of guru. His art, like his persona, was vatic and expansive. By nature and destiny I was more of a loner, a reflective type. The appropriate mode for him was epic, mine was lyric. As poets, we could scarcely be more different.

My meeting with Charles took place in Provincetown in—let's see—the summer of '59 or '60. Elise and I were living in a little studio shack on the beach, the Blanche Lazzell studio. It was just about dusk one evening after dinner when we heard a knock at our door. There in the sunset glow stood our friend Franz Kline, who had emerged from Black Mountain to play an important role in the Abstract Expressionist generation. Behind him tagged a big fellow, big and awkward and intense, towering over Franz, who resembled a sawed-off Ronald Colman. Each of them was lugging a case of beer. Obviously Franz planned to settle in for a long evening, as he tended to do. "You and Charles Olson should get together," he said to me. "Two poets from the same town."

Franz was one of the world's great nonstop storytellers, and as soon as we were seated he began reminiscing about his early years in Pennsylvania coal-mining country. Meanwhile, I was trying to talk to Charles: I remember asking him about his work and his association with Ezra Pound, who was no hero of mine. But it was difficult to conduct any kind of conversation, because Franz was determined to hold center stage, and the more beer he consumed the more voluble he became. I've forgotten most of the details and the connections, if there were any connections, but long past midnight he was reenacting a hometown junior baseball game, played next to the railroad tracks, that went into extra innings and might have gone on forever if the long ball he hit in his turn at bat hadn't landed providentially in the hopper car of a passing freight train—an automatic home run. Elise's eyes were closing and she was anxious to get to bed, but she couldn't because our bed was right there in the same room. Every now and then I caught her dozing off.

Hours later Franz was still going strong, recounting, in fits and starts between explosive bursts of laughter, how he had climbed up on the roof of his parents' house to repair a leak, when he was joined by an overly friendly calico cat that paid for its curiosity by getting stuck, all four paws, in a patch of black roofing cement and changing, out of fright, to a hissing and howling tarball. At this point Franz heightened the dramatic effect by pausing for a few minutes while he emptied the last can of beer. I could see through the window overlooking the bay that the night had passed and the day was breaking. What happened to that poor cat must remain untold, for suddenly Charles, who had been sitting beside me, silent and pale, struggled to his feet, lurched forward a step or two—I think he was looking for the bathroom—and fell flat on his face to the floor. Franz rose from his chair, stood over Charles, and placed one foot gently on his neck. "And so another Indian bit the dust," he intoned.

And so ended my one encounter with Charles Olson. We never did get to exchange a word about our Worcester childhoods.

FQ: I don't associate your poetry much with politics until about the time you start introducing your Worcester background, primarily in *The Testing-Tree*. And I see those two things curiously coming together in my mind, the sense of place becoming more solid in the later work and also the sense of politics coming in right at the same time.

SK: As a rule, my political poems are indirectly political—not polemic—"The Testing-Tree"* or "The Wellfleet Whale,"* for example. Though you can say there is political content in them, that is subsumed under a larger context, which I consider to be existential. If the substantive frame is large enough, there's room in it for political subcurrents, but the poem isn't written to prove the political point.

FQ: There are exceptions though to that rule, right? Like Wilfred Owen, for example, in "Dulce et Decorum Est."

SK: But as Owen said, the poetry is in the pity. It's not in the argument. This is what makes his war poems so painfully shattering. They come out of such passion, such depth of feeling, and they have the smell of the battlefield in them, too, don't forget, from having been composed, practically, on the scene. I doubt that he wrote those poems in order to convert people to pacifism. He wrote them out of the urgency of his need to express the deepest feeling he had.

JB: Do you think that's true even on the wider world scene, like with the Russian poets that you have translated? Let's say Voznesensky or Akhmatova. Do you think that sensibility carries over to them?

SK: In varying degree. Akhmatova was the poet who established the Russian model for the incorporation of the political event into the personal. She doesn't write a polemic on the evils of dictatorship; she writes of the imprisonment of her son, of standing in line outside the prison in the hope of learning something about his fate, of the loss of her friends, of the fear that poisons the air. It's all at the level of event—personal event— history personified in the experience of the maker. The declamatory rant of Mayakovsky seems to me scarcely readable anymore. And even with a poet of Neruda's stature, I have to suppose that time will nibble away at his overtly political rhetoric, though I don't have much doubt that the scale of his imagination will prove grand enough to withstand the assault. For myself, I have come to believe that the most wonderful thing to tell is the mystery and beauty of ordinary human existence. If you can tell what it feels like to be alive, then I think you have done what poetry can do better than any other art.

FQ: Another thing I have noticed going on in your poetry is that you seem to be moving more and more into the present.

SK: Present tense?

FQ: Present tense and immediacy, as if you are able to capture the day, as you say. It seems to me that it is the immediate day rather than the recollected day, as if your paintbrush, in a sense, is moving at a considerably faster speed to capture what's happening immediately in front of you. Do you feel that the present tense is becoming more central to your work?

SK: I don't consistently write in the present tense. My tendency is to resort to a more complicated syntax than that, as an instrument for exploring the layers of time. In fact, I resist the present tense anecdotal poem, the favorite product of poetry workshops. Poetry wants to be more than anecdotal. It wants to become history, it wants to become legend. And you can't do that by asserting, "I am walking down the street, I see a leaf in the gutter, the fall is coming, and my heart leaps." [Laughter.]

FQ: At that point you were going more into the Frank O'Hara sort of fringe, also what spun off from Frank O'Hara, right? But it seems that Jim Wright also had a closer connection with the present tense. One of the things I always noticed about his poetry was the present tense often being dominant. That's not anecdotal.

SK: No, it's not anecdotal because in those poems, like "Lying in a Hammock" or "A Blessing," the poet is moving through the day, forever the pilgrim, a stranger to himself, toward some spiritual insight, a moment of revelation, that will redeem the day. And this, I think, is the triumph of those poems: that moment of illumination puts everything that happened before in a new light, as if it belonged to a different time order.

JB: I keep coming back to what you spoke of earlier about writing from the core of your being and your central concerns, and I thought of something I read in your essay on Whitman, where you spoke of his creating the person who would write the poems. I am trying to reconcile those two ideas.

SK: They are aspects of the same process. You don't know who you are unless you create an identity out of the formless welter within you. You consolidate a being, and that's the center. That's the center out of which you function creatively.

FQ: When I take a look at the spacing of your books—1933, 1944, 1958, etc., about every fourteen years—and then when I look at these people who are shoveling books out about once every year, or every two or three years, or something like that, I can't help wondering at the disparity. I mean, does your external life prevent you from writing a lot?

SK: I don't think so. I don't separate my so-called external life from my work. It seems to be I'm the same person whether I'm typing at my desk, or fighting for my public causes, or grubbing in my garden, or attending a board meeting at the Fine Arts Work Center or at Poets House, or shopping at the A&P, or looking at the manuscript of a young poet who has come to see me. The modalities of the life itself are what sustains and replenishes my work. I'm probably as productive as I want to be or can be. I tend to brood about a poem for months—sometimes for years—until I feel it is ready to hatch. I try, in fact, to resist the temptation to write more poems than I feel compelled to write.

FQ: So that publication doesn't seem to be one of the essentials of your poetic experience?

SK: Publication isn't a major event for me. It's more of an afterthought. Actually, I have to force myself to send out poems that I have written. Sometimes I hold on to a new poem for years.

JB: There seems to be a rather firmly entrenched academic establishment in this country to which poets are drawn just to make a living. Do you think this has a negative influence on their work?

SK: The co-opting of poetry by the academy has made American poets functionaries of the system. They belong to it. And therefore, no matter how independent they profess to be, they have lost a portion of their mobility and freedom.

FQ: You have always sort of kept one foot in the academy and one foot out, it seems to me.

SK: Even that one foot in has been tentative. Until my middle years I had no academic connections whatsoever. My first teaching appointment, at Bennington, was in '46, so that I was twenty years out of school before I returned, and then my principle has been never to accept tenure. I have always operated on a year-to-year contract and usually as part-time faculty, meaning—as you know—the acceptance of slave wages. I have strong convictions about the relationship of the poet to the academy, and perhaps my central one is that if you start thinking of yourself as an academic and if you're on the payroll for life tenure, you may as well admit that you're a subject of the academic state. Almost every poet is now.

FQ: I was just thinking there are very few people who have managed to survive totally outside of the academy. I think there have been a couple.

SK: Very few, and they are becoming scarcer and scarcer because the track is clearly defined. You get out of college and then you enroll in a creative writing program, receive your graduate degree, and get yourself hired as a teaching assistant. And that's the track. It's pretty hard to escape it.

FQ: Yes, and you have no real human experience outside the academy to draw on.

SK: In which case you compensate for that poverty of experience by cultivating your verbal skills and technical finesse. You may even find an academic critic who will interpret your ambiguities for you and set you up as a postmodernist icon. The most influential contemporary criticism has almost persuaded us that no poetry is worth attention unless it requires a mediator.

FQ: One of the things I admire about Robert Francis's poetry is how you just don't have to explain it. You bring his work into the classroom for discussion and everybody just gets it.

SK: I know. It's disappointing! [Laughter.]

FQ: Exactly! I think that's the reason his work has been largely ignored by the academy. He certainly has enough good poems to show up in somebody's anthology and yet . . .

SK: He's not in any anthology?

FQ: No, not at all.

SK: But you know the big anthologies, the ones dependent on the approval of local school committees and college faculties, have become such indiscriminate grab-bags, in their effort to satisfy every vocal faction, that it's hard to take them seriously. Their standards for inclusion have become as much political, in the broad sense, as literary.

FQ: Have you ever had any of your poems set successfully to music?

SK: I've been interested in the process, but have had some reservations about the results. If the music tries to follow the temper of the poem—sob when the poem is sobbing and laugh when the poem is laughing—it's boring. I prefer something contrapuntal, to suggest a dialogue between the poetry and the music.

JB: You have had some collaborations with artists, such as Philip Guston.

SK: And with several others, including my wife, Elise Asher. Poetry resists illustration, but there's a long history of sympathetic collaboration between poets and painters. The secret is in the free exercise of parallel imaginations. But any combination of the arts is difficult.

FQ: Did you see that Anselm Kiefer exhibit in New York where he used lines from Celan's holocaust poetry embedded in his paintings?

SK: Yes, I did. That show really knocked me over. Some of my artist friends felt it was too ambitious, too grandiose, too heavy. I didn't think so at all. American art at the moment is so pale in comparison that I can understand why American painters would . . .

FQ: Feel a little jealous. [Laughter.] Did you ever spend any time abroad?

SK: I've lived in Italy and France, been to Russia several times, and Yugoslavia, Poland, Israel, Egypt, England, Africa. I've been around.

FQ: Well, I knew you'd been around! What was your longest stay?

SK: About a year each in Italy and France.

FQ: Do you think that had a strong effect on your writing?

SK: Only indirectly: It had a strong effect on *me*. I've written only a few poems out of my experiences abroad. There are things that may still emerge, but I can't say that anyone reading my poems would say, "This is a world traveler."

FQ: Were you ever tempted to leave this country and move over there?

SK: No. I have very deep American roots. This is the place where I feel the most friction—a creative necessity; where I care intensely about what's happening; where I have my causes to fight for. When you're abroad, you're more or less detached from local politics and current events. That's damaging, I think. To keep your conscience and your imagination alive, you need to feel that everything that happens is of consequence to you, that a crime in the streets or a crime of government is a crime against you. Another factor for me, personally, is that as a first-generation American—my mother had been here only fifteen years when I was born—my feeling about this country is deep and passionate: the defense of democratic values is the defense of my own existence. Not so long ago nearly all our poets of reputation came of old American families and Anglo-Saxon descent. In the ferment and creative explosion that followed World War I, the significant gesture was to live in London or Paris and become identified with the cosmopolitan avant-garde. For writers like Eliot or Pound the decision to uproot themselves was almost as comfortable as it was stylish: they had a secure sense of status. For a poet today it would be a more difficult move. There is an essential insecurity about one's own existence, and even about the existence of poetry.

FQ: That might also explain why Williams doesn't feel as pulled abroad, too, because of his Spanish mother and all of the rest of that.

SK: The mix of his ancestry became part of his legend. It was a liberating influence on him.

FQ: And again, with regard to Charles Olson, I think he would have agreed with you. He had a passionate belief in what he came to understand as the American Dream, and was also of recent immigrant status.

SK: In the background of the American imagination is the American Constitution, with its revolutionary insistence on the Rights of Man. We are still defending those rights and values, and we know they are in peril. We know, out of the history of our own time, that unless we care enough about them to fight for them that they are subject to destruction, even from within. And I think anyone who comes out of an immigrant household has an element of insecurity written into his genes.

FQ: How do you explain that group earlier in the century known as The Fugitives—poets like Robert Penn Warren and Allen Tate and John Crowe Ransom?

SK: They were attempting to preserve the values that belonged to the southern agrarian society, the society that developed out of an aristocratic slave economy. They didn't think of it in those terms: they believed they were defending a kind of aristocracy of values. Essentially what they were resisting was change—the change into the modern world. It was like trying to stop the tide. There was no way you could defend the southern agrarian tradition when southern agrarianism was itself being demolished in the wave of the new industrial invasion of the South. Cotton was no longer king, and the program of The Fugitives was an exercise in nostalgia. All literary movements, all art movements, are rooted in a social or societal condition, just as Romanticism was an outgrowth of the revolutionary euphoria of the late eighteenth century. There is no such thing as a separate aesthetic movement. People who yearn for a neoclassical return or a neoconservative revival in politics or in literature are really hankering to turn the clock back to a class-structured society and an aesthetic that conforms to it.

JB: Can you make sense of the "language poets" in that same light?

SK: I'm not an authority on their work, since I find most of it unreadable. I view them as deconstructionists of a sort, whose premise is that poetry, as a reflection of society, has become so corrupt and meaningless that it is no longer fit for use as an expressive or interpretive instrument. Their solution is to strip words away from contexts and syntax until they resemble abstract entities. Isn't that the end of literature?

FQ: Bob Hass has called them the "formalists of the left," and has said that if you were to draw a straight line from Marxism into poetry you would eventually arrive at the language poets, who think of themselves as leftist in their destruction of the sense of order in language.

SK: Fanatics of the right might equally want to deprive poetry of its soul. They would like to deny that poetry has anything to do with the mind's long struggle to set itself free.

JB: One of the essential elements of poetry then is that challenge to the state of things, the things that stand against one's own understanding and experience.

SK: There is no way you can separate poetry from history. History—the experience of the race—is the subject matter of poetry. Poetry wants to communicate what it feels like to be alive, a feeling that differs from generation to generation and yet extends in an unbroken line back to the beginning of the human adventure. It's an existential continuum. You can't cut it off suddenly at any point and say, "We're going to begin again." There is no way you can begin, you can only continue, and that's the never-ending story of art.

Provincetown /1989

Transcending the Self

by Grace Schulman

Stanley Kunitz: Now tell me about your project. I'm not quite sure what you're up to.

Grace Schulman: The idea has to do with the creation of the self in poetry, that "process of transformation" you observe in the poetry of Whitman. Is it a notion you have had about your own work as well?

SK: That's where the notion comes from.

GS: You told Chris Busa, for the *Paris Review* interview: "If you understand a poet's key images, you have a clue to the understanding of the whole work." I think of your early pond images—those cold dank pictures of the lost father—as growing more benign in the later work. Is that correct?

SK: I suppose I'm a more forgiving person now than I was in my youth. Maybe I'm less angry with myself.

GS: There must have been a great deal to work through—your father's suicide, your stepfather's death, the loss of your sisters, the failure of your first marriage . . .

SK: It wasn't until I began writing about the circumstances of my early years that I grasped the extent of my losses. And then I felt a certain exaltation in being able to address them.

GS: Did the absence of a father in your life have to do with the generous teacher you became? As a teacher, you have been a father to many of us.

SK: No doubt, I've wanted to become the father I never had.

GS: Another of the changes in the poems, early to late, is the attitude toward women. There's a genuine empathy in the later work.

SK: I suspect it was always there. Remember that I was brought up, like Dionysus, in the company of women—mother and two older sisters. It's true that I didn't fully appreciate my resourceful and strong-willed mother until I realized—too late, I fear—how brave and remarkable she was. I needed to resist her in order to establish my own identity. She keeps coming back to me, as if seeking an ultimate understanding.

GS: Are you aware of those images as they change?

179

SK: If I persist in summoning those images, it must be because I need to find out what they are trying to say to me.

GS: About the anger in the early poems: Your early vocational life, the struggle for survival, the years you spent editing reference works—all that must have been a factor.

SK: I wouldn't deny it, but that's not the whole story.

GS: There's a good deal of rage in *Passport to the War*. Was your personal anger about the army?

SK: Nearly all those poems were written before I was drafted. It was a time of monstrous violence and hatred. Fascism was everywhere on the march, and who could stop it? As a pacifist, I felt doubly helpless. And I had a premonition of the Holocaust. When people say they had no inkling of the nightmare, that's a lie. One knew what was happening. The taste of it was in the air.

GS: You have said that you are most at home in the country. Why do you live in the city now?

SK: Actually, Elise and I divide our time between New York and Cape Cod. Elise has her painting studio here and her gallery connections, and until recently I've been teaching at Columbia. I've adapted to the urban environment better than I expected, largely because of our many friends here and the undeniable stimulus that metropolitan cultural life provides. But still my imagination is more at home in the country and by the sea. I'm not a nature poet, but I am a poet of the natural world.

GS: I've wondered about your immersion in the visual arts. Dore Ashton told me that you did a collage for *A Joseph Cornell Album,* which she edited. I believe the work accompanied your poem "The Crystal Cage," which was dedicated to Joseph Cornell.

SK: I'll show it to you: the framed original is on my library wall. [He brings the work consisting of the poem, in his handwriting, flanked by cut-out images of an exposed staircase, steel girders and lattices, various biomorphic objects, a pair of upthrusting hands, a cat in harness, and the pensive head of a child.]

GS: It's intricate. Marvelous to see it. Did your marriage to Elise inspire your attraction to the visual arts?

SK: Contributed to it. I can trace my involvement back to my child-hood, when the public library and the Worcester Art Museum were my favorite sanctuaries.

GS: I know you love to work with your hands, and that there is a carpenter's world of images—houses, doors, windows—in the poems. But then, being a visual artist is another matter.

SK: I think of all the arts as related and wish I could work at them all. That makes me think of something else I can show you: it's an assemblage called "The Story of My Life." [He leads me to the dining room and points to a wooden box hung on the wall, probably an old till, with numerous compartments behind glass, each containing a miniature stage set of objects.]

GS: Amazing. Did you say those are the materials of your life?

SK: Found or acquired objects. Some bric-a-brac. Each arrangement is episodic and brings back special remembrances. Here are fossil thunder-stones in an evolutionary row, and you must read the legend behind them: "Yes, please." Here's a waltzing mouse out of one of my poems, and [point-ing to a wooden bug] my homage to Kafka. Easter egg. Hat pin. Then of course there had to be a cat. This is Celia, the late mistress of our house-hold. And notice the time [pointing to an old-style pocket watch]: five minutes to midnight.

GS: Where did you do this? In Provincetown?

SK: No, here in the city, some thirty years ago.

GS: You have wanted to be a visual artist?

SK: I still do. But how many lives does one have? Morbid introspec-tion is the poet's curse. There are times when I long for the externality of the visual artist's medium. Gardening is my alternative recourse. I work at my garden in Provincetown just as I would at a composition in sculpture or painting.

GS: Didn't you begin as a musician?

SK: My old violin is sleeping in my closet, long since abandoned. My first art. I studied it seriously until poetry possessed me. The revelation I had was that I needed to play my own music.

GS: I've wanted to ask you for some time whether you've been moved by Hebrew legend or by Hebrew poetry.

SK: Do you think I have been?

GS: Well, I know you've cared for Christian poets—Donne, Herbert, Hopkins—just as I have. Still, I find the Hebrew influence in your work, for example, in the poem "Open the Gates"*: "I stand on the terrible threshold." You know, there is a Hebrew prayer to "Open the Gates" just as the Temple gates are closing, in the *ne'ila,* or "closing," service of Yom Kippur. It's the most solemn time of them all.

SK: I was unaware of that. My religious upbringing was negligible. What influenced me most was the secular Jewish tradition, with its ethical emphasis. Socialist theory and liberal principles in general left their permanent mark on me. I am drawn to religious mythology of any persuasion, but resist and fear institutional religion. It was the drama of Christianity, not its dogma, that led me to the metaphysical poets. In my first father-poem, "For the Word Is Flesh," beginning "O ruined father dead, . . ." I evoked "the fierce wild cry of Jesus on the holy tree." That was in my early twenties.

GS: Did Dante lead you to the drama of Christianity? You have said there was a copy of the *Inferno* in your mother's library.

SK: My recollection is that I was reading the Gospels before I came to Dante.

GS: Did your visit to Jerusalem in 1980 affect your work? I don't find it, but I'm sure it's there at some level.

SK: I don't really know. Of course, what appears in the poems is only a fraction of the experience that went into them. The visit to Jerusalem shook me, and the fact that it hasn't yet emerged as recognizable subject-matter doesn't signify that I'm through with it. My imagination has a long fuse. It occurs to me that in "The Flight of Apollo,"* written years before, I had envisioned "new Jerusalems." The old Jerusalem, so ancient and beautiful, is ravaged by politics and hatred. I would like to believe, despite all the evidence to the contrary, that humanity is ready for the task of building new sacred places.

GS: If I may ask a technical question: Marianne Moore once quoted Williams as having said he gave up the long line because of his nervous nature. I know your nature is not nervous, but why did you relinquish the sonnet and the iambic pentameter quatrain?

SK: To set the record straight, I've written altogether less than a handful of sonnets, none since my first book of poems appeared, and that was sixty years ago! And I've never applied myself to other traditional forms, such as the sestina and villanelle. Quatrains once seemed to correspond with the pattern of my thought and syntax, but that's no longer true. My shorter line length, usually three strong stresses, with a good deal of variation, is simply an adjustment to my normal breath unit. The main difference between my early and late work is that along the way I've gotten rid of a lot of baggage, both psychological and rhetorical. I guess that for the person I have become there was too much order, too much artifice, in the universe of the high style.

GS: Your work shows an unusual familiarity with scientific lore. How important is modern science to you?

SK: For some time in this century it has become apparent that at their outermost limits the imagination of the scientist and that of the poet are converging. Speculative science has invaded the area of mystery where only poets and theologians had previously dared to enter. Who else these days is privileged to explore the metaphysics of chaos?

GS: Which of the sciences are you particularly interested in?

SK: Anthropology, biology, zoology, horticulture, oceanography, astronomy, astrophysics, cosmology—you name them! I'm only an amateur, but I read whatever I can lay my hands on in those fields. Sometimes I find that the information I'm not ready to digest is what stirs the mind the most.

GS: I sense a connection there with your concept of self-transcendence, to which I'd like to return. Could you elaborate on it a little? What is the relation to the work?

SK: As I see it, the first and primary act of the poetic imagination is to create the person who will write the poems. The persona you create is a projection of your daily self, inseparable from it, but significantly greater, more purposeful. If you live intensely enough, at the center of your being, you will eventually become that other. Survival depends on self-renewal. That's putting it in a nutshell!

GS: Your poems abound in archetypal images—the dark journey, death and rebirth, the quest, the fall. Is their presence the result of an aesthetic choice?

SK: I don't deliberately introduce them. They occur naturally. At a certain depth of exploration, private images—those that belong to the daily self—gravitate toward and cohere with the buried archetypes, everybody's heritage.

GS: You've read Jung, of course.

SK: And Freud as well. Along this line of questioning it may be relevant to note that I've never been analyzed myself. Critics at one point, with their mania for classification, tried to lump me with the so-called confessional school, but that was based on a misconception of my intent and practice. I want poems that don't tell secrets, but are full of them.

GS: "I am not done with my changes," you wrote, just over a decade ago. In your mid-eighties do you still feel that way?

SK: If I didn't I'd be dead—or sorry.

New York / February 1990

"I'm Not Sleepy"

by Esther Harriott

Esther Harriott: About sixty years ago, in the poem "I Dreamed That I Was Old," you wrote, "My wisdom, ripe with body's ruin, found / Itself tart recompense for what was lost / In false exchange." Your view of age is more cheerful now, isn't it?

Stanley Kunitz: When I wrote that poem in my early twenties, age and, of course, its companion, death, were terrifying prospects. They haunted me. I'm still not wholly reconciled to the fate of the body, but I can truthfully say that I've found more rewards and compensations in my mid-eighties than I ever expected. Above all, I never imagined that the blessings of love and friendship would endure so long.

EH: What are some of the other rewards and compensations?

SK: Just to be rid of the hangups and anxieties of your youth—that's a kind of blessing too. And then, there's an assurance that comes out of having learned so much about yourself, why you are here, what you have done, how much is left for you to do. There is a—I wouldn't call it serenity—but a feeling of relief that you haven't completely wasted your life. Maybe you can take a little pride in having triumphed over the many difficulties and disasters that beset you. As D. H. Lawrence said, "Look! We have come through!" There remains the nagging question as to how well you have used your resources, and there's a bit of comfort in being able to reply, "Not so well as I might have hoped, but maybe well enough to feel that there is time still to justify the life." The persons around me who have aged badly are the ones who don't feel justified. They can't forgive themselves for having abused or squandered their talent. When people lose their self-esteem, their moral center collapses.

EH: You speak of being able to say "Look! We've come through!" It's surprising how many of the artists and writers I've interviewed were critically neglected until relatively late in life.

SK: Including me.

EH: Including you. Would you say that perhaps the critical neglect was a factor in your continuing productivity? That it taught you to persevere?

SK: Neglect can kill. But from this vantage point I can see that the years of my deepest discontent, when I was working in the dark, were the

185

most seminal period of my creative life, a time of testing, self-questioning, self-renewal. I learned, as I think every artist must, to recognize my own flaws and limitations, to build on whatever strengths I had, and to affirm and reaffirm the worth of my endeavor. I came to understand that the challenge for poets in our society is to make something virtuous, even heroic, out of the marginality of our existence. It's a risky enterprise.

EH: Isn't this one of the advantages as you grow older—that you can afford to work on your own terms, to feel a freedom from critical opinion?

SK: In the end, there's really only a handful of persons whose opinions you care about.

EH: I'd like to go back to your earlier remark that in your youth you were haunted by the idea of death. Was that because of your father's suicide before you were born?

SK: I wondered how and why he did it. The terror of oblivion haunted my childhood. I dreaded falling asleep at night because of the fear of losing consciousness. I'm sure that affected my biological rhythm because, to this day, I hate going to sleep and fight it off as long as I can. I practically never go to bed before three or four in the morning.

EH: I've been trying to figure out when you *do* sleep, because you work at night and, in the summer, presumably you garden during the day, and you're active at the Fine Arts Work Center in Provincetown, and . . .

SK: Yes, but I have a long day. My writing day usually begins around nine or ten at night and then continues for as long as I can hang on.

EH: When do you sleep then? Off and on?

SK: No, I have a Puritan conscience about sleep, and napping would make me feel guilty. I can't even picture myself taking an afternoon snooze. So what do I do? Last night, say, I went to bed exactly at four forty-five. It then took me an hour before I could fall asleep, and I was up at eight-thirty. That's enough for me to get by on, though I usually want four or five hours. But that's enough. If I have five, I feel that I have slept out completely.

EH: So one of your great assets is that you have an extraordinary amount of energy, compared to people of any age.

SK: That's what my young friends say! [Laughs.]

EH: It's not only that you don't get that much sleep, but that . . .

SK: I'm not sleepy.

EH: Right. Do you attribute that energy to good genes or discipline or to being so engaged with your work and with the world?

SK: I don't think of it as a matter of discipline. My mother lived to age eighty-six and was wonderfully alert till her death. I keep going because of unfinished business. There's still work for me to do. For anyone who has a poem to write or a garden to cultivate, the days are never long enough. How could I ever be bored with existence?

EH: You have many friends in the arts, I know, both poets and painters.

SK: One of the sorrows of longevity is the loss of old friends. I've outlived most of my contemporaries. These days my companions tend to be younger than I, some of them much younger, including a number of former students. In many ways I feel closer to their generation than to my own.

EH: In terms of outlook?

SK: In terms of awareness and concerns. In any case, I'm more conversable with them. With the old, it seems to me that I have little to say. The normal subject of conversation with another octogenarian is pretty obvious. I have other things on my mind!

EH: But that wouldn't be the case, would it, if you were talking to an artist of your generation?

SK: Of course there are exceptions, but it's not uncommon for old artists—I mean in particular the celebrated ones—to retreat into themselves, to wrap themselves in their own mythology, to become, in short, iconic figures. You cannot establish contact with their secret life: it's buried too deep inside them.

EH: That's the penalty not only of age, but of fame, isn't it? Couldn't that also happen with a young superstar—not knowing where the myth leaves off and the true identity begins?

SK: It could, though that's not anything, I guess, for young poets to worry about nowadays. Superstars are creatures of the marketplace.

EH: I was thinking of someone like Andy Warhol.

SK: The success of his career, I've always felt, had some of the elements of a parody. It's undeniable that he created, as celebrities tend to do, a legend about himself, but in his case the legend was an artifact, assembled out of spare parts in what he ironically called his Factory. This isn't what Keats meant when he said that the poet's life is a continual allegory.

EH: What is it an allegory of?

SK: Of human destiny, I suppose. The artist isn't somebody special or exotic, but a representative human being. Coleridge said that the poet is one who puts the whole soul of man into activity. I think of it in a somewhat different way. I have this image of a house. We occupy this house, which is our bodily frame, and for most persons maybe three or four lights in the house are burning and the rest is in darkness. But the creative imagination calls for turning all the lights on, for the house to be ablaze with light. That's what one lives for, really—those moments when you feel that blazing luminosity within.

EH: Is there any way that those of us who are not creative artists can turn on all those lights? Is it a matter of being passionately engaged or curious?

SK: A lot of it has to do with the extent of one's curiosity and caring. What bothers me about so many people is how little curiosity they have about what's happening to others, what's happening in the world, what's happening right now, for example, in Eastern Europe, Israel, the Soviet Union. To me the day's news is terribly important. The first thing I do in the morning is read *The New York Times*. The imagination renews itself by intermeshing with the dynamics of history. If you feel you're irrelevant to history, you fester.

EH: But what is your feeling when you learn that in Eastern Europe or Israel or the Soviet Union there has been a regression to things like hypernationalism and old ethnic hatreds? Don't you despair about progress?

SK: It isn't a question of progress, it's a question of concern. I don't delude myself that people are getting any better. Perhaps the state of the individual has improved at the subsistence level, but the relative quotient of good to evil in the world in this century—a century that includes the Holocaust—has probably deteriorated. To stay human we need to understand that what happens to others is happening to us. That's what the moral imagination is all about.

EH: Did you know that Rollo May used you as an example in his book on creativity, *The Courage to Create*? He said that you wrote your poems out of rage. But I think he was quoting from your poem "The Thief"—"I write this poem for money, rage, and love"—which was rage directed at having your pocket picked, whereas he interpreted the rage as rage against death.

SK: Rollo was basing his conclusions on conversations we had more than twenty years ago. There certainly was a period when I raged against all sorts of things. I may have told him it was the idea of being mortal that offended me most. Perhaps it's still at the root of my persistence in staying alive. I want to outwit the enemy.

EH: Could it be that the feeling that there is still work to do contributes to longevity? That you must stay alive in order to finish it?

SK: I can't picture myself ever saying, "I have done everything I could. Now I'm going to sit in the sun and vegetate for the rest of my life."

EH: You have said that your work is to tell what it means to be living and dying at the same time. Your poems express an ambivalent attitude to death. On the one hand, there is the dread of it in "What of the Night?" when you tell the messenger—that is, death—"in a childish voice" that your father is not home. But in some of your other poems about death, there's an acceptance, almost an attraction. In "The Long Boat," for example, the phrase "conscience, ambition, and all that caring" suggests that death would be a relief from those burdens.

SK: That's a momentary surrender to fatigue on the part of the man in the death-boat, as it puts out to sea. It's not the crux of the poem. Do you recall the conclusion?—"As if it didn't matter / which way was home; / as if he didn't know / he loved the earth so much / he wanted to stay forever."

EH: You've said, "Anybody who remains a poet throughout a lifetime has a terrible will to survive." A *terrible* will?

SK: Yes, exactly. Fierce and terrible. How else would one hang on?

EH: In much of your writing you seem to hold a tragic view of life. And yet you also seem to be blessed with a sanguine temperament.

SK: I'll refer you to Aristotle's *Poetics* for an explanation of why the tragic imagination is more compatible with a sanguine temperament, as you put it, than with a melancholy or depressed one. The tragic view leads to exaltation, not to depression.

EH: You've written that you envy your painter friends because they're not working out of their insides all the time.

SK: My point there is that poetry is spun out of one's breath and tissue. It's an extraordinarily internal affair, more so than any other art, with the possible exception of music.

EH: Is writing essays a different kind of process?

SK: They're hard for me to write. I spend as much care on them as I do on a poem. Sometimes it's excruciating just to get the wording right. I'm not a fluent writer.

EH: Are you more fluent in writing poetry?

SK: To a degree. Expository prose bothers me more because I get so impatient with the bridges, the connections, in the course of plodding from sentence to sentence, paragraph to paragraph. I love the fact that in a poem you are free to leap from pole to pole with a flick of the tongue.

EH: But your prose is extraordinarily fluid. I think that the essays in *A Kind of Order, A Kind of Folly* are wonderful.

SK: That encourages me to proceed with my plan to put out a new and expanded collection. The old one has been out of print for some time. As it happens, I'm in the process now of negotiating contracts for three books—which shows you [laughing] how sanguine I am about the future.

EH: Do you think there has been a change in your style as you've grown older?

SK: Everybody says so. But I also think there is a continuity, an abiding principle.

EH: There has been a continuity in your themes and concerns, but what about the style itself? Do you think there is such a thing as a "late style"? You've said, "In my later years I have wanted to write poems that are simple on the surface, even transparent in their diction." The course of your poetic style reminds me of Yeats's development. In both cases the early poems are more decorative, the later ones simpler in form and more powerful.

SK: Yeats was one of my early heroes and I learned a lot from him.

EH: Doesn't he have some lines about this kind of thing? "I made my song a coat / Covered with embroideries / Out of old mythologies / . . . there's more enterprise / In walking naked"?

SK: Yes. His early poems were quite soft and misty. He didn't become great until he stepped out of the Celtic twilight and began to speak directly of his feelings about Ireland, about Maude Gonne, and the two themes he eventually spotted as imperative concerns for an old poet: namely, sex and death.

EH: Do you agree with Yeats on that?

SK: It depends on the interpretation of his terms. If you stretch his pair of themes to their referential limits they cover practically everything, the sacred as well as the profane.

EH: In your poem "Raccoon Journal" you speak of "the separate wilderness of age, / where the old, libidinous beasts / assume familiar shapes, / pretending to be tamed." I find that last phrase, "pretending to be tamed," particularly provocative. Would you care to comment?

SK: It's a moment of reversal in the action of the poem. Perhaps I'm saying,"Don't be deceived by this old man's mask of civility and resignation. There's a wilderness inside him. Those obstreperous intruders, the Snopes-like raccoons, may simply be coming home."

EH: The art historian Kenneth Clark said, "If the late style in art can teach us to develop a late style in life, it will have rendered us an incomparable service." Do you think there can be a relationship between art and life in that sense?

SK: I'm not sure of the sense. When Michelangelo was doing his sculpture or when Leonardo was painting, that was "late style" then. Renaissance art is no longer a late style, but it was a late style when it was being practiced. Do you follow me?

EH: Yes, I think I do, but aren't you talking about a school of art? I think Clark was talking about individual artists—the way Michelangelo's style changed in his later years.

SK: It isn't always true. It doesn't always change for the better. It's true of Yeats, at least the late Yeats that I care about. I have no great love for the early Yeats—the late Yeats is the one who speaks to me. But the late Wordsworth, for example, is probably a more representative example. We don't really expect poets to flourish into their seventies and beyond. We prefer them to comply with the romantic legend and die young. At least that's been true up to now. It may not be true tomorrow, given the spectacular advances in modern medical science. The famous poets of the next century may well be wiser and better Methuselahs. Theoretically, one's late style ought to be more universal than the style of one's egotistical youth.

EH: Egotistical youth? Do you think those two words go together?

SK: Almost inevitably.

EH: I've heard it said, and I don't agree with it, that poets are at their best in their twenties.

SK: That's when poetry is a glandular phenomenon. Your skin secretes it. Everything you touch glistens. At a later stage you have to go down into the depths for your poems, back to your origins, to the first stirrings of the self. You have to plunge as deep into your life as you possibly can, and then you have to fight your way back. The difference is substantial, and I do think it explains the distinction between early and late work. A poet of my age is a many-layered creature. Past, present, and future are all seething together in my mind. My poetry these days may look easy on the surface—transparent, as I like to say—but perhaps it has gained a certain elemental gravity as it keeps cutting through those time-layers, from childhood and youth through the eventful middle years to whatever remains for me to face, including, of course, the last brutal reality. That recognition saturates the text. It both taints and sweetens every word I write.

New York / May 1990

Appendix

A Sampling of Poems Discussed in the Text

ORGANIC BLOOM

The brain constructs its systems to enclose
The steady paradox of thought and sense;
Momentously its tissued meaning grows
To solve and integrate experience.
But life escapes closed reason. We explain
Our chaos into cosmos, cell by cell,
Only to learn of some insidious pain
Beyond the limits of our charted hell,
A guilt not mentioned in our prayers, a sin
Conceived against the self, So, vast and vaster
The plasmic circles of gray discipline
Spread outward to include each new disaster.
Enormous floats the brain's organic bloom
Till, bursting like a fruit, it scatters doom.

FATHER AND SON

Now in the suburbs and the falling light
I followed him, and now down sandy road
Whiter than bone-dust, through the sweet
Curdle of fields, where the plums
Dropped with their load of ripeness, one by one.
Mile after mile I followed, with skimming feet,
After the secret master of my blood,
Him, steeped in the odor of ponds, whose indomitable love
Kept me in chains. Strode years; stretched into bird;
Raced through the sleeping country where I was young,
The silence unrolling before me as I came,
The night nailed like an orange to my brow.

How should I tell him my fable and the fears,
How bridge the chasm in a casual tone,
Saying, "The house, the stucco one you built,
We lost. Sister married and went from home,
And nothing comes back, it's strange, from where she goes.
I lived on a hill that had too many rooms:
Light we could make, but not enough of warmth,
And when the light failed, I climbed under the hill.
The papers are delivered every day;
I am alone and never shed a tear."

At the water's edge, where the smothering ferns lifted
Their arms, "Father!" I cried, "Return! You know
The way. I'll wipe the mudstains from your clothes;
No trace, I promise, will remain. Instruct
Your son, whirling between two wars,
In the Gemara of your gentleness,
For I would be a child to those who mourn

And brother to the foundlings of the field
And friend of innocence and all bright eyes.
O teach me how to work and keep me kind."

Among the turtles and the lilies he turned to me
The white ignorant hollow of his face.

OPEN THE GATES

Within the city of the burning cloud,
Dragging my life behind me in a sack,
Naked I prowl, scourged by the black
Temptation of the blood grown proud.

Here at the monumental door,
Carved with the curious legend of my youth,
I brandish the great bone of my death,
Beat once therewith and beat no more.

The hinges groan: a rush of forms
Shivers my name, wrenched out of me.
I stand on the terrible threshold, and I see
The end and the beginning in each other's arms.

THE WAR AGAINST THE TREES

The man who sold his lawn to standard oil
Joked with his neighbors come to watch the show
While the bulldozers, drunk with gasoline,
Tested the virtue of the soil
Under the branchy sky
By overthrowing first the privet-row.

Forsythia-forays and hydrangea-raids
Were but preliminaries to a war
Against the great-grandfathers of the town,
So freshly lopped and maimed.
They struck and struck again,
And with each elm a century went down.

All day the hireling engines charged the trees,
Subverting them by hacking underground
In grub-dominions, where dark summer's mole
Rampages through his halls,
Till a northern seizure shook
Those crowns, forcing the giants to their knees.

I saw the ghosts of children at their games
Racing beyond their childhood in the shade,
And while the green world turned its death-foxed page
And a red wagon wheeled,
I watched them disappear
Into the suburbs of their grievous age.

Ripped from the craters much too big for hearts
The club-roots bared their amputated coils,

Raw gorgons matted blind, whose pocks and scars
Cried Moon! on a corner lot
One witness-moment, caught
In the rear-view mirrors of the passing cars.

GREEN WAYS

Let me not say it, let me not reveal
How like a god my heart begins to climb
The trellis of the crystal
In the rose-green moon;
Let me not say it, let me leave untold
This legend, while the nights snow emerald.

Let me not say it, let me not confess
How in the leaflight of my green-celled world
In self's pre-history
The blind moulds kiss;
Let me not say it, let me but endure
This ritual like feather and like star.

Let me proclaim it—human be my lot!—
How from my pit of green horse-bones
I turn, in a wilderness of sweat,
To the moon-breasted sibylline,
And lift this garland, Danger, from her throat
To blaze it in the foundries of the night.

END OF SUMMER

An agitation of the air,
A perturbation of the light
Admonished me the unloved year
Would turn on its hinge that night.

I stood in the disenchanted field
Amid the stubble and the stones,
Amazed, while a small worm lisped to me
The song of my marrow-bones.

Blue poured into summer blue,
A hawk broke from his cloudless tower,
The roof of the silo blazed, and I knew
That part of my life was over.

Already the iron door of the north
Clangs open: birds, leaves, snows
Order their populations forth,
And a cruel wind blows.

THREE FLOORS

Mother was a crack of light
and a gray eye peeping;
I made believe by breathing hard
that I was sleeping.

Sister's doughboy on last leave
had robbed me of her hand;
downstairs at intervals she played
Warum on the baby grand.

Under the roof a wardrobe trunk
whose lock a boy could pick
contained a red Masonic hat
and a walking stick.

Bolt upright in my bed that night
I saw my father flying;
the wind was walking on my neck,
the windowpanes were crying.

THE FLIGHT OF APOLLO

Earth was my home, but even there I was a stranger. This mineral
crust. I walk like a swimmer. What titanic bombardments in those
old astral wars! I know what I know: I shall never escape from
strangeness or complete my journey. Think of me as nostalgic,
afraid, exalted. I am your man on the moon, a speck of megalo-
mania, restless for the leap toward island universes pulsing beyond
where the constellations set. Infinite space overwhelms the human
heart, but in the middle of nowhere life inexorably calls to life.
Forward my mail to Mars. What news from the Great Spiral Neb-
ula in Andromeda and the Magellanic Clouds?

2

I was a stranger on earth.
Stepping on the moon, I begin
the gay pilgrimage to new
Jerusalems
in foreign galaxies.
Heat. Cold. Craters of silence.
The Sea of Tranquillity
rolling on the shores of entropy.
And, beyond,
the intelligence of the stars.

KING OF THE RIVER

If the water were clear enough,
if the water were still,
but the water is not clear,
the water is not still,
you would see yourself,
slipped out of your skin,
nosing upstream,
slapping, thrashing,
tumbling
over the rocks
till you paint them
with your belly's blood:
Finned Ego,
yard of muscle that coils,
uncoils.

If the knowledge were given you,
but it is not given,
for the membrane is clouded
with self-deceptions
and the iridescent image swims
through a mirror that flows,
you would surprise yourself
in that other flesh
heavy with milt,
bruised, battering towards the dam
that lips the orgiastic pool.

Come. Bathe in these waters.
Increase and die.

If the power were granted you
to break out of your cells,
but the imagination fails
and the doors of the senses close
on the child within,
you would dare to be changed,
as you are changing now,
into the shape you dread
beyond the merely human.
A dry fire eats you.
Fat drips from your bones.
The flutes of your gills discolor.
You have become a ship for parasites.
The great clock of your life
is slowing down,
and the small clocks run wild.
For this you were born.
You have cried to the wind
and heard the wind's reply:
"I did not choose the way,
the way chose me."
You have tasted the fire on your tongue
till it is swollen black
with a prophetic joy:
"Burn with me!
The only music is time,
the only dance is love."

If the heart were pure enough,
but it is not pure,
you would admit
that nothing compels you
any more, nothing
at all abides,
but nostalgia and desire,
the two-way ladder
between heaven and hell.

On the threshold
of the last mystery,
at the brute absolute hour,
you have looked into the eyes
of your creature self,
which are glazed with madness,
and you say
he is not broken but endures,
limber and firm
in the state of his shining,
forever inheriting his salt kingdom,
from which he is banished
forever.

ROBIN REDBREAST

It was the dingiest bird
you every saw, all the color
washed from him, as if
he had been standing in the rain,
friendless and stiff and cold,
since Eden went wrong.
In the house marked For Sale,
where nobody made a sound,
in the room where I lived
with an empty page, I had heard
the squawking of the jays
under the wild persimmons
tormenting him.
So I scooped him up
after they knocked him down,
in league with that ounce of heart
pounding in my palm,
that dumb beak gaping.
Poor thing! Poor foolish life!
without sense enough to stop
running in desperate circles,
needing my lucky help
to toss him back into his element.
But when I held him high,
fear clutched my hand,
for through the hole in his head,
cut whistle-clean . . .
through the old dried wound
between his eyes
where the hunter's brand
had tunneled out his wits . . .
I caught the cold flash of the blue
unappeasable sky.

THE ARTIST

His paintings grew darker every year.
They filled the walls, they filled the room;
eventually they filled his world—
all but the ravishment.
When voices faded, he would rush to hear
the scratched soul of Mozart
endlessly in gyre.
Back and forth, back and forth,
he paced the paint-smeared floor,
diminishing in size each time he turned,
trapped in his monumental void,
raving against his adversaries.
At last he took a knife in his hand
and slashed an exit for himself
between the frames of his tall scenery.
Through the holes of his tattered universe
the first innocence and the light
came pouring in.

THE PORTRAIT

My mother never forgave my father
for killing himself,
especially at such an awkward time
and in a public park,
that spring
when I was waiting to be born.
She locked his name
in her deepest cabinet
and would not let him out,
though I could hear him thumping.
When I came down from the attic
with the pastel portrait in my hand
of a long-lipped stranger
with a brave moustache
and deep brown level eyes,
she ripped it into shreds
without a single word
and slapped me hard.
In my sixty-fourth year
I can feel my cheek
still burning.

AN OLD CRACKED TUNE

My name is Solomon Levi,
the desert is my home,
my mother's breast was thorny,
and father I had none.

The sands whispered, *Be separate*,
the stones taught me, *Be hard*.
I dance, for the joy of surviving,
on the edge of the road.

THE TESTING-TREE

1

On my way home from school
   up tribal Providence Hill
      past the Academy ballpark
where I could never hope to play
   I scuffed in the drainage ditch
      among the sodden seethe of leaves
hunting for perfect stones
   rolled out of glacial time
      into my pitcher's hand;
then sprinted lickety-
   split on my magic Keds
      from a crouching start,
scarcely touching the ground
   with my flying skin
      as I poured it on
for the prize of the mastery
   over that stretch of road,
      with no one no where to deny
when I flung myself down
   that on the given course
      I was the world's fastest human.

2

Around the bend
   that tried to loop me home
      dawdling came natural
across a nettled field
   riddled with rabbit-life
      where the bees sank sugar-wells
in the trunks of the maples

and a stringy old lilac
    more than two stories tall
blazing with mildew
    remembered a door in the
        long teeth of the woods.
All of it happened slow:
    brushing the stickseed off,
        wading through jewelweed
strangled by angel's hair,
    spotting the print of the deer
        and the red fox's scats.

Once I owned the key
    to an umbrageous trail
        thickened with mosses
where flickering presences
    gave me right of passage
        as I followed in the steps
of straight-backed Massassoit
    soundlessly heel-and-toe
        practicing my Indian walk.

3

Past the abandoned quarry
    where the pale sun bobbed
        in the sump of the granite,
past copperhead ledge,
    where the ferns gave foothold,
        I walked, deliberate,
on to the clearing,
    with the stones in my pocket
        changing to oracles
and my coiled ear tuned
    to the slightest leaf-stir.
        I had kept my appointment.
There I stood in the shadow,
    at fifty measured paces,

of the inexhaustible oak,
tyrant and target,
  Jehovah of acorns,
    watchtower of the thunders,
that locked King Philip's War
  in its annulated core
    under the cut of my name.
Father wherever you are
  I have only three throws
    bless my good right arm.
In the haze of afternoon,
  while the air flowed saffron,
    I played my game for keeps—
for love, for poetry,
  and for eternal life—
    after the trials of summer.

4

In the recurring dream
  my mother stands
    in her bridal gown
under the burning lilac,
  with Bernard Shaw and Bertie
    Russell kissing her hands;
the house behind her is in ruins;
  she is wearing an owl's face
    and makes barking noises.
Her minatory finger points.
  I pass through the cardboard doorway
    askew in the field
and peer down a well
  where an albino walrus huffs.
    He has the gentlest eyes.
If the dirt keeps sifting in,
  staining the water yellow,
    why should I be blamed?
Never try to explain.

That single Model A
  sputtering up the grade
unfurled a highway behind
  where the tanks maneuver,
    revolving their turrets.
In a murderous time
  the heart breaks and breaks
    and lives by breaking.
It is necessary to go
  through dark and deeper dark
    and not to turn.
I am looking for the trail.
  Where is my testing-tree?
    Give me back my stones!

QUINNAPOXET

I was fishing in the abandoned reservoir
back in Quinnapoxet,
where the snapping turtles cruised
and the bullheads swayed
in their bower of tree-stumps,
sleek as eels and pigeon-fat.
One of them gashed my thumb
with a flick of his razor fin
when I yanked the barb
out of his gullet.
The sun hung its terrible coals
over Buteau's farm: I saw
the treetops seething.

They came suddenly into view
on the Indian road,
evenly stepping
past the apple orchard,
commingling with the dust
they raised, their cloud of being,
against the dripping light
looming larger and bolder.
She was wearing a mourning bonnet
and a wrap of shining taffeta.
"Why don't you write?" she cried
from the folds of her veil.
"We never hear from you."
I had nothing to say to her.
But for him who walked behind her
in his dark worsted suit,
with his face averted

as if to hide a scald,
deep in his other life,
I touched my forehead
with my swollen thumb
and splayed my fingers out—
in deaf-mute country
the sign for father.

THE SNAKES OF SEPTEMBER

All summer I heard them
rustling in the shrubbery,
outracing me from tier
to tier in my garden,
a whisper among the viburnums,
a signal flashed from the hedgerow,
a shadow pulsing
in the barberry thicket.
Now that the nights are chill
and the annuals spent,
I should have thought them gone,
in a torpor of blood
slipped to the nether world
before the sickle frost.
Not so. In the deceptive balm
of noon, as if defiant of the curse
that spoiled another garden,
these two appear on show
through a narrow slit
in the dense green brocade
of a north-country spruce,
dangling head-down, entwined
in a brazen love-knot.
I put out my hand and stroke
the fine, dry grit of their skins.
After all,
we are partners in this land,
co-signers of a covenant.
At my touch the wild
braid of creation
trembles.

THE ABDUCTION

Some things I do not profess
to understand, perhaps
not wanting to, including
whatever it was they did
with you or you with them
that timeless summer day
when you stumbled out of the wood,
distracted, with your white blouse torn
and a bloodstain on your skirt.
"Do you believe?" you asked.
Between us, through the years,
from bits, from broken clues,
we pieced enough together
to make the story real:
how you encountered on the path
a pack of sleek, grey hounds,
trailed by a dumbshow retinue
in leather shrouds; and how
you were led, through leafy ways,
into the presence of a royal stag,
flaming in his chestnut coat,
who kneeled on a swale of moss
before you; and how you were borne
aloft in triumph through the green,
stretched on his rack of budding horn,
till suddenly you found yourself alone
in a trampled clearing.

That was a long time ago,
almost another age, but even now,
when I hold you in my arms,
I wonder where you are.

Sometimes I wake to hear
the engines of the night thrumming
outside the east bay window
on the lawn spreading to the rose garden.
You lie beside me in elegant repose,
a hint of transport hovering on your lips,
indifferent to the harsh green flares
that swivel through the room,
searchlights controlled by unseen hands.
Out there is childhood country,
bleached faces peering in
with coals for eyes.
Our lives are spinning out
from world to world;
the shapes of things
are shifting in the wind.
What do we know
beyond the rapture and the dread?

THE WELLFLEET WHALE

A few summers ago, on Cape Cod, a whale foundered on the beach, a sixty-three-foot finback whale. When the tide went out, I approached him. He was lying there, in monstrous desolation, making the most terrifying noises—rumbling—groaning. I put my hands on his flanks and I could feel the life inside him. And while I was standing there, suddenly he opened his eye. It was a big, red, cold eye, and it was staring directly at me. A shudder of recognition passed between us. Then the eye closed forever. I've been thinking about whales ever since.

—Journal entry

1

You have your language too,
  an eerie medley of clicks
    and hoots and trills,
location-notes and love calls,
  whistles and grunts. Occasionally,
    it's like furniture being smashed,
or the creaking of a mossy door,
  sounds that all melt into a liquid
    song with endless variations,
as if to compensate
  for the vast loneliness of the sea.
    Sometimes a disembodied voice
breaks in, as if from distant reefs,
  and it's as much as one can bear
    to listen to its long mournful cry,
a sorrow without name, both more
  and less than human. It drags
    across the ear like a record
running down.

2

No wind, No waves, No clouds.
  Only the whisper of the tide,
    as it withdrew, stroking the shore,
a lazy drift of gulls overhead,
  and tiny points of light
    bubbling in the channel.
It was the tag-end of summer.
  From the harbor's mouth
    you coasted into sight,
flashing news of your advent,
  the crescent of your dorsal fin
    clipping the diamonded surface.
We cheered at the sign of your greatness
  when the black barrel of your head
    erupted, ramming the water,
and you flowered for us
  in the jet of your spouting.

3

All afternoon you swam
  tirelessly round the bay,
    with such an easy motion,
the slightest downbeat of your tail,
  an almost imperceptible
    undulation of your flippers,
you seemed like something poured,
  not driven; you seemed
    to marry grace with power.
And when you bounded into air,
  slapping your flukes,
    we thrilled to look upon
pure energy incarnate
  as nobility of form.
    You seemed to ask of us
not sympathy, or love,

or understanding,
    but awe and wonder.

That night we watched you
    swimming in the moon.
        Your back was molten silver.
We guessed your silent passage
    by the phosphorescence in your wake.
        At dawn we found you stranded on the rocks.

4

There came a boy and a man
    and yet other men running, and two
        schoolgirls in yellow halters
and a housewife bedecked
    with curlers, and whole families in beach
        buggies with assorted yelping dogs.
The tide was almost out.
    We could walk around you,
        as you heaved deeper into the shoal,
crushed by your own weight,
    collapsing into yourself,
        your flippers and your flukes
quivering, your blowhole
    spasmodically bubbling, roaring.
        In the pit of your gaping mouth
you bared your fringework of baleen,
    a thicket of horned bristles.
        When the Curator of Mammals
arrived from Boston
    to take samples of your blood
        you were already oozing from below.
Somebody had carved his initials
    in your flank. Hunters of souvenirs
        had peeled off strips of your skin,
a membrane thin as paper.
    You were blistered and cracked by the sun.

The gulls had been pecking at you.
The sound you made was a hoarse and fitful bleating.

What drew us, like a magnet, to your dying?
   You made a bond between us,
      the keepers of the nightfall watch,
who gathered in a ring around you,
    boozing in the bonfire light.
      Toward dawn we shared with you
your hour of desolation,
   the huge lingering passion
     of your unearthly outcry,
as you swung your blind head
    toward us and laboriously opened
      a bloodshot, glistening eye,
in which we swam with terror and recognition.

5

Voyager, chief of the pelagic world,
   you brought with you the myth
     of another country, dimly remembered,
where flying reptiles
    lumbered over the steaming marshes
      and trumpeting thunder lizards
wallowed in the reeds.
   While empires rose and fell on land,
     your nation breasted the open main,
rocked in the consoling rhythm
    of the tides. Which ancestor first plunged
      head-down through zones of colored twilight
to scour the bottom of the dark?
   You ranged the North Atlantic track
     from Port-of-Spain to Baffin Bay,
edging between the ice-floes
    through the fat of summer,
      lob-tailing, breaching, sounding,

grazing in the pastures of the sea
    on krill-rich orange plankton
        crackling with life.

You prowled down the continental shelf,
    guided by the sun and stars
        and the taste of alluvial silt
on your way southward
    to the warm lagoons,
        the tropic of desire,
where the lovers lie belly to belly
    in the rub and nuzzle of their sporting;
        and you turned, like a god in exile,
out of your wide primeval element,
    delivered to the mercy of time.
        Master of the whale-roads,
let the white wings of the gulls
    spread out their cover.
        You have become like us,
disgraced and mortal.

Biographical Note

Stanley Kunitz was born in Worcester, Massachusetts in 1905. After graduating from Harvard *summa cum laude* he began a long, varied career as poet, editor, essayist, translator, horticulturalist, and mentor of young poets. The poems of his later years recall Robert Lowell's praise of *The Testing-Tree* in 1971: "He again tops the crowd—he surpasses himself, the old iron brought to the white heat of simplicity."

The honors for his poetry include the Pulitzer Prize, Bollingen Prize, National Endowment for the Arts Senior Fellowship, Brandeis Medal of Achievement, Harriet Monroe Award, Guggenheim Fellowship, Ford Foundation Award, and Lenore Marshall Prize. He was designated the first State Poet of New York (1987–89) and awarded the Walt Whitman Citation of Merit. In 1992 he received the Centennial Medal from Harvard University.

He has edited the Yale Series of Younger Poets, served as consultant in poetry to the Library of Congress, and taught for many years in the graduate writing program at Columbia University. He is a founder of the Fine Arts Work Center in Provincetown, Massachusetts, a member of the American Academy of Arts and Letters, a chancellor of the Academy of American Poets, and founding president of Poets House in New York.

Kunitz has translated some of the major Russian poets. He has made extensive lecture and reading tours of the Soviet Union, Poland, the west coast of Africa, Israel, and Egypt; and he has participated in international poetry festivals in The Netherlands, Yugoslavia, Italy, Canada, and England. For most of his adult life he has been active in the civil liberties and peace movements.

His eightieth birthday was celebrated by festivals and exhibitions in Provincetown, Worcester, and New York. *A Celebration for Stanley Kunitz* (1986) included contributions from sixty-four fellow-writers. *Publishers Weekly* saluted him as "a man who is both great and modest, the epitome of all we would wish our poets to be."

Mr. Kunitz and his artist wife Elise Asher live in New York City and Provincetown, where he cultivates a renowned seaside garden.

Contributors' Notes

Jonathan Blunk tells us he is an independent radio producer, disc jockey, and amateur jazz musician.

Robert Boyers is a professor of English at Skidmore College and the founding editor of *Salmagundi*. He is the author of *Atrocity and Amnesia: The Political Novel Since 1945* (Oxford University Press) and *After the Avante-Garde: Essays in Art and Culture* (Penn State Press).

Christopher Busa is the editor and publisher of *Provincetown Arts*. He is co-editor of *The Erotic Works of D. H. Lawrence* (Avenol).

Cynthia Davis is a professor of English at Texas A & I University.

Louise Glück teaches at Williams College. She is the author of *Descending Figure* (Ecco Press), *Firstborn* (Ecco Press), and *The Triumph of Achilles* (Ecco Press). Her most recent book of poems is *The Wild Iris* (Ecco Press).

Esther Harriott is the author of *American Voices: Five Contemporary Playwrights in Essays and Interviews* (McFarland). She is an editor at The New York Public Library and writes book reviews for *New York Newsday*. Ms. Harriott is working on a book of interviews with creative artists over seventy-five.

Marie Howe received her M.F.A. from Columbia University. She has published a book of poems, *The Good Thief* (Persea), which won the National Poetry Series in 1987. She serves on the Fine Arts Work Center (Provincetown) Writing Committee and teaches at Tufts University.

Richard Jackson has published three collections of poems, *Part of the Story* (Grove Press), *Worlds Apart* (University of Alabama Press), and *Alive All Day* (Cleveland State University Press), and two books of criticism, *Acts of Mind: Conversations with Contemporary American Poets* (University of Alabama Press) and *The Dismantling of Time in Contemporary Poetry* (University of Alabama Press).

David Lupher conducted his interview while he was an undergraduate at Yale. He is a classics professor at the University of Puget Sound.

Susan Mitchell has published two volumes of poetry, *The Water Inside the Water* (Wesleyan University Press) and *Rapture* (HarperCollins). She was a fellow for two years at the Fine Arts Work Center in Provincetown. She is the Mary Blossom Lee Professor in Creative Writing at Florida Atlantic University.

Stanley Moss's books of poems include *The Skull of Adam, The Wrong Angel* (Macmillan), and *The Intelligence of Clouds* (Harcourt Brace Jovanovich). Forthcoming is a book of *New and Selected Poems*. He is the publisher and chief editor of The Sheep Meadow Press.

Bill Moyers is the well-known television journalist and producer. Moyers has served as deputy director of the Peace Corps, special assistant to President Johnson, and as a trustee of the Rockefeller Foundation. Recently, he was elected a fellow of the American Academy of Arts and Sciences.

William Packard teaches creative writing at New York University. He is the founder and editor of *The New York Quarterly*. His books include *The Poet's Craft* (Paragon) and *The Poet's Dictionary* (Harper & Row).

Fran Quinn is poet-in-residence at Butler University. His latest book is *Milk of the Lioness* (Bachrach, Coleman, and McCray). A new collection, *In a Dusty Room*, is in circulation.

Francine Ringold has edited *Nimrod* for twenty-five years. She is an adjunct professor of English and theater at the University of Tulsa. Her publications include three books: *Voices* (Myrtle Press), *Making a Mark: A Guide to Writing and Drawing for Senior Citizens* (Council Oak Books), and *A Magic Journey: Writing and Painting at Gatesway* (Coman and Associates).

Selden Rodman's credits include the following books he has edited: *One Hundred British Poets, One Hundred American Poems, One Hundred Modern Poems, South America of the Poets, Conversations with Artists*, and *Tongues of Fallen Angels* (New Directions).

Michael Ryan's first book, *Threats Instead of Trees*, won the Yale Series of Younger Poets award. His second book, *In Winter*, was selected for the National Poetry Series in 1981. He won the Lenore Marshall/Nation prize in 1987 for his book *God Hunger* (Viking). He is a professor of English at the University of California at Irvine.

Grace Schulman has published two books of poetry: *Burning Down the Icons* (Princeton University Press) and *Hemispheres* (Sheep Meadow Press). She is poetry editor of *The Nation* and a professor of English at Baruch College, CUNY. She is also the author of *Marianne Moore: The Poetry of Engagement* (University of Illinois Press), a critical book.

Caroline Sutton is a free-lance journalist

Daniel Weissbort founded the magazine *Modern Poetry in Translation* with Ted Hughes in 1965. He has published numerous translations and four collections of his own poetry, most recently *Fathers* (Northern House, Newcastle). He directs the Translation Workshop at the University of Iowa. His most recent translation is *The Poetry of Survival: Post-War Poets of Central and Eastern Europe*.

Stanley Kunitz: Selective Bibliography

Poetry and Prose:

Intellectual Things. New York: Doubleday, Doran, 1930.
Passport to the War: A Selection of Poems. New York: Holt, Rinehart, and Winston, 1944.
Selected Poems 1928-1958. Boston: Atlantic-Little, Brown, 1958.
The Poems of John Keats (ed.). New York: Crowell, 1965.
The Testing-Tree. Poems. Boston: Atlantic-Little, Brown, 1971.
The Terrible Threshold: Selected Poems 1940-1970. London: Secker & Warburg, 1974.
The Coat without a Seam: Sixty Poems 1930-1972. Northampton, MA: Gehenna Press, 1974.
Robert Lowell: Poet of Terribilità. New York: Pierpont Morgan Library, 1974.
A Kind of Order, A Kind of Folly: Essays and Conversations. Boston: Atlantic-Little, Brown, 1975.
From Feathers to Iron. Washington: Library of Congress, 1976.
The Lincoln Relics: A Poem. Port Townsend, Washington: Greywolf Press, 1978.
The Poems of Stanley Kunitz, 1928-1978. Boston: Atlantic-Little, Brown, 1979.
The Wellfleet Whale and Companion Poems. New York: Sheep Meadow Press, 1983.
Next-to-Last Things: New Poems and Essays. Boston: Atlantic-Little, Brown, 1985.
The Essential Blake (ed.). New York: Ecco Press, 1987.

Translations:

Voznesensky, Andrei. *Anti-Worlds and the Fifth Ace*. Trans. W. H. Auden, Stanley Kunitz et al. Ed. Patricia Blake and Max Hayward. New York: Schocken Books, 1967.
Yevtushenko, Yevgeny. *Stolen Apples*. Ed. Albert Todd. Trans. Stanley Kunitz et al. New York: Doubleday & Co., 1972.
Akhmatova, Anna. *Poems of Akhmatova*. Selected, Translated, and Introduced by Stanley Kunitz with Max Hayward. Boston: Atlantic-Little, Brown, 1973.
Drach, Ivan. *Orchard Lamps*. Ed. Stanley Kunitz and translated with others. New York: Sheep Meadow Press, 1978.

Yale Series of Younger Poets:

Kunitz, Stanley. Foreword. *Collecting Evidence*. By Hugh Seidman. Ed. Stanley Kunitz. New Haven: Yale University Press, 1970.
———. Foreword. *Lugging Vegetables to Nantucket*. By Peter Klappert. Ed. Stanley Kunitz. New Haven: Yale University Press, 1971.
———. Foreword. *Obscenities*. By Michael Casey. Ed. Stanley Kunitz. New Haven: Yale University Press, 1972.

Kunitz, Stanley. Foreword. *Field Guide*. By Robert Hass. Ed. Stanley Kunitz. New Haven: Yale University Press, 1973.

———. Foreword. *Threats instead of Trees*. By Michael Ryan. Ed. Stanley Kunitz. New Haven: Yale University Press, 1974.

———. Foreword. *Snow on Snow*. By Maura Stanton. Ed. Stanley Kunitz. New Haven: Yale University Press, 1975.

———. Foreword. *Gathering the Tribes*. By Carolyn Forché. Ed. Stanley Kunitz. New Haven: Yale University Press, 1976.

———. Foreword. *Beginning with O*. By Olga Broumas. Ed. Stanley Kunitz. New Haven: Yale University Press, 1977.

Reference Works Edited:

Tante, Dilly [Pseud.], ed. *Living Authors: A Book of Biographies*. New York: H. W. Wilson, 1931.

———. *Authors Today and Yesterday: A Companion Volume to Living Authors*. With Howard Haycraft. New York: H. W. Wilson, 1933.

Kunitz, Stanley J., ed. *The Junior Book of Authors: An Introduction to the Lives of Writers and Illustrators for Younger Readers*. With Howard Haycraft. New York: H. W. Wilson, 1934. 2nd ed. 1951.

———. *British Authors of the Nineteenth Century*. With Howard Haycraft. New York: H. W. Wilson, 1936.

———. *American Authors, 1600-1900: A Biographical Dictionary of American Literature*. With Howard Haycraft. New York: H. W. Wilson, 1938.

———. *Twentieth Century Authors: A Biographical Dictionary of Modern Literature*. With Howard Haycraft. New York: H. W. Wilson, 1942.

———. *British Authors before 1800: A Biographical Dictionary*. With Howard Haycraft. New York: H. W. Wilson, 1952.

———. *Twentieth Century Authors: First Supplement*. With Vineta Colby. New York: H. W. Wilson, 1955.

———. *European Authors: 1000-1900, A Biographical Introduction to European Literature*. With Vineta Colby. New York: H. W. Wilson, 1967.

Books Contributed To:

Kunitz, Stanley. "Poetry's Silver Age: An Improbable Dialogue." *Writing in America*. Ed. John Fischer and Robert B. Silvers. New Brunswick, New Jersey: Rutgers University Press, 1960.

———. "The Taste of Self" (on Theodore Roethke's "In a Dark Time"). *The Contemporary Poet as Artist and Critic*. Ed. Anthony Ostroff. Boston: Little, Brown, 1964.

———. "On 'Father and Son.'" Ibid.

———. "Out of the Edge." *Randall Jarrell 1914-1965*. Ed. Robert Lowell, Peter Taylor, and Robert Penn Warren. New York: Farrar, Straus, and Giroux, 1967.

————. Foreword. *Worcester Poets: With Notes toward a Literary History*. By Michael True. Worcester, Massachusetts: Worcester County Poetry Association, 1972.

————. "Where Joy Is" (prefatory note). *To Hold in My Hand: Selected Poems*. By Hilda Morley. New York: Sheep Meadow Press, 1983.

————. "Poet and State." *Poetry and Politics: An Anthology of Essays*. Ed. Richard Jones. New York: Quill, 1985.

————. "Jeremiah: The Fountain Overflows." *Congregation: Contemporary Writers Read the Jewish Bible*. Ed. David Rosenberg. New York: Harcourt Brace Jovanovich, 1987.

————. "James Brooks: Reflections." *James Brooks: The Early 1950s*. New York: Berry-Hill, 1989.

————. "Chariot" (poem). *Varujan Boghosian*. Dartmouth, New Hampshire: Hood Museum of Art, 1989.

Articles and Essays:

"Dilly Tante Observes." *Wilson Bulletin for Librarians* (title changed to *Wilson Library Bulletin*, 1939). Continued as "The Roving Eye" with initials "S.J.K." January 1928-March 1943.

Kunitz, Stanley. "From Queen Anne to the Jungle." Rev. of Edith Sitwell. *Poetry* 37 Mar. 1931: 339-345.

————. "Horace Gregory's First Book." *Poetry* 38 Apr. 1931: 41-45.

————. "Middle Way." Rev. of "AE" (George William Russell). *Poetry* 38 Aug. 1931: 276-80.

————. "Poetry of Conrad Aiken." *Nation* 14 Oct. 1931: 393-94.

————. "Poet of the War." Rev. of Wilfred Owen. *Poetry* 40 June 1932: 159-62.

————. "Six English Poets." *Poetry* 42 July 1933: 228-33.

————. "Honor of Doubt." Rev. of Harold Monroe. *Poetry* 44 June 1934: 162-64

————. "Enchanted Pilgrim." Rev. of Elder Olson. *Poetry* 45 Feb. 1935: 279-82.

————. "Lesson from Rilke." Rev. of Rilke trans. *Poetry* 45 Mar. 1935: 328-32.

————. "Between Two Worlds." Rev. of C. Day Lewis. *Poetry* 47 Dec. 1935: 158-62.

————. "Simplicity in Wonder." Rev. of W. H. Davies. *Poetry* 48 July 1936: 232-34.

————. "Poet's Duty." Rev. of C. A. Millspaugh. *Poetry* 50 Apr. 1937: 43-45.

————. "Learned in Violence." Rev. of Conrad Aiken. *Poetry* 50 May 1937: 103-6.

————. "The Single Conscience." Rev. of Mary Colum. *Poetry* 52 May 1938: 86-94.

————. "Profile of a Mask." Rev. of Horace Gregory. *Poetry* 58 June 1941: 152-56.

————. "Pangolin of Poets." Rev. of Marianne Moore. *Poetry* 59 Nov. 1941: 96-98.

———. "The Day is a Poem." Rev. of Robinson Jeffers. *Poetry* 59 Dec. 1941: 148-54.

———. "Pentagons and Pomegranates." Rev. of Louise Bogan. *Poetry* 60 Apr. 1942: 40-43.

Kunitz, Stanley. "In the Beginning." Rev. of *Five American Poets*. *Poetry* 60 July 1942: 215-19.

———. "A Tale of a Jar." Rev. of H.D. *Poetry* 70 Apr. 1947: 36-42.

———. "News of the Root." Rev. of Theodore Roethke. *Poetry* 73 Jan. 1949: 222-25.

———. "Bronze by Gold." Rev. of Gwendolyn Brooks and Annie Allen. *Poetry* 76 Apr. 1950: 52-56.

———. "Creative Writing Workshop." *Education* 73 Nov. 1952: 152-56.

———. "Seminar in the Arts." *Education* 73 Nov. 1952: 172-76.

———. "Five Points of the Compass." Rev. of Logan, Hall, Hutchinson, Woods, and Wales. *Poetry* 88 June 1956: 183-91.

———. "Careful Young Men." *Nation* 9 Mar. 1957: 200-201.

———. "Private Eye." Rev. of Kenneth Fearing. *Saturday Review* 29 June 1957: 25.

———. "Identity Is the Problem." Rev. of Lenore G. Marshall. *Saturday Review* 40 July 1957: 28.

———. "No Middle Flight." Rev. of John Berryman. *Poetry* 90 July 1957: 244-49.

———. "Poems Recorded by Richard Wilbur." *Evergreen Review* 8 Spring 1959: 201-2.

———. "American Poetry's Silver Age." *Harper's* 219 Oct. 1959: 173-79.

———. "Process and Thing: A Year of Poetry." *Harper's* 221 Sep. 1960: 96.

———. "New Books." *Harper's* 223 Aug. 1961: 86-91.

———. "The Taste of Self." *New World Writing* 19 1961: 106-14.

———. "The Cold War and the West." *Partisan Review* 29 Winter 1962: 40-42.

———. "Father and Son: A Rejoinder." *New World Writing* 20 1962: 211-15.

———. "Frost, Williams, and Company." *Harper's* 225 Oct. 1962: 100-103.

———. "Graves, Nemerov, Smith." *New York Times Book Review* 21 July 1963: 4.

———. "Robert Lowell: The Sense of a Life." *New York Times Book Review* 14 Oct. 1964: 34.

———. "Roethke: Poet of Transformations." *New Republic* 23 Jan. 1965: 23-29.

———. "Sea Son of the Wave." Rev. of *The Life of Dylan Thomas*, by Constantine Fitzgibbon. *New York Times Book Review* 31 Oct. 1965: 1.

———. "The Hartford Walker." *New Republic* 12 Nov. 1966: 23-26.

———. "A Sum of Approximations." *Translation* Winter 1973: 56-61.

———. "The Life of Poetry." *Antaeus* 37 Spring 1980: 149.

———. "Jean Garrigue: A Symposium." *Twentieth Century Literature* 29 Spring 1983: 13-18.

———. "The Layers." *Ironwood* Fall 1984: 71-74.

————. "Communication and Communion: A Dialogue." *Southern Review* Spring 1985: 404-14.

————. "Jack Tworkov." *Provincetown Arts* Aug. 1985: 5.

————. "At the Tomb of Walt Whitman." *American Poetry Review* Sep./Oct. 1985: 24-27.

————. "The Poet's Quest for the Father." *New York Times Book Review* 22 Feb. 1987: 1. Repr. in *Provincetown Arts* Annual Issue 1992.

————. "Gardening for Love." *New York Times Book Review* 11 Oct. 1987: 53.

————. "An Island Garden." *New York Times Book Review* 11 Dec. 1988: 28.

Interviews and Conversations:

Kunitz, Stanley. "A Conversation with Robert Lowell." *New York Times Book Review* 4 Oct. 1964. Repr. in Stanley Kunitz, *A Kind of Order, A Kind of Folly: Essays and Conversation*, 1975.

————. "Auden on Poetry: A Conversation with Stanley Kunitz." *Atlantic* 218 Aug. 1966: 94-102.

————. "A Conversation with Andrei Voznesensky." *New York Times Book Review* 16 April 1972. Repr. (fuller text) in *Antaeus* Summer 1972 and *A Kind of Order, A Kind of Folly*.

Russell, Robert. "The Poet in the Classroom." *College English* 28 May 1967: 580-86.

Lupher, David. "A Yale Lit Interview." *Yale Literary Magazine* 136 May 1968: 6-13.

Packard, William. "Craft Interview with Stanley Kunitz." *New York Quarterly* 1 Fall 1970: 9-22. Repr. in *The Poet's Craft: Interviews from The New York Quarterly*. Ed. William Packard. New York: Paragon, 1987. Previously in *The Craft of Poetry: Interviews from the New York Quarterly*, Ed. William Packard. New York: Doubleday, 1974.

Rodman, Selden. *Tongues of Fallen Angels*. New York: New Directions, 1972.

Boyers, Robert. " 'Imagine Wrestling with an Angel': An Interview with Stanley Kunitz." *Salmagundi* 22-23 Spring 1973: 71-83. Repr. as "An Interview with Stanley Kunitz." *Contemporary Poetry in America*. Ed. Robert Boyers. New York: Schocken Books, 1974.

Davis, Cynthia. "Interview with Stanley Kunitz." *Contemporary Literature* 15 Winter 1974: 1-14.

Ryan, Michael. "An Interview with Stanley Kunitz." *Iowa Review* 5 1974: 76-85.

Allen, Henry. "The Poet's Poet: Stanley Kunitz at the Library of Congress." *Potomac (Washington Post* supplement) 9 Jan. 1975: 10.

Slaughter, Adele. "Stanley Kunitz on 'The Science of the Night'." *Calvert* Spring 1975: 6-9.

Brantley, Robin. "A Touch of the Poet." *New York Times Magazine* 7 Sept. 1975: 80-83.

Loxterman, Alan, moderator. "Poetry in the Classroom: A Symposium with Marvin Bell, Donald Hall, and Stanley Kunitz." *American Poetry Review* 6 1977: 9-13.

Gross, Harvey. "Stanley Kunitz: Action and Incantation." *Antaeus* 30/31 Spring 1978: 283-95.

Busa, Christopher. "The Art of Poetry XXIX: Stanley Kunitz." *Paris Review* Vol. 24, no. 83 Spring 1982: 205-46. Repr. (revised) in Stanley Kunitz, *Next-to-Last Things: New Poems and Essays*.

Jackson, Richard. "Living the Layers of Time." *Acts of Mind: Conversations with Contemporary Poets*. Ed. Richard Jackson. Alabama: University of Alabama Press, 1983.

"Stanley Kunitz Addresses New York Poets at Gracie Mansion." *Envoy* No. 44 and 45 23 Sept. 1983: 3.

Busa, Christopher. "Stanley Kunitz: A Poet in His Garden." *Garden Design* Winter 1984-85: 46-47, 92.

Sutton, Caroline. "PW Interviews: Stanley Kunitz." *Publishers Weekly* 228 20 Dec. 1985: 67-68.

"A Poet's Garden." *House Beautiful* Apr. 1986: 106.

Weissbort, Daniel. "Translating Anna Akhmatova." *Translating Poetry*. Ed. by Daniel Weissbort. Iowa City: University of Iowa Press, 1989.

Ringold, Francine. "Lighting the Lamp." *Nimrod* April 1991: Vol. 34, no. 2 Spring/Summer 1991: 71-3

Index

"Abduction, The," 145, 151, 153, 161, 219
Adams, Léonie, 50, 74, 137, 138
Air Transport Command, 23
Akhmadulina, Bella, 109
Akhmatova, Anna, 40, 64, 89, 90, 99-116, 165, 172
A Kind of Order, A Kind of Folly, 129, 131, 147, 148, 150, 151
"Ambergris," 6
Ammons, A. R., 148
Andrews, Roland, 80
"An Old Cracked Tune," 69, 120, 158, 211
Apollo II, 163
Apollon, 104
"Approach to Thebes, The," 36, 54, 96
Aristotle, 189
"Around Pastor Bonhoeffer," 18
"Artist, The," 36, 54, 209
"As Flowers Are," 39
Asher, Elise, 22, 26, 29, 30, 123, 166, 170, , 171, 176, 180
Ashton, Dore, 180
Atlantic Monthly Press, 67, 75, 99, 123, 125, 141
Auden, W. H., *ix, x, xi, xii,* 9, 10, 47, 125
Azores, The, 121

Babbitt, Irving, 56
Bach, Johann Sebastian, 77
Bacon, Francis (painter), 26
Bangladesh, 28
Baudelaire, Charles, 40, 90, 109
Beatles, The, 6
Beat Poetry, 27, 47
Buteau Family, The, 166
Beck, Emily Morison, 125
Beethoven, Ludwig van, 24
Benét, William Rose, 22
Bennington College, 23, 51, 79, 82, 120, 125, 174
Berryman, John, 48, 53, 90
"Beyond Reason," 33
Bishop, Elizabeth, 20, 51, 148

Blake, William, 4, 6, 12, 24, 32, 33, 42, 49, 62, 71, 86, 96, 97, 126, 161, 168
Bloom, Harold, 71
Bly, Robert, 44
Bogan, Louise, 50, 74
Bohr, Niels, 82
Bonhoeffer, Dietrich, 18, 91
Borges, Jorge Luís, 27
Brandeis University, 125
Brooks, Cleanth, 10
Buddha, 25
Busa, Christopher, *xi,* 147, 150, 154, 179
Byron, Lord George Gordon, 157

Camp Monroe, 23
Carroll, Lewis, 24
Casey, Michael, 53
Caucasus Mountains, 108
Cavafy, C. P., *ix*
Celan, Paul, 176
"Change," 92, 93, 148
Chaucer, Geoffrey, 151
Chekhov, Anton, 136
Chesterton, G. K., 27
Clark, Kenneth, 191
Clark University, 20, 81, 87
Cloud of Unknowing, The, 76
Coat without a Seam, The, 31, 37
Cohen, Leonard, 63
Coleridge, S. T., 59, 93, 94, 95, 97, 98, 188
Columbia University, 125, 137, 138, 145, 153, 180
Conrad, Joseph, 71
Contemporary Poet as Artist and Critic, The, 11, 45
Cornell, Joseph, 180
Cornell University, 169
Crane, Hart, 53
"Crystal Cage, The," 180
cummings, e. e., 21, 57
"Customs-Collector's Report, The," 58

Dante, *xi,* 25, 64, 69, 86, 144, 151, 152
"Dark and the Fair, The," 39

Daryal Gorge, 108
Davies, Sir John, 9
Davison, Peter, 125
Death Valley, 86
Debs, Eugene V., 167
"Deciduous Branch," 16
de Kooning, Willem, 84
de la Mare, Walter, 129
Dial, The, 22, 47, 62
Dickens, Charles, 20, 69
Dickinson, Emily, 131, 132
Dine, Yetta Helen, 19, 20, 21, 68, 69, 123,
    124, 150, 160, 161, 166, 167, 179
Dionysus, 179
Dixon, R. W., 132
Donne, John, 4, 42, 71, 126
Doré, Gustave, 69, 86
Doubleday, Doran, 125
Dry Tortugas, 144
Duchamp, Marcel, 148
Dugan, Alan, 16
Dylan, Bob, 63, 83

East Prussia, 19
Eliot, T. S., *x, xi*, 4, 42, 47-50 53, 55, 56,
    57, 65, 72, 132, 136, 168, 169, 177
"End of Summer," 13, 162, 202
*European Authors, 1000-1900: A Biograph-
    ical Dictionary of European Literature*, 16

"Father and Son," 11, 45, 70, 71, 161,
    179-80, 196
Federalist Papers, The, 28
Ferguson, Margaret, 92
Fine Arts Work Center, 16, 17, 53, 84,
    153, 168, 174, 186
"Fitting of the Mask, The," 35
Fitts, Dudley, 12
"Flight of Apollo, The," 25, 94, 163, 182,
    204
Florida, 144, 145, 154
"For the Word is Flesh," 15
Fort Jefferson, 144
Francis, Robert, 175
Freud, Sigmund, 95, 147, 184
Frost, Robert, *xi*, 27, 55, 65, 78, 129, 168

Gauguin, Paul, 162
Gay, Robert, 21

"Geometry of Moods," 97
Georgia, 18, 93
Ghana, 83
Gibbon, Edward, 69
Gilbert, Jack, 169
Ginsberg, Allen, 27, 28, 53
Goddard, Dr. Robert H., 81
Goethe, Johann Wolfgang von, 69
Gonne, Maud, 191
Goya, Francisco, 24
Graham, Martha, 120
"Green Ways," 37, 38, 95, 151, 201
Greenwich Village, 7, 123
Gregor, Arthur, 99
Guggenheim Fellowship, 75, 123
"Guilty Man, The", 35, 96
Guston, Philip, 84, 123, 149, 175

Haley, Alex, 83
Hardy, Thomas, 47, 129, 164
Harrison, Jane Ellen, 132
Hart, Moss, 169
Harvard University, 15, 21, 22, 56, 57,
    79, 81, 125, 169, 170
Hass, Robert, 53, 178
Hayward, Max, 40, 89, 99-116
"Hemorrhage, The," 68
Herbert, George, 4, 42, 71, 126
Herrick, Robert, 15, 21
Hiroshima, 27
Hitler, Adolph, 18, 81, 91
Holocaust, The, 180
Holt, Rinehart, and Winston, 75, 125
Homer, 25
Hopkins, Gerard Manley, *xi*, 4, 11, 15, 42,
    47, 48, 57, 71, 77, 126, 131, 132, 169
Horace, 136
Hound and Horn, 62
House Beautiful, 141
Humphries, Rolfe, 74

"I Dreamed That I Was Old," 185
"Image-Maker, The," 152, 154
Intellectual Things, 4, 22, 32, 34, 35, 41,
    50, 56, 57, 74, 96, 125, 146
Israel, 28, 29, 176, 188

James, Henry, 104, 145
Jarrell, Randall, 51, 54

Jeffers, Robinson, 81
Jerusalem, 182
Jesus, 25, 36, 68, 71, 149, 151
"John Harvard," 21
Jones, Lewis Webster, 79
"Journal for My Daughter," 92, 97
Joyce, James, 53, 54, 57, 70, 169
Jung, Carl, 11, 52, 65, 70, 95, 184

Kabbalah, 146
Kafka, Franz, 27, 40, 181
Kaufman, George S., 169
Keats, John, 15, 42, 43, 91, 126, 131, 133, 157, 170, 188
Kiefer, Anselm, 176
King, Martin Luther, 87
"King of the River," 41, 70, 95, 205
Kinnell, Galway, 26
Kipling, Rudyard, 27, 62, 156
Kittredge, George Lyman, 56
Kizer, Carolyn, 169
Klappert, Peter, 53
Kline, Franz, 84, 170, 171
Kunitz, Solomon Z., 19, 20, 68, 69, 97, 124, 160, 179, 186

"Lamplighter: 1914," 141
Lao-tse, 71
Lawrence, D. H., 77, 185
Lawrence, Seymour, 125
Leibniz, Gottfried Wilhelm, 152
Levertov, Denise, 48
Lewis, R.W.B., 87
Lincoln, Abraham, 13, 28, 155
"Long Boat, The," 142, 189
Longfellow, Henry Wadsworth, 156
Lowell, Amy, 62, 123
Lowell, Robert, 39, 41, 51, 53, 103, 123, 149, 170
Lowes, John Livingston, 56

MacDowell Colony, 84
Macmillan Publishers, 99
Macon, GA, 18, 93
Mailer, Norman, 26, 121
Malraux, André, 3
"Man Upstairs, The," 65
Mandelstam, Osip, 52, 109
Marvell, Andrew, 56

Maryland, 144
Matisse, Henri, 26
May, Rollo, 188, 189
Mayakovsky, Vladimir Vladimirovich, 172
Mayflower Compact, The, 121
McKuen, Rod, 63
McLuhan, Marshall, 63
Melville, Herman, 6
"Mens Creatrix," 32, 146
Merwin, W. S., 109
Mexico, 18
Michelangelo, 25, 191
Milton, John, 63
Moore, Marianne, 22, 57, 62, 75, 182
Moses, 71
Motherwell, Robert, 84, 121, 123
"Motion of Wish," 33, 146
"Mound Builders, The," 5, 17, 18, 93
Mozart, Wolfgang Amadeus, 25, 77
Mudd, Dr. Samuel, 144
"Mulch, The," 58
"My Sisters," 128-131, 135

Nash, Ogden, 125
National Endowment for the Arts, 16, 123
Neruda, Pablo, 27, 172
Nerval, Gérard de, 132
Nevada, 86
New Hope, PA, 23, 49, 166, 169
New Republic, The, 22
New School for Social Research, 125
Newton, Isaac, 25
New York City, 7, 16, 117, 123, 125, 141, 155, 166, 167, 169
New York Quarterly, The, 12
New York School, The, 44
New York Times, The, 163, 188
Next-to-Last Things, 123, 133, 141, 144-146, 148, 149, 151-154
"Night Letter," 35, 72
Nixon, Richard, 48

Ocmulgee National Monument, 93
O'Hara, Frank, 173
Olson, Charles, 10, 20, 170, 171, 177
"Open the Gates," *xii*, 38, 52, 86, 94, 150, 151, 182, 198
"Organic Bloom," 146, 147, 195
Owen, Wilfred, 72

The Paris Review, 68, 131, 135, 179
Parker, Dorothy, 169
Parker, Frankie, 22
Pascal, Blaise, 52
Passport to the War, 4, 34, 35, 39, 63, 75, 125, 180
Pasternak, Boris, 55, 107
Paz, Octavio, 27
Pearce, Helen, 22
Picasso, Pablo, 26, 48, 54
Pierian Sodality, 22
Piston, Walter, 22
Plath, Sylvia, 51, 55, 90
Plato, 33, 34, 93, 145
"Poem," 11
Poetry, 22, 50, 123
Poets House, 174
Pope, Alexander, 48
"Portrait, The," 68, 69, 160, 210
Post, Martin, 21
Pound, Ezra, 47, 48, 53, 55, 56, 65, 89, 168, 170, 177
"Proteus," *xiii*
"Prophecy on Lethe," 38
Proust, Marcel, 57
Provincetown, MA, *xiii*, 16, 19, 30, 53, 68, 73, 84, 117, 121, 123, 149, 155, 165, 168, 170, 181, 182, 186
Pulitzer Prize, 72, 117, 123, 168

Queens College, 125
"Quinnapoxet," 161, 216
Quinnapoxet, 141, 166

"Raccoon Journal," 145, 146, 153, 191
Ransom, John Crowe, 10, 177
Read, Sir Herbert, 47, 48
Reagan, Ronald, 135
Riley, James Whitcomb, 156
"River Road," 49, 58, 74
"Robin Redbreast," 58, 85-86, 94, 208
Robinson, Edwin Arlington, 65, 168
Roethke, Theodore, *ix, xii, xii*, 8, 15, 23, 26-27, 41, 42, 48, 49-51, 52, 61, 65, 71, 74, 75, 78, 79, 169, 170
Rosenthal, M. L., 42
Rothko, Mark, 23, 24, 36, 54, 84
"Round, The," 150
Russell, Bertrand, 86

Russia, 19, 40, 69, 100, 175
Russian Revolution, The, 167

Sacco-Vanzetti Trial, 80
Saturday Review of Literature, 22
Schwartz, Delmore, *xii*, 132, 133
"Science of the Night, The," 76, 82, 96
Scylla and Charybdis, 132
Seattle, WA, 23
Seidman, Hugh, 44, 53
Selected Poems: 1928-1978, 36, 37, 38, 40, 41, 75, 94, 125
Senegal, 83
Service, Robert, 156
Sexton, Anne, 90
Shakespeare, William, 25, 69
Shaw, Bernard, 86
Shelley, Percy Bysshe, 157
Sidney, Sir Philip, 136
"Single Vision," 95-6
"Snakes of September, The," 117, 124, 149, 152, 218
Snodgrass, W. D., 51
Snyder, Gary, 27
Socrates, 145
Solzhenitsyn, Aleksandr, 5
Spenser, Edmund, 44
Stalin, Josef, 107
Stanley Steamer, 141
Stevens, Wallace, *xi*, 37, 49, 55, 65, 168
Stevenson, Robert Louis, 27

Tate, Allen, 51
Tennyson, Alfred, Lord, 15, 42, 156
The Testing-Tree, 36, 40, 41, 57, 65, 68, 72, 73, 85, 171
"Testing Tree, The," 41, 58, 78, 86, 166, 172, 212
Thackeray, William Makepeace, 20
"Thief, The," 189
Thomas, Dylan, 46, 47, 83
Thomas, Norman, 167
Thompson, Lawrance, 27
"Three Floors," 85, 160, 203
Tobey, Mark, 23
Tolstoy, Leo, 20, 69
Torah, 150
Twentieth Century Authors: First Supplement, 16

Ungaretti, Giuseppe, 109
United Nations, The, 128
Universalist Church, 26
University of Washington, 86, 125, 169

Valéry, Paul, *x*, 28, 94
Vermeer, Jan, 129
Vermont, 26
"Very Tree," 33, 146
Vietnam War, The, 4, 5, 48, 53
Virgil, 25
Voznesensky, Andrei, 5, 40, 64, 89, 90, 172

Wagoner, David, 169
"War Against the Trees, The," 24, 30, 73, 199
Warhol, Andy, 187
Warren, Robert Penn, 10, 177
Washington, George, 15, 155
"Wellfleet Whale, The," 6, 149-151, 172, 221
Welty, Eudora, 128
"What of the Night?", 189
Whitehead, Alfred North, 81
Whitman, Walt, 133, 173, 179
Whittier, John Greenleaf, 156
Wilbur, Richard, 125, 158
Williams, William Carlos, *xi, xiii*, 49, 55, 65, 168, 177, 182

H. W. Wilson Company, 21, 79, 80, 125
Wilson, Woodrow, 14, 28
Winters, Yvor, 10, 22
Wittgenstein, Ludwig, 131
Worcester Art Museum, 181
Worcester Classical High School, 12, 21
Worcester, MA, 19, 20, 43, 69, 78, 79, 81, 87, 121, 124, 127, 155, 161, 165, 166, 167, 170
Worcester Telegram, The, 21, 79, 80
Wordsworth, William, 15, 20, 42, 92, 97, 127, 132, 133, 134
World War I, 141, 166
World War II, 22, 75, 96
Wormwood Hill, CT, 16, 22, 73, 166, 169
Wright, James, 169, 173
Wylie, Elinor, 50

Yale Series of Younger Poets, 12, 22, 44, 53, 67, 85, 87, 170
Yale University, 87
Yeats, W. B., *xi*, 15, 36, 42, 47, 55, 64, 102, 151, 164, 166, 180
Yevtushenko, Yevgeny, 3, 5, 89
Yom Kippur, 182
Yucca Flats, 86

Zabel, Morton Dauwen, 22